THE POWER OF PICTURES IN CHRISTIAN THOUGHT

The use and abuse of images in the Bible and theology

ANTHONY C. THISELTON

First published in Great Britain in 2018

Society for Promoting Christian Knowledge
36 Causton Street
London SW1P 4ST
www.spck.org.uk

British Library Cataloguing-in-Publication Data
A catalogue record for this book is available from the British Library

ISBN 978–0–281–07886–8
eBook ISBN 978–0–281–07887–5

Typeset by Falcon Oast Graphic Art Ltd, www.falcon.uk.com
First printed in Great Britain by Ashford Colour Press
Subsequently digitally reprinted in Great Britain

eBook by Falcon Oast Graphic Art Ltd, www.falcon.uk.com

Produced on paper from sustainable forests

Contents

Preface

This book is written from the heart. In Christian teaching and preaching we need more pictures and illustrative presentations to make concepts and images more powerful, vivid, clear and convincing. This would be in no way to water them down. This book is not part of the current fashion of promoting 'stories', as if these were *alternatives* rather than *supplements* to ideas or biblical expositions.

Indeed if we look at biblical precedents, clearly the teaching of Jesus is full of pictorial examples from everyday life, especially in his parables. It becomes apparent in our Part 2, however, that the epistles of Paul abound no less in pictures, images and analogies often to illustrate the most complex ideas. The whole Bible, including the book of Revelation, provides a feast of visual representations.

However, pictures may also seduce and mislead us. It quickly emerged that this book could not simply be written from the heart, but called for the full engagement of the head also. For many are not only helped, but also misdirected, by pictures. In some circles people claim to receive pictures from God, which, they suggest, invite or direct individuals or churches to act on what they suppose the picture conveys. Everything depends, however, not only on the genuineness of the claim that *God* has given the picture, but also on how the picture has been *interpreted.*

At this point the homely observations of the sophisticated philosopher Ludwig Wittgenstein come boldly into play. He is known for his defence of the 'picture' theory of language, especially in his earlier work. But he also emphasized that pictures can be *variously* interpreted. For example, in a two-dimensional picture apparently of an elderly man walking uphill leaning on his stick or cane, could he, in fact, be sliding backwards downhill? There are not two pictures, but one. The picture can be interpreted in more than one way. Wittgenstein and others provide numerous examples of potentially ambiguous pictures, even if their single meaning seems self-evident at first sight. His examples include Jastrow's duck-rabbit, the Necker cube (we can see a glass cube in various ways, including as an open box), radio circuitry, what a triangle might represent, photographs, and many more instances.

Yet Wittgenstein is not alone in exposing the radical consequences of different points of view. In hermeneutics Chladenius long ago demonstrated the importance of 'points of view'. In more recent times **point of view** has become increasingly important in literary theory. Robert Alter, for example, has shown the importance of different points of view in parallel narratives which were once dismissed as contradictory sources. In Part 1 we warn readers that an element of thinking in philosophy, hermeneutics and literary theory is required if we want a full understanding of the issues. A study of symbols and metaphors necessarily completes this exploration.

Part 2 focuses entirely on biblical examples. We examine Old Testament uses of pictures, symbols and metaphors, including uses of prophetic symbolism, where sometimes actions further supplement pictures. It is self-evident that Jesus drew pictures and images in abundance from Galilean rural and household life. He was a master teacher. The possible surprise is that Paul also used so very many analogies, images and pictures, even if usually from the city rather than the countryside. Whether Paul or a Pauline disciple wrote the Pastoral Epistles, these, too, provide useful illustrations from practical, everyday life. The book of Revelation provides a feast of pictures, images and visual representations which deserve attention. But all of this underlines our double argument. On the one hand pictures remain powerful, vivid and necessary. On the other hand their correct and careful interpretation is equally necessary; otherwise they will simply mislead and seduce us.

Hence Part 3 seeks to apply this twofold positive and negative argument to Christian communication today. We reaffirm that 'one picture is worth a thousand words', but also stress that understanding requires great care and honesty. We suggest some counter-examples from Gnostic writings, from some (not all) mediaeval and post-mediaeval mystics and from some (not all) modern, often local, 'charismatic' groups. We also consider post-biblical interpretations of some of the biblical writings, including the book of Revelation, and the genuine needs of modern preaching and teaching. Both the positive and negative arguments of this book hang together coherently, and have immense practical effect. I am not aware of other studies which make the same dual case.

I am most grateful for the help of those to whom I owe a special debt. Most of all, once again I am very grateful to Revd Stuart Dyas, with the help of his wife, Revd Dr Dee Dyas, not only for corrections to typographical errors, but also for suggesting numerous improvements in vocabulary and style. Their advice has been invaluable, especially on mediaeval and post-mediaeval mystics. Their notice of errors or clumsy phrasing and vocabulary has been meticulous, and valuable in improving clarity and meaning.

Anthony C. Thiselton, FBA

About the author

Anthony C. Thiselton is Emeritus Professor of Christian Theology in the University of Nottingham, and Emeritus Canon Theologian of Leicester and of Southwell and Nottingham. Dr Thiselton has taught in five British universities, including Bristol and Durham, and in numerous universities overseas. He is a Fellow of King's College and of the British Academy. He holds four doctorates and has published some 27 books and nearly 90 research articles. On Sundays he ministers at St Mary's, Attenborough.

Abbreviations

1QS	*Rule of the Community* (Dead Sea Scrolls)
ANF	Ante-Nicene Fathers
BDAG	Danker, F. W., Bauer, W., Arndt, W. F., and Gingrich, F. W. *Greek-English Lexicon of the New Testament and Other Early Christian Literature.* 3rd edn. Chicago, 2000
BDB	Brown, F., Driver, S. R., and Briggs, C. A. *The New Hebrew and English Lexicon.* Lafayette, 1980
CUP	Cambridge University Press
ExpTim	*Expository Times*
Int	*Interpretation*
JBL	*Journal of Biblical Literature*
JSNT	*Journal for the Study of the New Testament*
JSNTSup	Journal for the Study of the New Testament: Supplement Series
LCC	Library of Christian Classics. Philadelphia, 1953–
LXX	Septuagint
NCB	New Century Bible
NIGTC	New International Greek Testament Commentary
NovT	*Novum Testamentum*
NovTSup	Supplements to Novum Testamentum
NPNF	Nicene and Post-Nicene Fathers
NTS	*New Testament Studies*
OUP	Oxford University Press
SBLDS	Society of Biblical Literature Dissertation Series
SJT	*Scottish Journal of Theology*
SNTSMS	Society for New Testament Studies Monograph Series
TDNT	*Theological Dictionary of the New Testament.* Edited by G. Kittel and G. Friedrich. Translated by G. W. Bromiley. 10 vols. Grand Rapids, 1964–76
WBC	Word Biblical Commentary
WUNT	Wissenschaftliche Untersuchungen zum Neuen Testament

Part 1

PHILOSOPHICAL, HERMENEUTICAL AND LITERARY

1

The power of pictures, visual images and symbols

One picture is worth a thousand words

It is often said that a picture is worth a thousand words. Probably this axiom first appeared in exactly this form in 1911 in a newspaper in America.[1] The slightly different phrase, 'One look is worth a thousand words', appeared at a similar time in 1913.[2] The exact original phrase reappeared in 1918 in an advertisement for the *San Antonio Light*.[3] The Russian writer Ivan Turgenev (1818–83) had earlier written, 'The drawing shows me at one glance what might be spread over ten pages in a book.'[4] Dawn Grider provided visual representations of Jon Egah's sermons by drawings of the cross, the empty tomb, hands raised in worship, and so on. The images provide concepts more instantly than pages of complex words, whether spoken or written.

More than this, pictures are instantly memorable. Many regular Christian worshippers may not be able to explain the contrast in Paul and Luther between faith or grace and 'works'. But, as Timothy Dudley-Smith writes, they 'know exactly what they mean by singing:

> Nothing in my hand I bring,
> Simply to thy cross I cling'.[5]

He then quotes R. W. Dale of Birmingham as saying, 'Let me write the hymns of a Church, and I care not who writes the theology.'

Visual representations seem immediately to solve the problem of inadequate attention-spans. We can either glance at a picture or contemplate it over time. Pictures often convey emotions, and may appeal

---

1 Tess Sanders (ed.), 'Speakers Give Sound Advice', *Syracuse Post Standard* (28 March 1911), p. 18.
2 Advertisement for Piqua Auto Supply House, in Piqua, Ohio, USA.
3 War advertisement, *San Antonio Light* (10 January 1918), p. 6.
4 Ivan Turgenev, *Fathers and Sons* (1862), ch. 16. This is Bazarov's remark to Anna Sergeyevna (Eng., e-books, University of Adelaide, 2016).
5 Timothy Dudley-Smith, *A Functional Art: Reflections of a Hymn Writer* (Oxford: OUP, 2017), p. 4.

to deep-seated commitments, as when many people may identify with brand images or national flags. This applies not only to food or groceries, but also to institutions ranging from universities to corporate manufacturing companies. Pictures may make us feel patriotic, excited, disgusted or curious. These may be divided, at least in part, by generational differences. Magazines are notorious for exploiting pictures and images, often to attract allegiance and purchasing habits. They provide readers with immediate self-involving focus. We may take a flag for granted, until we find ourselves in foreign parts, or in the midst of a war.

Whatever the complexities of the relation between printed or written prose and visual images, we cannot but notice the difference between telling and showing; between hearsay report and eyewitness testimony, and between speaking about a subject and beholding its content directly. Furthermore, these two styles of representation appear to belong to two different cultures and generations. One is the world of books and the academy; the other is the more popular culture of images, today partly separated by ageing, youth and generational differences. Today's generation grows up with mobile phones, digital tablets and television; yesterday's generation often had rooms full of books and encyclopaedias. It is tempting to perceive one as the legacy of the past, and the other as the promise of the future. The American politician Ralph Waldo Emerson (1803–82) called his political party 'the Party of the Future', on the ground that some people see everything good as future, and everything bad as past.

The arrival in force of the digital era reinforces many of these arguments. Martin Veravsky has argued that reading a book of 500 pages may take 30 hours, whereas a film of the book would normally convey its content within about two hours. It will provide more information per minute than the written book. The film also normally combines the two senses of seeing and hearing, whereas the written word appears to use only one of the senses. Students today have generally ceased to amass libraries of books as their parents used to do, and spend their time consulting visual media in varied forms. The significance of these remarks applies not so much to efficiency in the use of time, as instant access. What is significant is being able to grasp content as a *whole in a moment*. Several writers compare the Greek concept of vision with the Hebrew prioritizing of the ear. In spite of blatant oversimplification and dated, serious misunderstandings and flaws, Boman emphasized this basic contrast in his book *Hebrew Thought Compared with Greek*.[6]

[6] Thorlief Boman, *Hebrew Thought Compared with Greek* (Eng., London: SCM, 1954),

Visual representation is often more memorable than lines of print. Even among those who are not theists or Christians, the Johannine imagery of the Good Shepherd and the Vine, and the Lucan images of the Prodigal Son and the Lost Sheep remain unforgettable as visual images for many.[7] The book of Revelation depicts the tree of life, and God's wiping away tears from every eye. We shall exemplify many more memorable physical images in Part 2, below.

Photography has greatly enhanced the expansion of visual imagery and experience. The film critic André Bazin claimed concerning the nineteenth century, for the first time 'An image of the world is formed automatically, without the creative intervention of man . . . Photography affects us like a phenomenon of nature'.[8]

Nevertheless many argue that pictures and visual images cannot fully convey meaning without the context or tradition of verbal texts which surround them. Martin Jay in his impressive volume, *Downcast Eyes: The Denigration of Vision in Twentieth-Century French Thought*, has provided one of the most striking and accurate accounts of the relation between visual perception and the printed or written word, together with critiques by a host of philosophers and historians of culture.[9] He pays careful attention to both sides of the debate.

Jay notes the ubiquity of visual metaphors, which may be either an aid or an obstacle to our knowledge of reality. This judicious double-sightedness constitutes a theme of our book also. On the one hand, many cultures have been 'dominated by vision: microscopes, telescopes, cameras and cinema'.[10] On the other hand, Judaism expressed suspicion of idolatry, and Islamic thought rejected figural representation. The Iconoclastic Controversy of the eighth century and the Cistercian monasticism of St Bernard constitute counter-movements to visual representation. In the modern period, Henri Bergson, Jean-Paul Sartre, Maurice Merleau-Ponty, Emmanuel Levinas, Michel Foucault, Roland Barthes and Jacques Derrida also represent this strong counter-movement. In France, Jay

---

throughout. However, this has been radically and rightly criticized by James Barr, *The Semantics of Biblical Language* (Oxford: OUP, 1961), pp. 46–79, 96–100, and throughout, especially when Boman confuses concepts with the *use* of concepts, and also the significance of comparative languages.

7 John 10.11–18; and Luke 15.3–7 and 11–32.

8 André Bazin, 'The Ontology of the Photographic Image', in Jean Renoir (ed.), *What Is Cinema?* (Berkeley: University of California Press, 1967), p. 13.

9 Martin Jay, *Downcast Eyes: The Denigration of Vision in Twentieth-Century French Thought* (Berkeley: University of California Press, 1993).

10 Jay, *Downcast Eyes*, p. 3.

points out, a preoccupation with fashion, cinema and pictures seems to have become reversed.[11] Thus the French philosopher Jacques Ellul (1912–94) has developed a strong argument *against* visual images in his book *The Humiliation of the Word*.[12] He writes as a member of the French Reformed tradition. He argues that technology has downgraded the written word, and led to the visual often having priority over the conceptual. Hegel comments, 'The situation of the word in our society is deplorable.'[13] Ours, he says, is a culture in which *sight* has triumphed over the experience of *hearing*.

While we provide detailed exploration of biblical examples in the second part of this book, an initial glance at pictorial metaphors in the Bible readily makes the point. The Methodist scholar Vincent Taylor underlined the power and memorable influence of the phrase 'the blood of Christ' for Christians of several traditions. He wrote:

> To explain the allusions to 'blood' as synonyms for 'death' is mistaken. One can hardly fail to be conscious of a loss of meaning if instead of 'being justified *by his blood*' (Romans 5:9), we read 'being justified in Christ crucified'.[14]

Taylor provides a multiplicity of such examples, and more recent authors could be also be cited. More recently Fleming Routledge has commented on 'the blood of Christ'. She quotes George Hunsinger:

> Christ's blood is a metaphor that stands primarily for the suffering love of God. It suggests that there is no sorrow God has not known, no grief he has not borne, no price he was unwilling to pay, in order to reconcile the world to himself in Christ.[15]

One of the best-known historical examples of this emphasis on the visual comes from John Foxe's *Book of Martyrs*, first published in 1563, as *Acts and Monuments*, but subsequently published as *Foxe's Book of Martyrs* over several further editions, notably in 1570, 1576 and 1583. The influence of this book was massive, especially after Elizabeth I (1558–1603) ordered a copy of it to be placed in every cathedral in England. Many

---

11 Jay, *Downcast Eyes*, pp. 10, 14 and 15..

12 Jacques Ellul, *The Humiliation of the Word* (Grand Rapids: Eerdmans, 1985).

13 Quoted in Ellul, *The Humiliation of the Word*, p. 155.

14 Vincent Taylor, *The Atonement in New Testament Teaching* (London: Epworth Press, 1940), p. 92.

15 Fleming Routledge, *The Crucifixion: Understanding the Death of Jesus Christ* (Grand Rapids: Eerdmans, 2015), p. 283.

parish churches followed suit, with the result that in most churches the three books officially on display were the Bible, the Book of Common Prayer and *Foxe's Book of Martyrs.* The latter traced the persecution of 'Protestant' believers from the time of John Wycliffe (1330–84) through the reign of Catholic Queen Mary (1553–8), whose reign the book described as 'horrible and bloody'. It aimed to expose the wickedness of Catholic 'idolatry', and to describe in the most lurid fashion the suffering of the Protestant martyrs.

The key to the book's influence and success, however, depended largely on its numerous woodcuts provided by Foxe's printer, John Day. These 153 or so visual illustrations depicted the suffering of martyrs burned at the stake (including Cranmer, Ridley and Latimer). Many were tortured in various ways of the utmost cruelty, and many suffered unspeakable humiliations. The power of this vivid visual representation became an unchallengeable model of the principle of the power of pictures.

Visual representation from Plato to Descartes and today

The reverse was the case, Jay argues, from Parmenides and Plato to Descartes. Erich Auerbach (1892–1957), the eminent German philological and literary critic, adopted the opposite approach to that of Ellul in his book *Mimesis,* in which he discusses visual representation from the ancient world to modern times. He wrote, 'Clearly outlined, brightly and uniformly illuminated, men and things stand out in a realm where everything is visible.'[16] He is here discussing Homer, and Jay notes Hellenic affinity with the visible form, from Parmenides to Plato. In Plato, he argues, 'truth' was embodied in the *eidos,* or eternal timeless idea, in contrast to the empirical world. His image of the cave and its shadows illustrates the value and limitations of perception through the senses. For Plato *theōria* (Greek for *contemplation*) 'created an opportunity for the philosopher to see behind the spectacle to the true beauty'.[17]

The Greek privileging of vision, Jay continues, led to Aristotle's notion of metaphor as 'to see our likeness'.[18] In spite of early Christianity's suspicion of images, the Incarnation stood at the centre of Christian faith as the embodiment of God in human form. Aristotle also regarded Greek

[16] Erich Auerbach, *Mimesis: The Representation of Reality in Western Literature* (Eng., Princeton: Princeton University Press, 1953), p. 2 (1967 edn, p. 3).

[17] Robyn J. Whitaker, *Ekphrasis, Vision, and Persuasion in the Book of Revelation* (WUNT 2, 140; Tübingen: Mohr, 2015), p. 55.

[18] Aristotle, *Poetics,* 1459 A.

phantasia as something imagined, a mental picture or a vision. Verity Platt comments, '*Phantasia* is thus represented as . . . the power of the mind itself to visualize and communicate with god.'[19] In the mediaeval era Thomas Aquinas (1225–74), Dante (1265–1321) and Meister Eckhart (1260–*c.*1325) stressed the importance of visual representation. Aquinas quotes Augustine as saying that the mind acquires knowledge of corporeal things through the bodily senses, and similarly the mind can know bodily things also.[20] He distinguished between *veneration* of images in iconolatry and *worship* of images in idolatry. Norman Bryson argued that the stained-glass windows of Canterbury Cathedral placed visual imagery at the service of the biblical and historical narratives that they illustrated.[21] Renaissance art also contributed to this visual emphasis.

The climax of visual representation and imagery, however, comes in the philosophy of René Descartes (1596–1650), especially in his *Discourse on Method* (1637). He believed that the vision of the eye was 'the most comprehensive and the noblest' of the senses. Jay comments, 'The grip of ocularcentrism was perhaps nowhere as evident as in France, the culture whose recent reversal of attitudes is thus perhaps all the more worthy of study.'[22] He speaks of 'the stubborn world of Cartesian philosophy', and adds, 'Descartes was a quintessentially visual philosopher, who tacitly adopted the position of a perspectivalist painter using *camera obscura* to produce an observed world.'[23] The American philosopher Richard Rorty called it 'the paradigm of the visual model: the intellect inspects entities modelled on retinal images', and this becomes the basis of 'modern' epistemology, that is, of 'representations which are in the mind'.[24] In his more recent book, *Truth and Progress*, Rorty called Descartes' philosophy 'an unfortunate bit of residual Aristotelianism'.[25]

One aspect of Descartes' concern with visual representation can be seen in his interest in optical instruments devised for the improvement of

---

[19] Verity Platt, 'Virtual Visions: *Phantasia* and the Perception of the Divine in the Life of Apollonius of Tyana', in E. L. Bowie and J. Elsner (eds), *Philostratus* (Cambridge: CUP, 2009), p. 152.

[20] Aquinas, *Summa Theologiae* (Eng., [60 vols.] London: Eyre and Spottiswoode, 1963, vol. 12), Pt 1, Qu. 84, art. 2.

[21] Norman Bryson, *Word and Image: French Painting of the Ancient Regime* (Cambridge: CUP, 1981), p. 1.

[22] Jay, *Downcast Eyes*, p. 69.

[23] Jay, *Downcast Eyes*, p. 69.

[24] Richard Rorty, *Philosophy and the Mirror of Nature* (Princeton: Princeton University Press, 1979), p. 45.

[25] Richard Rorty, *Truth and Progress: Philosophical Papers*, vol. 3 (Cambridge: CUP, 1998), p. 113.

vision. This can be seen in his longer edition of his *Discourse on Method, Optics, Geometry, and Meteorology*, in which he calls sight the noblest of the senses.[26] Jay traces the influence of Descartes on visual representation to John Locke and the Enlightenment with certain modifications. Descartes aimed at 'certain' truths, which could not be doubted.[27] In effect, this is an individualist rationalism. It places the self and its reflection and vision as the starting point of philosophical thought. Descartes' dualism of mind and body also gave privilege to mental reflection, and its capacity to view ideas and images.

Descartes strongly influenced John Locke (1632–1704), and his *Essay Concerning Human Understanding* (1690). Although Locke represented the tradition of British empiricism, in contrast to rationalism, he also sought 'certain' knowledge, in contrast to second-hand opinion. Yet he rejected Descartes' notion of 'innate ideas'.[28] In Book II of his *Essay* he argued that an 'Idea is the Object of Thinking', and that 'All Ideas come from Sensations or Reflection'.[29] 'Experience', he argued, may directly perceive objects in the world through the senses, even if the mind combines them as it reflects upon them. Thus human experience perceives the 'primary' qualities of objects (solidity, extension, mobility and so on), and 'secondary' qualities (colours, sounds, tastes and so on).[30] In the process of apprehending sense-perceptions, he used the well-known analogy between the mind and a blank sheet of paper (Lat., *tabula rasa*). After its perception, reflection may process raw data. His empiricist successor George Berkeley (1685–1753) stressed senses and ideas more strongly, while David Hume (1711–76) stressed senses and fleeting perceptions.

Jay also accorded to the thinkers of the Enlightenment a broad emphasis on visual representation, but with counter-currents suggesting dialectic between visual expression and writing or hearing. Voltaire (1694–1778) asked, 'What is an idea?', and answered, 'It is an image that paints itself in my brain . . . I've ideas only because I've images in my head.'[31] 'Idea' is thus an internal representation of objects as visual experiences. Jay comments, 'The Cartesian attitude toward vision [was] not abandoned

---

[26] René Descartes, *Discourse on Method, Optics, Geometry, and Meteorology* (Cambridge, MA: Hackett Publishing, 2001), p. 65. More accessible editions include René Descartes, *Discourse on Method and the Meditations* (London: Penguin, 1968).

[27] Descartes, *Discourse on Method* (1968 edn), pp. 33, 38 and 43.

[28] John Locke, *An Essay Concerning Human Understanding* (2 vols, Oxford: Clarendon Press, 1894), Essay I. 4. 3.

[29] Locke, *Essay* II. 1. 1 and II. 1. 2.

[30] Locke, *Essay*, II. 8, 9 and 10.

[31] Voltaire, *Philosophical Dictionary* (Eng., New York: Knopf, 1924 and 1972), p. 256.

in eighteenth-century France.'[32] Similarly the Scottish 'Common Sense' philosopher Thomas Reid (1710–96) wrote, 'Of all the faculties called the five senses, sight is without doubt the noblest.'[33] He also appealed to the discoveries of Sir Isaac Newton, and to the extreme minuteness and great speed of the eye. By contrast, he argued, the ear was less reliable, often depending on hearsay.

Other Enlightenment thinkers include Denis Diderot (1715–84), chief editor of *The Encyclopédie*, art critic, and friend of Friedrich Grimm and Jean-Jacques Rousseau (1712–78). He wrote also an essay on painting, which was praised by Goethe. His contribution to visual art included his special appreciation of Jean-Baptiste Greuze (1725–1805) the painter. In philosophy he at first followed Voltaire, but later became an atheist and materialist. Rousseau also explored visionary projection. Yet both Diderot and Rousseau expressed hostility to the seductive power of images, citing them as commending visual representation, but also providing what Jay called 'counter-currents to Enlightenment ocularcentrism in its dominant form', that is, reservations about direct visual representation.[34] Diderot also emphasized the special power of touch, as well as commenting on seeing an object, admiring it, experiencing it and desiring to possess it as an instantaneous emotion.

The notion of visual representation largely survived until the second half of the nineteenth century. Then several factors tended to challenge its dominance. In new technology, optics showed the increasing complexity of visual retinas and sight, and the increasing role of the brain or mind in shaping what was actually seen. In philosophy, Friedrich Nietzsche (1844–1900) collapsed any clear distinction between truth and interpretation, while in company with Ludwig Feuerbach (1804–72), Karl Marx (1818–83) and Sigmund Freud (1856–1939) he seemed to abolish any notion of a 'God's eye' view of the world, in spite of Hegel. Kierkegaard had satirized Hegel as 'contemplating the eternal' and viewing reality 'theocentrically'.[35] Most clearly of all, Henri Bergson (1859–1941) expounded the role of process, change and time, as if to dethrone timeless and static visual representation of sight. The Continental hermeneutical tradition from Chladenius to Heidegger further demonstrated the

[32] Jay, *Downcast Eyes*, p. 85.

[33] Thomas Reid, *An Enquiry into the Human Mind on the Principles of Common Sense* (Edinburgh: Bell & Greech, 1801), p. 152, and e-book (2015), p. 48.

[34] Jay, *Downcast Eyes*, p. 98.

[35] Søren Kierkegaard, *Concluding Unscientific Postscript* (Eng., Princeton: Princeton University Press, 1974), p. 190.

multiform nature of visual aspects or points of view, and dimensions of time and duration. The whole movement exposed the crucial importance of time and history. In Nietzsche's language it questioned the earlier assumption of 'immaculate perception'.[36]

We shall develop the details of this anti-visual approach in the next chapter. However, we may first introduce the positive and negative role of Ludwig Wittgenstein (1889–1951). An unduly simplistic understanding of Wittgenstein often suggests that in his early period of the *Tractatus* he simply held a 'picture theory' of language, whereby 'A proposition is a picture of reality'.[37] Many years later, he recalls in the *Philosophical Investigations*, 'A *picture* held us captive. And we could not get outside it, for it lay in our language, and language seemed to repeat it to us inexorably.'[38] In the *Tractatus* he writes, 'We picture facts to ourselves.'[39] The pictorial nature of propositions first occurred to Wittgenstein when he learned about the practice of representing traffic accidents in a law-court through the use of toy cars and dolls. It then looks as if in the *later* writings, visual representations or pictures can remain useful *only if they serve particular applications*, or are subservient to words. However, Kristóf Nyíri, Anthony Kenny and a host of other thinkers have shown that a profound ambiguity runs through Wittgenstein, so that he both affirms and denies the value of 'pictures'.[40]

Meanwhile we may note that in his Preface to the *Investigations* Wittgenstein suggests that his thoughts represent 'albums' rather than an extended prose essay. Albums are more like snapshots than essays. Later he lists examples of 'A multiplicity of language-games', which include 'Constructing an object (a drawing)'. [41] In a footnote to this section he writes, 'Imagine a picture representing a boxer in a particular stance.' Such a picture has many possible uses: to tell someone how to stand, to describe how someone once took his stand, and so on. Similarly in his

[36] Friedrich Nietzsche, *Thus Spoke Zarathustra* (London: Penguin, 1961), p. 149.

[37] Ludwig Wittgenstein, *Tractatus Logico-Philosophicus* (Eng. and Ger., London: Routledge & Kegan Paul, 1922 and 1961), 4.01.

[38] Ludwig Wittgenstein, *Philosophical Investigations* (Eng. and Ger., Oxford: Blackwell, 1958), sect. 115.

[39] Wittgenstein, *Tractatus*, 2.1.

[40] For example, Kristóf Nyíri, 'Wittgenstein's Philosophy of Pictures', Conference Paper at the HIT Centre, University of Bergen, December 2001, and 'Images and Metaphor in the Philosophy of Wittgenstein', Paper at the 33nd International Symposium, *Image and Imaging in Philosophy, Science and Arts*, Kirchberg, Austria, August 2010; and Anthony Kenny, *Wittgenstein* (London: Penguin, 1973), especially pp. 224–7.

[41] Wittgenstein, *Philosophical Investigations*, sect. 23.

discussion of the seeing of a cube, Wittgenstein admits that it can be understood in various ways, but adds: 'What really comes before our mind when we understand a word? – Isn't it something like a picture? – Can't it *be* a picture?' He remarks in the same section:

> Suppose that a picture does come before your mind when you hear the word 'cube', or see the drawing of a cube? In what sense can this picture fit or fail to fit a use in the word 'cube'? . . . I have purposely so chosen the example that it is quite easy *to imagine a method of projection* according to which the picture does fit after all. The picture of the cube did indeed *suggest* a certain use to us, but it was possible for me to use it differently.[42]

In this section Wittgenstein adds another footnote (b):

> I see a picture; it represents an old man walking up a steep hill leaning on a stick. – How? Might it not have looked just the same if he had been sliding downhill in that position? Perhaps a Martian would describe the picture so.

When Wittgenstein later talks about human gestures and signpost arrows, admittedly he says that how we use them is decisive for their meaning, but he does not reject their validity as pictures. He asks, 'How does it come about that this arrow *points*?'[43] What gives meaning to arrows or gestures is the complementary dual action of both the picture and our *use* of it. We could not function without *both* visual representation *and* particular human uses of it.

Part 2 of the *Investigations* was even more detailed and positive about pictures. Wittgenstein introduced the idea of a 'picture-object'. He discussed, for example, 'picture-faces' and remarked,

> In some respects I stand towards it as I do towards a human face. I could study its expression, can react to it as the expression of a human face. A child can talk to the picture-men or picture-animals, can treat them as it treats dolls.[44]

On the same page and in the same section Wittgenstein discussed the famous picture of the so-called duck-rabbit, which may be seen either as a rabbit's head looking upwards or as the head of a duck pointing sideways.

---

42 Wittgenstein, *Philosophical Investigations*, sect. 139 (his italics).
43 Wittgenstein, *Philosophical Investigations*, sects 432 and 454.
44 Wittgenstein, *Philosophical Investigations*, Pt 2, xi, p. 194.

It is possible to see this *as* the head of either a rabbit or a duck, depending on our initial interpretation of the picture.

Wittgenstein distinguished between the 'dawning' of an aspect and the 'continuous seeing' of an aspect. Continuous seeing often makes possible the sight of both aspects. Donald D. Evans has drawn on this picture or analogy of '*seeing as*' in his section on 'Onlooks'. I have also used this extensively in the context of Paul's account of seeing Christian believers as righteous when God justifies them by grace through faith.[45] Wittgenstein wrestled with the significance of his philosophy of pictures and the dawning of an aspect for the whole of section 2. xi, which amounts to more than 20 pages. Nyíri concludes, 'From the *Philosophical Investigations* there does not emerge a unified philosophy of pictures.'[46]

Wittgenstein's *Philosophical Grammar* and his *Zettel* contained more on pictorial meaning. In *Philosophical Grammar* he wrote, 'Anything can be a picture of anything, if we extend the concept of picture sufficiently.'[47] Thus, 'A diagram representing the inside of a radio receiver' will be merely 'a jumble of meaningless lines' to one person, but 'a significant picture' to another.[48] Wittgenstein wrote further, 'A blueprint serves as a picture of the object which the workman is to make from it. – And here we might call the way in which the workman turns such a drawing into an artefact, "the method of projection".'[49] The struggle over the role of pictures continues in the *Zettel*. He reflects,

> At that moment the thought was before my mind.' – And how? – 'I had this picture.' – So was the picture the thought? No; for if I had just told someone the picture, he would not have got the thought. The picture was the key. Or it *seemed* like a key.[50]

Some five sections later Wittgenstein comments, 'I understand the picture exactly as I could model it – I understand this description exactly. I could make a drawing from it.'

He continues: 'In many cases we might set it up as a criterion of

[45] Donald Evans, *The Logic of Self-Involvement* (London: SCM, 1963) pp. 124–44; and Anthony C. Thiselton, *The Two Horizons* (Grand Rapids: Eerdmans, 1980), pp. 415–22, and *Systematic Theology* (Grand Rapids: Eerdmans, 2015), pp. 371–73.

[46] Nyíri, 'Wittgenstein's Philosophy of Pictures', p. 4.

[47] Ludwig Wittgenstein, *Philosophical Grammar* (Berkeley: University of California Press, 1974), p. 163.

[48] Wittgenstein, *Philosophical Grammar*, p. 176.

[49] Wittgenstein, *Philosophical Grammar*, p. 213.

[50] Ludwig Wittgenstein, *Zettel* (Oxford: Blackwell, 1967), sects 239 and 240.

understanding, that one had to be able to represent the sentence in a drawing.'[51] Wittgenstein then remarks, 'The significant picture is what can not merely be drawn, but also represented plastically. And saying this would make sense.'[52] Further, he comments, 'Asked "What image have you?", one can answer with the picture.'[53] He discusses films, painted pictures, and sculptures, together with such gestures as shrugging one's shoulders, head-shakes, nods and so on.[54] Anthony Kenny sums up the point when he writes, 'All these passages seem to suggest that the picture theory needs supplementing, rather than that it is false; that the theory of "meaning as use" is a complement rather than a rival to the picture theory.'[55] This is why Wittgenstein remains an essential thinker both in the present chapter and in the chapter after next. Many more philosophers can now be cited today who endorse and develop this approach, including Judith Genova, Ernst H. Gombrich, and many others.[56] Judith Genova writes, 'To the extent that we think in language, we think in pictures.'[57]

Pictures, symbols and archetypes: emotions and participation

Up to now we have noted primarily the nature and extent of visual imagery. But we have not yet fully explored the *power* of pictures and visual images and symbols (except perhaps in the first section of this chapter). Joseph Campbell (1904–87), known for his work in comparative mythology and comparative religion, argued, 'A symbol is an energy-evoking and directing agent.'[58] One source of the power of symbols is the way in which they involve human emotions, as Tolstoy emphasized, the imagination, as Croce stressed, and the unconscious, according especially to Jung, and to varying extents Bevan, Tillich, Ricoeur, Fawcett and Dillistone.

---

51 Wittgenstein, *Zettel*, sect. 245.

52 Wittgenstein, *Zettel*, sect. 246.

53 Wittgenstein, *Zettel*, sect. 621.

54 Wittgenstein, *Zettel*, sect. 651.

55 Kenny, *Wittgenstein*, p. 226.

56 Judith Genova, 'Wittgenstein on Thinking: Words or Pictures?', in Roberto Casati and Graham White (eds), *Philosophy and the Cognitive Sciences* (Kirchberg am Wechsel, 1993), pp. 63–167; and *Wittgenstein: A Way of Seeing* (London: Routledge, 1995); Ernst H. Gombrich, *Art and Illusion: A Study in the Psychology of Pictorial Representation* (London: Phaidon Press, 1960); W. J. T. Mitchell, *Picture Theory* (Chicago: University of Chicago Press, 1994).

57 Genova, 'Wittgenstein on Thinking', p. 166.

58 Joseph Campbell, *The Flight of the Wild Gander: Explorations in the Mythological Dimension: Selective Essays, 1944–68* (Novato, CA: New World Library, 1969), p. 143.

Usually, however, symbols, like metaphors, involve some kind of visual imagery by implication. One of many examples is pressed by Dillistone. He regards the Christian sacraments as symbols which include visible expression.[59] They transcend merely descriptive language and its limits.

Many non-academics, as well as psychologists, talk of symbols as releasing energy necessary to bring about a task. They sometimes talk of what they call 'pathways of energy' over time, even across generations. Mere words, many say, fall short, when we try to describe or express deeply personal, emotional experiences. These writers stress that symbols express many different layers of meaning, beyond the literal. One example of this more popular approach is that of Peter Dean, *The Power of Symbols* (2010). He argues that 'hidden energies' lie embedded in symbols and images: 'They radiate a power which can be felt by everybody', and he aims 'to unearth the hidden energies within these symbols'.[60] Symbols, he argues, remain alive, however old they are. He cites Jung's claim that dreams are the most powerful example of symbols: 'They penetrate our unconscious'.[61] After his introduction on the perceived power of symbols, he discusses specific examples of symbols in prehistoric, Celtic, Egyptian, Graeco-Roman, Indian and Chinese cultures.

Carl Gustav Jung (1875–1961) was one of the three classic founders of psychoanalytical psychology, together with Sigmund Freud and Alfred Adler. He argued for the importance of the 'collective' unconscious, especially as a major source of collective symbols and archetypes. He regarded symbols as prior to the formulation of concepts. Like Paul Ricoeur, he thinks of symbols as 'double-meaning' expressions. Through symbol, Jung thinks that we can gain access to our 'shadow side', which we may otherwise have suppressed. In this respect, Jung, Tillich and Ricoeur regard symbols as integrating the wholeness of human life. Indeed Tillich regards fragmentation of the self as 'demonic'. Unlike Freud, Jung regards religion as grounded in the depths of the self. Jung expounded human 'life force', and beneath the personal unconscious, he argued, there lay a deeper and more important layer that contained the entire psychic heritage of humankind. Jung made much of this 'collective unconscious', which, he says, had been hinted at by his earlier childhood dreams and experiences. The symbols, he said, of psychotic patients had occurred in myths and fairy tales from all around the world. In his book of 1912,

---

[59] Frederick W. Dillistone, *Christianity and Symbolism* (London: Collins, 1955), pp. 169–284.

[60] Peter Dean, *The Power of Symbols* (William Pitt & Foursquare Books, 2010; e-book, 2013), p. 7.

[61] Dean, *The Power of Symbols*, p. 8.

Transformations and Symbols of the Libido, Jung replaced Freud's concept of libido and sexual drive or desire with a much broader concept of undifferentiated psychic energy, arguing that this energy could 'crystallize' into the universal symbols contained in dreams and myths. Much of his psychology, however, also elaborated theoretical hypotheses; for example, he saw the hero's slaying of the dragon as representing the struggle of the adolescent ego for deliverance from parental dominance. For Jung, the purpose of life was 'individuation', which involves pursuing one's own vision of the truth, and, in so doing, realizing one's fullest potential as a human being.

In 1913, Jung and Freud broke off their relationship. Jung saw the 'collective unconscious' as a collection of symbols that were shared by every human being but retained at the unconscious level. The symbols of the collective unconscious emerge through dreams across a number of generations. Jung also urged that symbols could remain living or could die. If, for example, the symbol of the cross dies for a Christian, it ceases to retain its transformative power. Other aspects of Jung's work included his classification of human beings into introverted and extraverted types, and the classification of people into thinkers, feelers, and those who stressed intuition or sensation.[62] This became the basis for the so-called Myers-Briggs tests of temperament.

Paul Tillich (1886–1965) was very much indebted to Jung. Tillich had been Professor at Frankfurt, but with the rise of Adolf Hitler in Germany, Reinhold Niebuhr invited him to the USA, where he spent 16 years as Professor at Union Theological Seminary, New York. He moved to Harvard from 1955 to 1962, but thereafter remained in Chicago until his death in 1965. His major work was the three-volume *Systematic Theology*, although he also wrote a number of more popular books, including *The Courage to Be*, *The Shaking of the Foundations*, *The Protestant Era*, *Dynamics of Faith* and *Theology of Culture*. These were all directed at different kinds of readers. In *The Theology of Culture* he wrote, 'Most of my writings . . . try to define the way in which Christianity is related to secular culture.'[63] His three-volume *Systematic Theology* was structured around a theology of correlation. Five 'questions' from a secular culture were correlated with five 'answers' from Christian faith. Thus in volume 1 questions about human reason were correlated with 'answers' about revelation. Throughout, answers relating to God can be formulated only as symbols that point to God, for God, Tillich insists, is *beyond* conceptual thought. He claims:

[62] Carl G. Jung, *Psychological Types* (London: Routledge, 1971).

[63] Paul Tillich, *Theology of Culture* (Oxford: OUP, 1964) p. vi.

'The method of correlation . . . makes an analysis of the human situation . . . and it demonstrates that the symbols used in the Christian message are the answers to these questions.'[64]

Tillich's most succinct summary of the function of symbols came in *Dynamics of Faith.* (1) Like signs, symbols, he said, point beyond themselves. (2) But differently from signs, the symbol 'participates in that to which it points'.[65] He compared the *participatory* role of the flag, which 'participates in the power and dignity of the nation'. (3) 'It opens up levels of reality which otherwise are closed to us'.[66] It reveals levels of reality that cannot be reached in any other way. Tillich compares 'pictures and poems' in this respect. (4) Symbol, he urges, unlocks dimensions and elements of the soul which correspond to the otherwise hidden dimensions and elements of reality. The symbol 'opens up hidden depths of our own being'.[67] (5) Symbols grow out of the collective unconscious; they cannot be chosen by an individual at will. (6) Thus they grow and die independently of some individual desire. The symbol of 'king', he suggested, depends on time and culture for its power. Religious symbols transcend the realm of finite reality. Symbols are distinctive in combining ultimacy and concreteness. He concludes, 'God is the basic symbol of faith.'[68]

Symbols, however, are innumerable. They are derived, Tillich argued, from our daily experience. Like David Strauss, he believed that symbols are combined as stories, and may often be derived from myth. But he also invited 'demythologization', or, better, what Childs and Caird call 'broken myth', that is, images that were once mythological, but now perform a different function.[69] Tillich insisted that a symbol is not identical with a myth. Symbols are unique. Tillich wrote, 'Symbols of faith cannot be replaced by other symbols.'[70]

In the case of religious symbols, these help us to distinguish between symbols of the Ultimate, and conceptual formulations of what is merely penultimate. A crude concept of God, for example, which one learned perhaps in Sunday School, or through bad church teaching, must not be

---

[64] Paul Tillich, *Systematic Theology* (3 vols, Chicago: University of Chicago Press, and London: Nisbet, 1953, 1957 and 1963), vol. 1, p. 70.

[65] Paul Tillich, *Dynamics of Faith* (London: Allen & Unwin, 1957), p. 42; cf. pp. 41–43.

[66] Tillich, *Dynamics of Faith*, p. 42.

[67] Tillich, *Dynamics of Faith*, p. 43.

[68] Tillich, *Dynamics of Faith*, p. 47.

[69] Tillich, *Dynamics of Faith*, p. 50; and B. S. Childs, *Myth and Reality in the Old Testament* (London: SCM, 1962), p. 42; George B. Caird, *The Language and Imagery of the Bible* (London: Duckworth, 1980), pp. 219–42.

[70] Tillich, *Dynamics of Faith*, p. 53.

confused with 'A representation of that which is unconditionally beyond the conceptual sphere'.[71] To worship a distorted picture of God is tantamount to idolatry, so ignorance must be countered by training.

In his *Systematic Theology* Tillich insisted that only the statement that 'God is being-itself is a non-symbolic statement'.[72] As in *Dynamics of Faith*, he also insisted that symbol is different from sign, especially in its capacity to participate in what it symbolizes. Like a sign, however, it can use finite experience to point to the Ultimate.[73] In *Systematic Theology*, volume 2, Tillich regards descriptions of Jesus as also symbolic. His 'Christological symbols' include: 'Son of David, Son of Man, Heavenly Man, Messiah, Son of God, Kyrios, Logos', and others.[74] In his third volume he especially explores the symbol 'the kingdom of God' as the answer to the question of the meaning of history.[75]

In his essays, 'The Visual Arts' and 'Contemporary Visual Arts', Tillich recalled how 'The visual arts became my hobby in the trenches of the First World War as an antidote to the enormous ugliness of life near the front'; they opened up 'the aesthetic realm'.[76]

Edwyn Bevan (1870–1943) was an older contemporary of Tillich. He taught at King's College, London, received doctorates of Letters and Law from Oxford and St Andrews, and wrote at least 30 books on comparative religion and related subjects. He was a Fellow of the British Academy, and his books ranged from *Stoics and Sceptics* (1913) and *Hellenism and Christianity* (1921) to *Symbolism and Belief* (1938) and *Holy Images* (1940). In *Symbolism and Belief* he considered especially the religious symbols of height, time, duration and light for God.[77]

Bevan shared some features in common with Tillich, including especially his 'feeling for the beautiful'. But unlike Tillich and Jung, he had emphatic suspicions about 'symbols without conceptual meaning'. Bevan rightly cited the work of William James, who observed on the basis of his experience in psychology that 'mad people' (nowadays the mentally ill or mentally challenged)

---

71 Paul Tillich, 'The Religious Symbol', in S. Hook (ed.), *Religious Experience and Truth* (Edinburgh: Oliver & Boyd, 1962), p. 303.

72 Tillich, *Systematic Theology*, vol. 1, p. 164.

73 Cf. Tillich, *Systematic Theology*, vol. 1, pp. 264–77.

74 Tillich, *Systematic Theology*, vol. 2, p. 125; cf. pp. 125–30.

75 Tillich, *Systematic Theology*, vol. 3, p. 381.

76 Paul Tillich, printed in Tillich, *On Art and Architecture* (New York: Crossroad, 1989), pp. 126 and 127; cf. pp. 45–80 and 126–38.

77 Edwyn Bevan, *Symbolism and Belief* (London: Allen & Unwin, 1938), pp. 28–81, 82–124, 125–50 and 206–30.

> may see the things around them charged with a meaning which is sinister and terrifying. They have no idea what they are afraid of, but as they look at a table or a door they are horribly afraid . . . The visible thing is characterised purely by the emotion it produces.[78]

This, Bevan asserts, is caused 'by the absence of any intellectual content', for example, in a state of ecstasy.[79] He admits that symbols point beyond themselves, but they are not necessarily non-conceptual. Symbols are always 'more than mere emotion'.[80]

Bevan anticipates parts of Tillich's work in comparing 'sexual feeling' and the importance of 'the whole', although he admits that we cannot know 'the whole' about God. On the other hand, to claim that the statement 'God is love' is merely symbolic is needless. Bevan writes from a deep knowledge of classical culture and of many cultures outside Europe.

Frederick W. Dillistone (1903–93) wrote several books on symbols including *Christianity and Symbolism* and *The Power of Symbols*. He was Professor at Wycliffe College, Toronto (1945–52), Dean of Liverpool Cathedral (1956–63) and Fellow of Oriel College, Oxford (1964–70). In *Christianity and Symbolism*, he explores symbols in the light of the Church, and enquires how the power of symbols can be restored for those who have come to find them meaningless. He was influenced by Suzanne Langer and Martin Foss, among others. The symbol, he argues, may 'touch off' a response, just as signs can, but symbols also 'go beyond signs by making possible the conception of an object'.[81] He especially explores the Christian sacraments as 'an outward and visible reality'.[82] Symbols, he argues, can be natural or can derive their power from custom and tradition.[83] He quotes C. Day Lewis as stating, 'Freshness, intensity, and evocative power', or emotions and even participation, are part of symbolism.[84] Like metaphors, symbols extend meanings, but they also maintain a constant interrelationship between various levels of experience, including the subconscious, archetypal and even the analogical.[85]

Like Bevan, Dillistone explored the symbolism of time. He noted that Plato and Aristotle regarded time as a 'defect of the universe'.[86] The Greeks

---

78 Bevan, *Symbolism and Belief*, p. 275; cf. pp. 275–96.
79 Bevan, *Symbolism and Belief*, p. 276.
80 Bevan, *Symbolism and Belief*, p. 287.
81 Dillistone, *Christianity and Symbolism*, p. 33.
82 Dillistone, *Christianity and Symbolism*, p. 15.
83 Dillistone, *Christianity and Symbolism*, p. 19.
84 Dillistone, *Christianity and Symbolism*, p. 21.
85 Dillistone, *Christianity and Symbolism*, p. 36.
86 Dillistone, *Christianity and Symbolism*, p. 81.

for the most part thought of 'God' as Eternal Timelessness. The Hebrews, however, he said, had 'a very different attitude'.[87] They stressed the quality of particular moments in time. One example would be the renewing of the covenant at particular times.[88] The observance of the Sabbath became a symbol that all time belonged to God. As Oscar Cullmann later observed, Christians regarded the main concept of time as the linear one of God's purposes of promise and fulfilment, while a subsidiary liturgical scheme survived which celebrated symbolic moments throughout the Christian year.[89] Dillistone, like Tillich, spoke of symbolism and wholeness, and also of symbolic action. He also discussed the symbolism of water in the context of Christian baptism. More controversial, however, was his connection of the water of baptism with his statement, 'There is ample evidence from the psycho-analytical investigation to show that water is the commonest archetypal image of the unconscious.'[90] His comments about water as having the 'open and obvious property of cleansing and purifying' must be modified in the light of Rudolf Schnackenburg's careful exposition of baptism in the thought of Paul.[91] Nor will everyone be content today with his distinctions between the Greek cultural tradition, the Roman cultural tradition, the Hebraic cultural tradition and the Jerusalemite cultural tradition; but all will endorse his emphasis on the Eucharist or Holy Communion as a covenantal symbolic visible act in memory of Jesus.[92] He argued that such a visible symbol cannot become outmoded as long as it is seen as a symbol of life-through-death.

Dillistone entitled his second major book on symbols *The Power of Symbols*, which was written much later in life.[93] His central thesis was 'the enormous importance of symbols'.[94] Again he acknowledged debts to Paul Tillich and Suzanne Langer, and to many others, including especially Ernst Cassirer, *The Philosophy of Symbolic Forms*. He also mentioned Mircea Eliade, Edmund Leach, Philip Wheelwright, and Erwin Goodenough, *Jewish Symbols in the Greco-Roman Period*.[95] He endorsed Goodenough's

---

[87] Dillistone, *Christianity and Symbolism*, p. 83.

[88] Dillistone, *Christianity and Symbolism*, p. 85.

[89] Dillistone, *Christianity and Symbolism*, pp. 95–105.

[90] Dillistone, *Christianity and Symbolism*, p. 183.

[91] Dillistone, *Christianity and Symbolism*, p. 193; and Rudolf Schnackenburg, *Baptism in the Thought of St Paul* (Oxford: Blackwell, 1964), throughout.

[92] Dillistone, *Christianity and Symbolism*, pp. 264–84.

[93] Frederick W. Dillistone, *The Power of Symbols* (London: SCM, 1986).

[94] Dillistone, *The Power of Symbols*, p. 1.

[95] Erwin Goodenough, *Jewish Symbols in the Greco-Roman Period*, vol. 4 (New York: Pantheon Press, 1953).

distinction between the denotative or literal and the connotative or associative. (We shall look later at Janet Martin Soskice on the denotation of referential metaphors, in Chapter 4.) He concluded, 'We find widespread agreement that the symbol is a powerful instrument to extend our vision, to stimulate our imagination and to deepen our understanding.'[96] As before, he acknowledged his dependence on Bevan, whose work he described as 'balanced and suggestive'.[97] He noted that Coleridge anticipated Tillich in stating that a symbol actually partakes (or *participates*) in the reality which it renders intelligible. Symbols, he argued, are especially visible, audible and often tangible. He expounded symbol as visual and dramatic, and as usually entailing self-transcendence. Following these more general comments, he examines such symbolic concepts as the body, new birth, food, land, clothes, the Jewish Passover and the Christian Eucharist, all of which open up 'vistas of new possibilities within another order of existence'.[98]

In the second part of his book Dillistone considered the contributions to symbolism of several philosophers and theologians. David Tracy, in *The Analogical Imagination*, argues that symbolism can extend the scope of literal speech. He considered the work of Ernst Cassirer, in which it was argued that in contrast to the dilemmas of the human predicament, symbols help humankind to live 'so to speak in a new dimension of reality'.[99] Dillistone concluded, 'Symbolic forms provide security and stability; some point forward to new discoveries and free enterprise.'[100] He again discussed Paul Tillich, whom we examined above. Finally he considered Paul Ricoeur, commenting, 'The visual can often be of immense help in the task of interpretation, and it is even open to question whether words were in fact the earliest means of symbolic communication.'[101] Under this heading he considered transcendence and self-transcendence with particular reference to Karl Jaspers. In a later section he examined symbolism in the Bible, which constitutes Part 2 of this book.

Paul Ricoeur (1913–2005), a French philosopher and specialist in hermeneutics and language, represented a more judicious approach than many others. He recognized the *creativity* of symbols and metaphors,

---

[96] Dillistone, *The Power of Symbols*, p. 13.

[97] Dillistone, *The Power of Symbols*, p. 23.

[98] Dillistone, *The Power of Symbols*, p. 35; cf. pp. 39–75.

[99] Dillistone, *The Power of Symbols*, p. 129; and Ernst Cassirer, *An Essay on Man* (New Haven: Yale University Press, 1944), p. 24.

[100] Dillistone, *The Power of Symbols*, p. 121.

[101] Dillistone, *The Power of Symbols*, p. 129.

which constituted part of their power. He also considered symbol and metaphor explicitly in relation to each other. Ricoeur recognized 'double meaning' and multi-level effects of symbols, and like Jung and Tillich took account of the unconscious. Nevertheless he approached the subject with a broader agenda and multi-disciplinary tools, and integrated this with a more informed and sophisticated approach to language and metaphor. In Chapter 3, we consider Ricoeur on symbol and especially metaphor.

Ricoeur studied philosophy at the Sorbonne in Paris in 1934, and was in early days influenced by the Catholic existentialist philosopher Gabrielle Marcel (1889–1973). In 1939 his academic career was interrupted by the Second World War, during which, as a prisoner of war, he studied German philosophy in Germany, especially that of Karl Jaspers, Edmund Husserl and Martin Heidegger. After the war he taught at the University of Strasbourg (1948–54), the only French university with a Protestant Faculty of Theology. Over the years he produced an impressive stream of published works, of which the most important magisterial volumes are *Time and Narrative* and *Oneself as Another*, and, almost as important, but still seminal, *Freud and Philosophy*.[102]

In 1956 Ricoeur produced *The Symbolism of Evil*.[103] He expressed one of his major convictions about the nature of symbol in the aphorism which also occurs in his later writings: 'Symbols give rise to thought'.[104] He urged that symbols have three dimensions: first, the cosmic, that relates to the world; second, the psychical that relates to dreams and imagination; and third, the poetic, which relates to modes of expression. Symbols have both a literal sense and also point beyond themselves. Hence he uses such biblical examples as a **stain** or **burden** as symbols of evil and guilt. *Stain* and *burden* are at first metaphors drawn from everyday life, but they also become symbols when they point beyond themselves to denote theological and moral realities. A primary symbol of evil is **defilement**, which is experienced subjectively as terror. He also considers the symbol of **sin**, which is an act and disposition against God. The symbol '**the wrath of God**' suggests that sin constitutes a broken relationship with God, in contrast to sin as simply missing a target. Divine *wrath* is not a permanent characteristic of God, but is called forth when humankind thinks and acts in ways contrary to God's will. He associated these two aspects with

[102] Paul Ricoeur, *Time and Narrative* (Eng., 3 vols, Chicago and London: University of Chicago Press, 1984–88; *Oneself as Another* (Chicago: University of Chicago Press, 1992); and *Freud and Philosophy: An Essay on Interpretation* (Eng., New Haven: Yale University Press, 1970).

[103] Paul Ricoeur, *The Symbolism of Evil* (Eng., Boston: Beacon Press, 1967 and 1969).

[104] Ricoeur, *Freud and Philosophy*, p. 543.

respectively the covenant (on relations with God) and the law and commandment. Ricoeur rightly stressed the communal aspect of all these terms, and their correlation with such positive symbols as redemption or 'buying back'. Symbols, for Ricoeur, always constitute a surplus of meaning beyond the literal meaning. In the second part of his book, he considered the relation between symbol and myth, which he regarded as a species of symbol.

Ricoeur developed his view of symbolism further in his book *Freud and Philosophy*. He was fully aware of the contrast between reductive explanations in language and constructive retrievals of the original meaning of symbol. Freud had regularly focused on dreams, which he called 'models of disguised, substitutive, and fictive expressions of human wishing or desire'.[105] From Freud, Ricoeur drew his notion of dreams and symbols as **double-meaning** expressions, which require an *interpretation*. This led him to see the crucial importance of hermeneutics. Freud had used the term 'overdetermination' to denote the inter-mixture or overlapping of multi-significations, which exhibit 'richness' or 'plurivocal' language.[106] Dreams, as they are accounted (the dream account or dream content), are not exactly the same as the dream-as-dreamt ('the dream thoughts'). Dreams often recount a 'condensation' of the dream itself, which is itself 'brief, meagre, and laconic', and often involves 'displacement', in which images become transformed or 'scrambled'.[107] Hence Ricoeur asserted, 'To interpret is to understand a double meaning.'[108]

In this light Ricoeur expressed one of his major theses about interpretation:

> Hermeneutics seems to me to be annotated by this double motivation: willingness to suspect, willingness to listen; vow of rigour, vow of obedience. In our time we have not finished doing away with idols, and have barely begun to listen to symbols.[109]

In other words, symbols are often our path to truth; but this is not invariably the case. Yet the sheer power of symbols is never doubted. For good or ill they are transformative, and convey a surplus of meaning beyond the literal. Symbols hide and reveal; they disguise and show; they conceal and disclose.

---

[105] Ricoeur, *Freud and Philosophy*, p. 5.
[106] Ricoeur, *Freud and Philosophy*, p. 19.
[107] Ricoeur, *Freud and Philosophy*, p. 93.
[108] Ricoeur, *Freud and Philosophy*, p. 8.
[109] Ricoeur, *Freud and Philosophy*, p. 27 (italics part his, part mine).

Metaphors also extend meaning beyond the literal and are also transformative. Ricoeur built his developed work on metaphor on the prior work of Monroe Beardsley (1915–85), Philip Wheelwright (1901–70) and Max Black (1909–88).[110] We shall defer this subject, however, until we discuss metaphor in a subsequent chapter.

In 1970 Thomas Fawcett published *The Symbolic Language of Religion.* He lectured at the University of Chester in the days when it was still a College of Education. He took up Daniélou's definition of symbol as affording us access through the visible world into a higher plane of being.[111] He also insisted on its 'multiplicity of signification', and argued that 'The maintenance of a symbol over a long period of time is some indication of the satisfactory nature of the symbol.'[112] Yet in his last chapter he recognized the decline of symbols, which he associated with a mythological world-view. He argued that humankind 'has lost something which it had once possessed'.[113] Meanwhile we question his over-ready association of symbol with myth. Our discussion of metaphor will bring out the creative power of metaphors, rather than literal writing, more than ever.

---

[110] Paul Ricoeur, *Interpretation of Meaning: Discourse and the Surplus of Meaning* (Fort Worth: Texas Christian University Press, 1976), p. 49.

[111] Thomas Fawcett, *The Symbolic Language of Religion* (London: SCM, 1970), p. 30.

[112] Fawcett, *The Symbolic Language of Religion*, p. 35.

[113] Fawcett, *The Symbolic Language of Religion*, p. 122.

2

The seduction of pictures and images under certain conditions

Negative reactions to 'the picture theory of language'

In spite of saying many positive things about pictures and visual imagery, Wittgenstein remained adamant that by cumulative argument the meaning of a picture is not self-evident; it can be *variously understood* to mean different things. Admittedly in Chapter 1, however, we drew on Wittgenstein's account of the *plausibility* of a picture theory of language. He had counted as pictures, Anthony Kenny writes,

> not only paintings, drawings, photographs, and other obviously pictorial representations in two dimensions, but also maps, sculptures, three-dimensional models, even such things as musical scores and gramophone records. His theory is perhaps best regarded as a theory of representation in general.[1]

One classic example of this approach was when, as we noted, during the period of the *Tractatus,* he realized that a complex legal dispute about a traffic accident could be clearly portrayed by a series of toy cars, model lorries (or trucks) and so on. By this means Wittgenstein believed that language depicted facts. He wrote, 'There must be something identical in a picture and what it depicts, to enable the one to be a picture of the other at all'.[2] Thus, he said, 'A picture can depict any reality whose form it has.'[3]

On the other hand, very soon Wittgenstein began to entertain doubts about the *comprehensiveness* of this theory of meaning. One obvious starting point is his belief that ostensive definition (i.e. defining things by pointing to them) is ambiguous and achieves relatively little. An ostensive definition is an explanation of the meaning of a word in such statements as 'This is an elephant', by demonstration and gestures such as pointing.

---

1 Anthony Kenny, *Wittgenstein* (London: Penguin, 1973), p. 54.

2 Ludwig Wittgenstein, *Tractatus Logico-Philosophicus* (Eng. and Ger., London: Routledge & Kegan Paul, 1922 and 1961), 2.161.

3 Wittgenstein, *Tractatus*, 2.171.

Wittgenstein often associated this view with Augustine, although it also has a place in John Locke and Bertrand Russell. Ostensive definition allows us to project names on to objects. But Wittgenstein soon became aware of a problem: this theory accounts for *only certain types* of words. Early in the *Investigations*, he stated that this approach may be appropriate, 'but only for this narrowly circumscribed region, not for the whole of what you are claiming to describe', and soon introduced the term 'language-game' to denote 'language and the actions into which it is woven'.[4] Language functions in as varied a set of ways as the varied functions of different tools in a toolbox, or levers and handles in a locomotive cabin.[5] Even in his interim *Blue Book*, he declared, 'Our craving for generality has another main source: our preoccupation with the method of science . . . This leads the philosopher into complete darkness.'[6]

A little later Wittgenstein compared the difficulty of applying ostensive definition to such utterances as 'giving orders and obeying them; describing the appearance of an object or giving its measurements; constructing an object from a description; speculating about any event'; or more specifically using words other than nouns, such as 'Away! Help! or No!'[7] He concluded, 'An ostensive definition can be variously interpreted in *every* case.'[8] This is exactly what he says about pictures. How we interpret a picture depends on a multiplicity of circumstances. For example, he says, 'Point to a piece of paper. – And now point to its shape – now to its colour – now to its number . . . How did you do it?'[9] This method is like pointing to a king on a chessboard, and saying, 'This is called a king', when Wittgenstein wants to define it in terms of its *use* in the rules of the game.[10] Ostensive definition is static and abstract, as when 'Language goes on holiday'.[11] It seeks to explain meaning 'outside a particular language-game'.[12]

In Part 2 of the *Investigations*, Wittgenstein expounded a subtle distinction between interpreting pictures and seeing them in various ways.

---

4 Ludwig Wittgenstein, *Philosophical Investigations* (Eng. and Ger., Oxford: Blackwell, 1958), sects 3 and 7.

5 Wittgenstein, *Philosophical Investigations*, sects 11 and 12.

6 Ludwig Wittgenstein, *The Blue and Brown Books: Preliminary Studies for the Philosophical Investigations* (Oxford: Blackwell, 2nd edn, 1969), p. 18.

7 Wittgenstein, *Philosophical Investigations*, sects 23 and 27.

8 Wittgenstein, *Philosophical Investigations*, sect 28.

9 Wittgenstein, *Philosophical Investigations*, sect. 33.

10 Wittgenstein, *Philosophical investigations*, sect. 35.

11 Wittgenstein, *Philosophical Investigations*, sect. 38.

12 Wittgenstein, *Philosophical Investigations*, sect. 47.

He drew on the famous drawing of a 'duck-rabbit' by Joseph Jastrow (1863–1944), a Polish-American psychologist, who worked on perception and optical illusion. In this drawing, the head in the picture can be seen either as the head of a rabbit looking upwards, or as the head of a duck looking to the left. In Wittgenstein's view 'I must distinguish between the "continuous seeing" of an aspect and the "dawning" of an aspect'.[13] In 'continuous seeing', someone might always see the picture as the head of a rabbit (or, in other circumstances, as a duck). People usually see the object *as* a duck or *as* a rabbit.

Nevertheless Wittgenstein did not identify *seeing as* with *interpreting* in every respect. Indeed I have elsewhere used *seeing as* in distinctive terms in the context of justification by grace through faith. For God to see humankind in one instance as sinning, and at another time as righteous, cannot constitute a contradiction, because these examples of 'seeing as' are *not statements* but *verdicts, declared in different contexts.* Context is also crucial for Wittgenstein. In the course of a detailed five-page discussion of aspect-perception, Hans-Johann Glock comments:

> The concept of seeing an aspect . . . is a state . . . Interpretation is an action . . . There is no possibility of being mistaken about seeing an aspect; aspect-seeing is a state; in particular it has genuine duration . . . Noticing an aspect is placing what we perceive in another context.[14]

But he admits that the contrast may overlap, and is blurred. We do not *describe* our perception of different aspects; we simply *express* them as 'avowals'. 'Aspect-dawning' or 'change of aspect' (Ger., *Aufleuchten eines Aspekts* or *Aspektwechsel*) was crucially important for Wittgenstein. Glock declares, 'Between 1947 and 1949 it dominates his work, partly under the influence of Köhler's Gestalt psychology.'[15] Wolfgang Köhler (1887–1967) was a German psychologist who (with others) founded the *Gestalt* school of psychology, which emphasized wholeness of vision, in contrast to an analysis of its parts.

Wittgenstein begins section 2, xi, of the *Investigations* by introducing the hollow cube framed by wires, which was first introduced by Louis

---

[13] Wittgenstein, *Philosophical Investigations*, Pt 2, xi, p. 194.

[14] Hans-Johann Glock, 'Aspect-Perception', in *A Wittgenstein Dictionary* (Oxford: Blackwell, 1996), pp. 38 and 39.

[15] Glock, 'Aspect-Perception', p. 37; cf. pp. 36–40; and Wittgenstein, *Philosophical Investigations*, Pt 2, xi, pp. 193–229; Ludwig Wittgenstein, *Remarks on the Philosophy of Psychology* (2 vols, Oxford: Blackwell, 1980), throughout; and *Last Writings on the Philosophy of Psychology* (2 vols, Oxford: Blackwell, vol. 1, 1982), throughout; (and vol. 2, 1992), pp. 12–17.

Albert Necker in 1832 to illustrate optical illusion. The cube may be seen as one in which the lower left or upper right appears as its front side. This 'Necker cube' is regularly used to illustrate optics. Wittgenstein observed: 'We see the illustration now as one thing now as another.'[16] Jastrow's duck-rabbit comes next. To see this differently has nothing to do with the picture, but depends on the context and training with which it is viewed: perhaps 'point of view'.[17] Third, he considered puzzle-pictures, from meaningful aspects and so on, but are these marginal cases of pictures? He states that an inner picture can be misleading. Any 'explanation' is not a report: 'It is forced from us.'[18] He added, 'The circumstances decide whether, and what, more detailed specifications are necessary.'[19] Next, he considered representations of a triangle, styles of paintings, and 'three-dimensional seeing'.[20] Then he returned again to 'seeing faces', with their role in life. What forces 'seeing' from us is our perception of the system to which it belongs.[21]

Clearly we could follow more of Wittgenstein's many examples. But it has become high time to see how these observations apply especially to Christian thought. The tendency to see meaning in mental pictures became prominent among many mediaeval mystics and many modern Charismatics. The twelfth-century mystic Hildegard of Bingen (1098–1179) experienced many visions which conveyed 'pictures', for example of light as representing Christ, fire and flashes as representing the Holy Spirit, red, burning fire, and so on.[22] Catherine of Siena (1347–80) provides more striking examples. Richard Foster and James Smith comment that Catherine's work 'involved the use of metaphor . . . Ladders, castles and dark nights – all had been employed as ways of describing the indescribable . . . Catherine adopts the metaphor of a bridge . . . as the way to heaven'.[23] The bridge has three steps or stairs, which represent aspects of Christ's work.[24] Julian of Norwich (1342–1416) includes 16 *Revelations of*

[16] Wittgenstein, *Philosophical Investigations*, 2, xi, p. 193.

[17] Wittgenstein, *Philosophical Investigations*, 2, xi, p. 195.

[18] Wittgenstein, *Philosophical Investigations*, 2, xi, p. 197.

[19] Wittgenstein, *Philosophical Investigations*, 2, xi, p. 199.

[20] Wittgenstein, *Philosophical Investigations*, 2, xi, p. 202.

[21] Wittgenstein, *Philosophical Investigations*, 2, xi, p. 208.

[22] Hildegard of Bingen, *Scivias;* short for *Scito vias Domini* (Eng., Abbey of Regina Laudus, 1990), 2.2 and 3.8.

[23] Richard J. Foster and James B. Smith (eds), *Devotional Classics: Selected Readings* (San Francisco: Harper, rev. edn, 1990), p. 264; cf. pp. 264–70.

[24] Catherine of Siena, *The Dialogue of Catherine of Siena* (Eng., London: Kegan Paul, Trench, Trübner, 1907), sect. 11.

Divine Love, or *Showings*, which often include pictorial representations, and Margery Kempe (*c.* 1373–1458) of King's Lynn, Norfolk, is especially noted for the experience of mystical visions in visual form.[25] Some of Margery Kempe's pictures become speculative, but Julian and Hildegard are sufficiently embedded in biblical and church tradition to offer reasonably controlled expositions of pictures. (These examples are discussed at greater length in Chapter 10.) A greater problem is raised by some current or local Charismatic practices, especially when 'pictures' concern not the great events of redemption, but personal guidance for churches or individuals (also discussed in Chapter 10). Here Wittgenstein's warnings about the need for context or tradition and training for 'seeing' pictures in accordance with truth come into their own. Yet even Wittgenstein, as Kenny, Kristóf Nyíri and Glock have indicated, is not entirely consistent or lacking ambiguity. Representation is one thing; representation in accordance with *truth* takes us one step further.

If any reply is needed might we not say that Wittgenstein's examples are often such borderline cases as puzzle-pictures, optical illusions and aspect-perceptions? This is relevant, but does not adequately answer his concerns about ostensive definitions or other types of pictures. On Wittgenstein's picture of 'an old man walking up a steep hill, leaning on a stick', he asked: 'Might it not have looked just the same if he had been sliding downhill in that position?'[26] This is no puzzle-picture or optical illusion. He further asked:

> Can what we grasp *in a flash* accord with the use, fit, or fail to fit, it? And how can what is present to us in an instant, i.e. what comes before our mind instantanteously, match a prolonged or habitual use?[27]

The notion of seeing a picture '*in a flash*' tends to rip the picture out of any prior training or context. Indeed time constitutes one of the major elements that we need to consider when we consider the truth or possible seduction of pictures.

Most of Wittgenstein's detailed comments about aspect-perception come from his *Philosophy of Psychology*, which we have noted, but not expounded. However, the most significant observations from this source were reprinted as *Philosophical Investigations*, Part 2, from which we have

---

[25] Julian of Norwich, *Revelations of Divine Love* (London: Penguin, 1998), pp. 50–1; and Lynn Staley (ed.), *The Book of Margery Kempe* (Kalamazoo, MI: Mediaeval Institute Publications, 1996), Bk 1.

[26] Wittgenstein, *Philosophical Investigations*, sect. 139 (b).

[27] Wittgenstein, *Philosophical Investigations*, sect. 139 (Wittgenstein's italics).

gathered plentiful comments.[28] Here he speaks of 'Seeing a geometrical drawing as a glass cube or as an inverted open box . . . or, again, seeing a triangle . . . as a mountain, as a wedge, as an arrow or pointer, as an overturned object . . .'[29] This concerns not only seeing three-dimensional objects, but contexts which invite comparisons. Wittgenstein was explicit in observing visual comparisons, as Severin Schroeder notes.[30] Indeed 'seeing' that involves perceiving likeness is what Schroeder calls a second meaning of 'seeing'. It is impossible to see a shape as a mountain, or as a face of this or that person, unless one can bring to the issue some prior experience of life. Schroeder insists, 'Wittgenstein appears to shift between two different accounts of aspect perception.'[31] Thus to see a person, object or visual representation, in some genuinely meaningful way for life, surely involves more than some abstracted instantaneous picture.

The debate about aspects or 'points of view' in hermeneutics

(1) An earlier debate about 'points of view' occurred not in philosophy but in hermeneutics. **Johann Martin Chladenius** (1710–59) wrote *Introduction to the Correct Interpretation of Reasonable Discourses and Writings* (1742) in which he developed this notion of 'point of view' (Ger., *Sehe-Punkte*). He suggested that a comprehensive account of all details relating to the background, context, and the writer's intention should be known before a text or letter could be fully understood.[32] Thus far he gave a historical, objective, account of interpretation, in accord with Enlightenment expectations. He insisted that to understand a writing and to understand a writer are identical.[33] If, after reading a discourse, we ask for an interpreter, this shows that we have not yet fully understood the writing.

In his Chapter 6, Chladenius points out that 'Different people perceive what happens in the world differently'.[34] The cause of the difference is that

---

[28] Most come from Wittgenstein, *Philosophy of Psychology – A Fragment*, published in the fourth edition of *Philosophical Investigations* (Oxford: Blackwell, 2009), sects 111–366.

[29] Wittgenstein, *Philosophy of Psychology – A Fragment*, sect. 116, p. 193, and sect. 162, p. 200.

[30] Wittgenstein, *Remarks on the Philosophy of Psychology* (2 vols., Oxford: Blackwell, 1980), sect. 317; and Severin Schroeder, 'A Tale of Two Problems: Wittgenstein's Discussion of Aspect Perception', in J. Cottingham and P. M. S. Hacker (eds), *Mind, Method, and Morality: Essays in Honour of Anthony Kenny* (Oxford: OUP, 2010), pp. 352–71.

[31] Schroeder, 'A Tale of Two Problems', p. 357.

[32] Johann Martin Chladenius, *Introduction to the Correct Interpretation of Reasonable Discourses and Writings* (Eng., Düsseldorf: Stern-Verlag, 1985), p. 176.

[33] Chladenius, *Correct Interpretation*, ch. 4, p. 159.

[34] Chladenius, *Correct Interpretation*, ch. 6, p. 308.

of different viewpoints. Potentially this may appear to yield contradictions. But this would be to reach 'premature conclusions'.[35] Nietzsche, of course, did draw such conclusions. But, Chladenius argued, the event or writing cannot be contradictory. The interpreter must persevere in testing and examining viewpoints until he has made sufficient comparisons either to do justice to more than one interpretation, or to exclude another as false or mistaken.[36] He believed in the possibility of universal or objective interpretation, in spite of limited points of view by individuals. The principle remains, however, that extrinsic thinking and other viewpoints must be applied to a single point of view. In the terms of our debate, one isolated glance on the part of a lone individual cannot be enough to reach genuine or complete understanding of a picture. What we see from a limited, finite, point of view must be compared with what is known from other sources.

(2) Even **Friedrich Schleiermacher** (1768–1834), the next major successor in hermeneutics, admitted the need for preliminary understanding (often called 'pre-understanding', Ger., *Vorverständnis*), but allowed for this to give way for a more complete understanding in careful dialogue with the text to be understood. He wrote, 'The understanding of a given statement [*Rede*] is always based on something prior, of two sorts – a preliminary knowledge of human beings, a preliminary knowledge of the subject matter.'[37] Indeed, he also wrote, 'In interpretation it is essential that one be able to step out of one's own frame of mind into that of another.'[38] Like Chladenius, he aimed at 'the coinherence of the universal and the particular in every word-meaning which this view presupposes can be called the individuality of meaning'.[39] Complete understanding does not come in a flash: 'Complete knowledge always involves an apparent circle, that each part can be understood only out of the whole to which it belongs, and vice versa.'[40] A 'divinatory' understanding of any object or text or picture must be complemented by a comparative method, which involves study, thinking and patience.[41] In the case of visual representation, this implies that an initial glimpse will not be adequate for full understanding of what is portrayed.

[35] Chladenius, *Correct Interpretation*, ch. 6, p. 314.
[36] Chladenius, *Correct Interpretation*, ch. 6, pp. 324–31.
[37] Friedrich Schleiermacher, *Hermeneutics: The Handwritten Manuscripts* (Eng., Missoula: Scholars Press, 1977), p. 59.
[38] Schleiermacher, *Hermeneutics*, p. 42.
[39] Schleiermacher, *Hermeneutics*, p. 32.
[40] Schleiermacher, *Hermeneutics*, p. 123.
[41] Schleiermacher, *Hermeneutics*, p. 150.

(3) **Friedrich Nietzsche** (1844–1900) and **Wilhelm Dilthey** (1833–1911) may be said to come next in a chronology of hermeneutical theorists, but move in polar opposite directions in discussing points of view. Nietzsche despairs of any coherent knowledge or understanding, while Dilthey aims in principle at a more objective 'science' of hermeneutics, for the *Geisteswissenschaften* or 'human sciences', in contrast to the natural sciences. Nietzsche took very seriously the finite historically conditioned situation of each individual, who could never attain an overview of the whole. In this respect he replicated Søren Kierkegaard's existentialist perspective. There appeared to Nietzsche to be no way of overcoming this radical limitation. Yet he realized that many individuals deeply claim to possess a wider knowledge of truth. Hence he wrote, 'Truth is that kind of error without which a certain species of human being cannot live.'[42] In the same aphorism he wrote, 'All that exists consists of interpretations.' Truth, he said, consists of illusions which we have forgotten are illusions. Belief in God, he said, is a fiction that enables us to transcend a point of view. Hence he wrote, 'We shall never be rid of God so long as we still believe in grammar.'[43] If God is dead, as Nietzsche believed, everything is permitted, and 'objective' truth lies beyond us. What began as perspectivalism ended as radical scepticism. To some extent it can be argued that Martin Heidegger and some or perhaps many sociologists retain a flavour of it.

On the other hand Wilhelm Dilthey did not follow this path. He was Professor at Basel and Berlin, and an ardent admirer of Schleiermacher. In hermeneutics he formed a link between Schleiermacher and Heidegger and Gadamer, except that Gadamer criticized him for offering too 'scientific' or 'objective' an account of hermeneutics. First, he developed the theme of Chladenius and Hegel on reason, while recognizing, with Heidegger, that all knowledge and understanding is *historically conditioned.* Second, with Herder and Schleiermacher, he sought to replace Hegel's emphasis on reason by an emphasis on *life* (*Leben*) or 'lived experiences'. He commented on Descartes, Locke, Hume and Kant, 'In the veins of the knowing subject *no real blood flows*.'[44] Third, he looked for some quasi-system which would do justice to the '*connectedness*' (Ger., *Zusammenhang*) behind various experiences in life. The aim is for the interpreter to 're-live' (Ger., *nacherleben*) the experience of the other by stepping out of his or her shoes to exercise sympathy or transposition

[42] Friedrich Nietzsche, *Complete Works* (18 vols, London: Allen & Unwin, 1909 to 1913), vol. 15: *The Will to Power*, vol. 2, aphorism 481.

[43] Nietzsche, *Complete Works*, vol. 12: *The Twilight of the Gods*, p. 22, aphorism 5.

[44] Wilhelm Dilthey, *Gesammelte Schriften*, vol. 5 (Leipzig: Teuber, 1927), p. 4 (his italics).

(*Hineinversetzen*) with the other.[45] Elsewhere he concluded, 'Understanding [*Verstehen*] is a rediscovery of the "I" in the "You".'[46]

In the end, the significance of Dilthey's work for visual imagery and pictures is that he dismissed sheer introspection as a reliable route to understanding, and replaced this by 'connectedness' or *inter-subjective judgement* and agreement as the way forward. Only by means of wider cross-communication than the isolated self could *any understanding of 'pictures'* be reached.

(4) In terms of chronology, the next major hermeneutical theorist was **Martin Heidegger** (1889–1976). He also dominated German philosophy from around 1923 to the late 1960s. His major work was *Being and Time* (Ger., 1927; Eng., 1962). He shared seminars on hermeneutics and philosophy with Bultmann, Gadamer and Jonas. It is debated whether his work underwent a 'turn' in the 1930s, but his subsequent writings reflected a change of mood such as his *Introduction to Metaphysics* (1959). Although he rejected the specific term, he is generally thought of as the main philosopher of existentialism, perhaps together with Kierkegaard and Sartre. All understanding, he argued, takes place within the framework of time.

There is little doubt that Heidegger subordinated the visual to the written. Hans Jonas wrote, 'The suppressed side of "hearing" gets a hearing after the long ascendancy of "seeing" and the spell of objectification which it cast upon thought.'[47] Martin Jay adds, 'His hostility to the heliocentric rationalism of Platonism was no less explicit, as was his rejection of the dualism of subject and object entailed by the privileging of vision.'[48] This especially shows itself in Heidegger's major distinction between 'presence-at-hand' (*Vorhandenheit*) and 'readiness to hand' (*Zuhandenheit*).[49] The latter can be used without visualizing it first. To conceive of objects as merely present at hand is a secondary or *derived* mode of conceptualizing.[50] The old-fashioned 'pseudo-scientific' way of seeing the world as an objective visual entity has gone out of fashion since W. Heisenberg, Max Born and Paul Dirac. Understanding, in Heidegger, is existential, and is an *a priori*, prior to cognition. Hence 'Dasein' (the thinking, feeling,

45 Wilhelm Dilthey, *Dilthey: Selected Writings* (Cambridge: CUP, 1976), pp. 226–7.

46 Dilthey, *Selected Writings*, p. 298.

47 Hans Jonas, *The Phenomenon of Life: Toward a Philosophical Biology* (Chicago: Northwestern University Press, 1982, reprinted 2001) p. 240.

48 Jay, *Downcast Eyes*, p. 270.

49 Martin Heidegger, *Being and Time* (Eng., Oxford: Blackwell, 1962), p. 67.

50 Anthony C. Thiselton, *The Two Horizons: New Testament Hermeneutics and Philosophical Description* (Grand Rapids: Eerdmans, 1980) p. 155, and pp. 151–8.

situated-in-history subject) has possibilities before it knows them. Thus, for Heidegger, it has 'potentiality-for-Being' (Ger., *Seinkönnen*).[51] Further, he said:

> Interpretation is grounded in something we have in advance – in a fore-having [*Vorhabe*] . . . something we see in advance – a foresight [*Vorsicht*] . . . It is grounded in something we grasp in advance – in a fore conception [*Vorgriff*] . . . and interpretation is never a presuppositionless apprehending of something presented to us.[52]

This takes us back to the hermeneutical circle of F. Ast and Schleiermacher. Heidegger wrote:

> If we see this circle as a vicious one and look out for ways of avoiding it . . . Then the act of understanding has been misunderstood from the ground up . . . The 'circle' in understanding belongs to the very structure of meaning.[53]

On this basis the notion of innocently beholding and understanding a picture in one moment becomes subordinated to a more complicated process of thinking and understanding.

Heidegger's later thought emerged after his so-called 'turn' (*Kehre*), in which he spoke increasingly of disclosure through poetry and art. He wrote concerning time, that it 'had ceased to be anything other than velocity, instantaneousness, and simultaneity'.[54] By contrast we must wait 'if necessary for a whole lifetime' for a revelation of Being.[55] This is very different from glancing at a picture or visual image.

(5) We may mention briefly the contribution of **Rudolf Bultmann** (1884–1976) to hermeneutics, although his emphasis on hearing rather than seeing remains less explicit than in Heidegger and Gadamer. This appears, for example, in his essay 'Adam, Where Art Thou?'[56] Here he sets in contrast the Greek notion of 'thoughtful contemplation' without regard to time with the Hebrew concept of living and eventful encounter with God in an event.[57] Nevertheless Bultmann is less negative towards visual

[51] Heidegger, *Being and Time*, p. 183.
[52] Heidegger, *Being and Time*, pp. 191–2 (Ger. p. 150).
[53] Heidegger, *Being and Time*, pp. 194–5 (his italics).
[54] Martin Heidegger, *Introduction to Metaphysics* (Eng., New Haven: Yale University Press, 1959), p. 38.
[55] Martin Heidegger, *On the Way to Language* (Eng., New York: Harper & Row, 1971), p. 108.
[56] Rudolf Bultmann, 'Adam, Where Art Thou?', in Bultmann, *Essays Philosophical and Theological* (Eng., London: SCM, 1955), pp. 119–32.
[57] Bultmann, *Essays*, pp. 124–6.

representation and art than some, as we can see from his essay 'Jewish Old Testament Tradition'.[58] However, he attacks the notion of 'objectification' throughout his work on 'myth' and elsewhere.[59] God, he said, is not merely a given object, but can be known in existential encounter. Moreover, the notion of word as 'event' characterized his writings, and permeated the thought of his pupils such as Ernst Fuchs, who spoke of hearing the word of God as a 'language-event' (*Sprachereignis*).[60] Certainly he emphasizes address and hearing in the Hebrew, not Greek, tradition. Humankind must listen in silence for the call of Being or God.[61]

(6) The next influential writer on hermeneutics was **Hans-Georg Gadamer** (1900–2002), former protégé and colleague of Heidegger, but with distinctive ideas of his own. In his magisterial work *Truth and Method*, he wrote, 'To hear and obey someone [*auf jemanden hören*]' means 'openness to the other', which is the basis of hermeneutical understanding.[62] We must detach ourselves, he wrote, 'from the Cartesian basis of modern science . . . and . . . from Greek thought' to hear the word addressed to us.[63] He was even more explicit in his autobiographical reflections. He wrote:

> Hermeneutics is above all a practice . . . It is the heart of all education that wants to teach us how to philosophize. In it *what one has to exercise above all is the ear*, the sensitivity for perceiving . . . that reside(s) in concepts.[64]

Jay has expounded this further.[65] 'Listening' to the text in openness for conversation and dialogue is crucial, but could not readily be so possible from visual apprehension.

(7) The most recent influential and towering thinker on hermeneutics is **Paul Ricoeur** (1913–2005). He wrote so much on symbol and metaphor that he cannot be said to oppose visual communication. In contrast to

---

[58] Bultmann, *Essays*, pp. 262–72.

[59] Bultmann, 'The Problem of Hermeneutics', in *Essays*, pp. 243–61, and 'New Testament and Mythology', in Hans-Werner Bartsch (ed.), *Kerygma and Myth* (2 vols, London: SCM, 1953), vol. 1, pp. 1–44.

[60] Ernst Fuchs, *Hermeneutik* (Tübingen: Mohr, 1970), pp. 103–7 and throughout.

[61] Ernst Fuchs, *Studies of the Historical Jesus* (London: SCM, 1964), p. 129.

[62] Hans-Georg Gadamer, *Truth and Method* (2nd Eng. edn, London: Sheed & Ward, 1989), p. 361.

[63] Gadamer, *Truth and Method*, p. 461.

[64] Hans-Georg Gadamer, 'Reflections on My Philosophical Journey', in Lewis E. Hahn (ed.), *The Philosophy of Hans-Georg Gadamer* (La Salle, IL: Open Court, 1997), p. 17 (my italics).

[65] Martin Jay, 'The Rise of Hermeneutics and the Crisis of Ocularcentrism' in *Force Fields: Between Intellectual History and Cultural Critique* (New York: Routledge, 1993), pp. 99–113.

Gadamer, just as he saw 'explanation' and 'understanding' as complementary, so he gives a fully positive account of seeing and hearing. We consider Paul Ricoeur further in Chapter 3. Meanwhile, the purpose of this chapter has not been to say that visual representation is valueless, but to confirm that visual representation is *not infallible*; it can even seduce us and mislead us, if it is wrongly interpreted. Its meaning is far from self-evident, apart from specific traditions and contexts.

The captivating power of images when seen as 'part of our language'

We may return to Wittgenstein, in spite of his sometimes ambiguous attitude towards pictures and visual communication. It is well known that when he recalled his earlier period of the *Tractatus*, he complained, 'A *picture* [*ein Bild*] held us captive. And we could not get outside it, for it lay in our language and language seemed to repeat it to us inexorably.'[66] Strictly, here 'picture' means a conception, but *Bild* also means picture or visual representation, because it concerns the picture of language expounded in the *Tractatus*. He commented that the plausibility and dominance of this model remained with him. Earlier he explained, 'The *pre-conceived idea* of crystalline purity can only be removed by turning our whole examination round.'[67]

One of many reasons for this feeling of captivity is that, Wittgenstein asserted, 'Meaning something is like attaching a label to a thing.'[68] This seems to be an innocent and obvious way of understanding meaning. But it applies only, he later said, to simplified forms of life, such as his language-game of two builders, in which one calls to the other such instructions as 'Slab!' and so on.[69] By contrast he later defined language-games as activities, with which he compared 'the multiplicity of the tools in language and of the ways they are used with the multiplicity of kinds of words and sentence'.[70] Language features not only nouns but also verbs such as 'commanding, questioning, recounting, chatting', which are 'as much a part of our natural history as walking, eating, drinking, playing'.[71]

---

[66] Wittgenstein, *Philosophical Investigations*, sect. 115 (his italics).
[67] Wittgenstein, *Philosophical Investigations*, sect. 108 (his italics).
[68] Wittgenstein, *Philosophical Investigations*, sect. 15.
[69] Wittgenstein, *Philosophical Investigations*, sects 19–20.
[70] Wittgenstein, *Philosophical Investigations*, sect. 23.
[71] Wittgenstein, *Philosophical Investigations*, sect. 25.

Again he shows the inadequacy of ostensive definition.[72] The tendency of someone who seeks to learn language and meaning is to say, 'There *must* be', but Wittgenstein urged patient and careful watching and understanding the various language-games which people put into action.[73] He examined the ostensive definition of the schematic drawing of a cube; but this can be more than one thing. An ostensive definition, he said, 'can be variously interpreted in every case'.[74] Thus, he concluded,

> The ideal, as we think of it, is a shakeup. For you can never get outside it; you must always turn back . . . Where does this idea come from? It is like a pair of glasses on our nose through which we see whatever we look at. It never occurs to us to take them off.[75]

Thus in this section of his observations, he concluded, as we saw, 'A *picture* held us captive.'[76] Any philosophical result seems to be 'running its head up against the limits of language'.[77]

Thus, as Wittgenstein has suggested, we must turn our enquiry round. His constant theme was to ask how language *engages* with life. He observed, 'The confusions which occupy us arise when language is like an engine idling, not when it is doing work.'[78] He still included examples of the various possible interpretations of pictures, but then turned his attention to reading and training, and then to numbers.[79] He then considered imagining various forms of language-game, after which he concluded, 'The common behaviour of mankind is the system of reference by means of which we interpret an unknown language.'[80] He added, '"But surely you can see . . ." – that is just the characteristic expression of someone who is under the compulsion of a rule.'[81] Wittgenstein then proceeded to develop some profound comments about the logical grammar of language which expressed pain, in one case, and love, in another, in the course of his attack on 'private' (i.e. unteachable) language. Love has meaning only when it is manifested in life. He asked, 'Could someone have a feeling of ardent love or hope for the space of one second – no matter what preceded

72 Wittgenstein, *Philosophical Investigations*, sect. 28; cf. sects 29–42.
73 Wittgenstein, *Philosophical Investigations*, sect. 66 (his italics).
74 Wittgenstein, *Philosophical Investigations*, sect. 28.
75 Wittgenstein, *Philosophical Investigations*, sect. 103.
76 Wittgenstein, *Philosophical Investigations*, sect. 115 (his italics).
77 Wittgenstein, *Philosophical Investigations*, sect. 119.
78 Wittgenstein, *Philosophical Investigations*, sect. 133.
79 Wittgenstein, *Philosophical Investigations*, sects 156–78 and 179–94 respectively.
80 Wittgenstein, *Philosophical Investigations*, sect. 206.
81 Wittgenstein, *Philosophical Investigations*, sect. 231.

or followed this second . . . The surroundings give it its importance.'[82] We can understand how understanding language entails far more than glancing at a picture. But we can also understand why Wittgenstein felt the captivating power of looking at language under an oversimplified generalizing model.

On the other hand Wittgenstein also recognized the reverse of this experience, or perhaps a complementary limitation. This concerns what he called 'aspect blindness'. He wrote, 'The "aspect-blind" will have an altogether different relationship to pictures from ours.'[83] For example, a spectator may view actors in historical costume as acting a historical play, but still perceive them *as* actors, without experiencing them *as persons in the play.* They may even recognize a photograph as a likeness of a friend, but still see it *as* a photograph, not *as the friend* who was photographed. Some have seen this as an emotional 'blindness'. In such cases, however, the picture does not fulfil its intended function; it proves to be ineffective.

Nevertheless, writers are still divided about Wittgenstein's attitude to pictures. W. J. T. Mitchell argues:

> Wittgenstein's iconophobia and the general anxiety of linguistic philosophy about visual representation may also be a sign that a pictorial turn is taking place . . . A philosophical career that began with a 'picture theory' of meaning . . . ended with the appearance of a kind of iconoclasm, a critique of imagery that led [Wittgenstein] to renounce his earlier pictorialism.[84]

Others claim the reverse of this. Kristóf Nyíri regards Wittgenstein as suggesting that pictures can be 'natural' carriers of meaning, that is. not needing special interpretation.[85] Our emphasis on the need for the interpretation of pictures or visual representations, however, is not a universal demand, but a plea that in many cases this is necessary.

---

[82] Wittgenstein, *Philosophical Investigations*, sect. 583; cf. Ludwig Wittgenstein, *Zettel* (Oxford: Blackwell, 1967), sect. 491 and sect. 594.

[83] Wittgenstein, *Philosophy of Psychology – Fragments*; reprinted as *Philosophical Investigations*, Part 2, para. 258, p. 214.

[84] W. J. T. Mitchell, *Picture Theory* (Chicago: University of Chicago Press, 1994), pp. 12–13.

[85] Kristóf Nyíri, 'Image and Metaphor in the Philosophy of Wittgenstein', *Image and Imaging in Philosophy, Science and the Arts* (Symposium: Kirchberg, 8–14 August 2010), p. 8; cf. pp. 1–15; cf. also William M. Ivins, *Prints and Visual Communication* (Cambridge, MA: Harvard University Press, 1953).

3

Pictures, metaphors and symbols

Types of metaphors: ornamental, creative and interactive

Virtually every major philosophical and theological thinker on metaphor agrees that ornamental metaphors have no place in serious thought, except as literary or rhetorical devices. Ornamental metaphors do not convey new truth, but only improve stylistically, or make more vivid, truths with which we are already familiar. One of the earlier familiar classics was Lakoff and Johnson, *Metaphors We Live By*. They define metaphor in the following way: '*The essence of metaphor is understanding and experiencing one kind of thing in terms of another.*'[1] Janet Martin Soskice points out that definitions of metaphor have been offered since the pre-Socratic philosophers, and especially since Aristotle. Indeed Heraclitus is said to have coined the metaphor 'the river of time', which Wittgenstein demonstrated had misleading consequences. Time as a flowing river suggests questions that we cannot answer, such as 'Where did the past go to?'[2] The history of metaphor runs throughout history, from the Ancient Greeks to Paul Ricoeur and Soskice.

Soskice has classified types of metaphors in a helpful way.[3] (1) Everyday metaphors include such figures of speech as 'neck of the bottle' or 'mouth of the river'. Most of these are now 'dead metaphors', thinned down by frequent use. (2) She rightly dismisses the decorative or substitution theory of metaphor as reducing it to 'no more than translating from a prior and literal understanding into an evocative formulation'.[4] It is akin to translating 'He is a fox' into 'He is cunning'. In the case of *substitution* metaphors, these are metaphors with which we could easily dispense

---

1 George Lakoff and Mark Johnson, *Metaphors We Live By* (Chicago: University of Chicago Press, 1980), p. 5 (their italics).

2 Ludwig Wittgenstein, *Philosophical Investigations* (Eng. and Ger., Oxford, Blackwell, 1958), sect. 89.

3 Janet Martin Soskice, *Metaphor and Religious Language* (Oxford: Clarendon Press, 1985), pp. 24–53.

4 Soskice, *Metaphor*, p. 25.

by simply *substituting literal speech* for the metaphor. (3) Soskice rejects equally theories of emotive effect. Particular metaphors often add emotional self-involvement to what is said. Such theories, she observes, are tantamount to older emotive theories of religious language, for example in Logical Positivism, and would exclude scientists and theologians from using metaphor. (4) She considers 'incremental' theories, which make possible new cognitive meanings.[5] These include Beardsley's 'Controversion' theory, which allows for metaphorical twists, Black's 'interactive' theory, which is stronger, and her 'Interanimation' theory, which she expounds. She draws on I. A. Richards' notion of **vehicle** and **tenor** (discussed below shortly) to explain a tension between the two implied worlds of meaning, and then stresses how metaphor can be both *creative* and *cognitive*.[6]

Even Paul Ricoeur acknowledged that in his voluminous work on metaphor he drew on earlier writers including Beardsley and Wheelwright in the 1950s, and Max Black in the 1960s.[7] Monroe Beardsley (1915–85) was an American philosopher who specialized in aesthetics. Philip Wheelwright (1901–70) was also an American philosopher and literary theorist. Max Black was educated in Britain, but moved to the USA to specialize in the philosophy of language. They produced a number of seminal works on symbol and metaphor.

Ricoeur published *The Rule of Metaphor* entirely on metaphor, but also discussed symbol and metaphor together in his *Interpretation Theory*.[8] Both symbol and metaphor produce a 'surplus of meaning'; both produce 'a double-meaning'; and both yield an open 'extension of the meaning of a name'.[9] When he defined the nature and function of metaphor he excluded the notion of substitution for a literal term (as Soskice does), insisting, rather, that it provides a 'transformation, which imposes a sort of twist on the words'.[10] Its relation to what would be called the literal meaning is *interactive*. In such cases, metaphor brings together two

---

5 Soskice, *Metaphor*, pp. 32–51.

6 Soskice, *Metaphor*, pp. 47–51.

7 Monroe Beardsley, *Aesthetics: Problems in the Philosophy of Criticism* (Indianapolis: Harcourt, Brace & World, 1958; reprinted 1981); and Philip Wheelwright, *The Burning Fountain: A Study in the Language of Symbolism* (Tulamore: Midland Books, 1954); Max Black, *Models and Metaphors: Studies in Language and Philosophy* (Ithaca: Cornell University Press, 1962), and as editor the multi-authored book *The Importance of Language* (Englewood Cliffs, NJ: Prentice-Hall, 1963).

8 Paul Ricoeur, *The Rule of Metaphor: Multi-disciplinary Studies of the Creation of Meaning in Language* (London: Routledge & Kegan Paul, 1978); and *Interpretation Theory: Discourse and the Surplus of Meaning* (Fort Worth: Texas University Press, 1976), especially pp. 45–70.

9 Ricoeur, *Interpretation Theory*, pp. 45 and 49.

10 Ricoeur, *Interpretation Theory*, p. 50.

separate 'worlds' or universes of discourse. Similarly *symbol* brings together two dimensions, or two universes of discourse, one linguistic and the other non-linguistic.[11] Symbols, Ricoeur argued, 'cannot be exhaustively treated by conceptual language . . . There is more in symbol than in any of its conceptual equivalents'. [12] In this respect he stood near to Tillich, although he showed more judicious caution than Tillich. Metaphor, like symbol, 'represents the extension of the meaning of a name through deviation from the literal meaning of words'.[13] It 'imposes a sort of twist on the words'.[14]

In *The Rule of Metaphor* Ricoeur asserted, 'Metaphor presents itself as a strategy of discourse that, while preserving and developing the creative power of language, preserves and overlaps the *heuristic* power wielded by *fiction*.'[15] To Roman Jakobson's notion of 'split-sense', he added **split-reference**. This may lead to fictional re-description. He begins from Aristotle's notion of 'giving a thing a name that belongs to something else'.[16] But it also involves movement, and much more than mere 'substitution'.[17] *Creative* metaphor is not the mere substitution of what we know already for purposes of ornament or decoration. Its power derives in part from being able to express *more than* literal language can express. Like Kierkegaard on 'indirect' language, and Bakhtin on 'polyvalent' language, this 'surplus of meaning' adds power to what otherwise might not have been communicated. Unlike the decline of the power of metaphor in dead metaphor, living metaphor brings together creatively two universes of discourse. Ricoeur calls this 'the intersection of spheres of discourse'.[18]

Ricoeur drew on Wheelwright and others for this 'tensive' view of metaphor. Wheelwright wrote, 'The essence of metaphor consists in the nature of the tension which is maintained among the heterogeneous elements brought together in one commanding image or expression.'[19] Tension occurs through the interaction between what the rhetorician I. A. Richards (1893–1973) called the **tenor** and the **vehicle** of the two 'worlds' of a metaphor. The vehicle is the object whose attributes are borrowed; the tenor is the attributes which are ascribed to it. Wheelwright took this

---

11 Ricoeur, *Interpretation Theory*, pp. 53–4.

12 Ricoeur, *Interpretation Theory*, p. 57.

13 Ricoeur, *Interpretation Theory*, p. 49.

14 Ricoeur, *Interpretation Theory*, p. 50.

15 Ricoeur, *The Rule of Metaphor*, p. 6 (Ricoeur's italics).

16 Aristotle, *Poetics*, 1456 B, 10.

17 Ricoeur, *The Rule of Metaphor*, p. 19.

18 Ricoeur, *The Rule of Metaphor*, pp. 295–303.

19 Wheelwright, *The Burning Fountain*, p. 101.

over.[20] Allen Tate called this 'intensive meaning'; others called it 'extended meaning'. Among rhetorical critics C. S. Lewis (1898–1963), scholar, poet and novelist, distinguished between 'the metaphor which we invent to teach by . . . the Master's metaphor' and 'the metaphor from which we learn . . . the Pupil's metaphor'.[21] Lewis suggested that the Master's metaphor might be used to teach those who perceived the world as a two-dimensional flat land (eventually corrupted to 'Flalansferes') to learn to see it as a three-dimensional sphere. He compares this to the philosophical Master's metaphor as teaching Kant through the analogy of seeing everything as blue, because they saw everything through blue spectacles (eventually corrupted to 'Bluspells').[22]

In the following essay in Black's book Owen Barfield (1898–1997), philosopher of law, and poet, made the same point about the creative extension of meaning through metaphor in his essay 'Poetic Diction and Legal Fiction'.[23] Barfield allows new terms to be used in such fields as the inheritance of property, and so on. With J. R. R. Tolkien (1892–1973), Lewis and Barfield formed the 'Inklings' as an informal group of literary theorists and writers at Oxford. In place of 'transformation' Barfield uses '*Tarnung*', to indicate 'hiding one meaning in another'.[24] Legal fiction, he said, comes into being when we need to extend language to say what strictly it cannot say. Ordinary words are given an extended meaning with a fictional twist. For example, 'Fictitious ownership, which we call trusteeship, has been strong enough to have other fictions erected on it.'[25] He illustrated this from new terms used in the field of the inheritance of property. By such means legal fictions provide a deep feeling of liberation.

As we have noted, in his essay 'Metaphor and Symbol' Ricoeur underlined extension of meaning by observing that both symbol and metaphor constitute double-meaning expressions and provide surplus of meaning. Sometimes they offer a 'productive use of ambiguity', and always yield 'extension of meaning'.[26] Then Ricoeur reaches an important conclusion. He declares, '*Thus a metaphor does not exist in itself, but in and through an*

[20] Wheelwright, *The Burning Fountain*, p. 103.

[21] C. S. Lewis, 'Bluspells and Flalansferes', in Black (ed.), *The Importance of Language*, p. 39; cf. pp. 36–50.

[22] Lewis, 'Bluspells and Flalansferes', pp. 43–6.

[23] Owen Barfield, 'Poetic Diction and Legal Fiction', in Black (ed.), *The Importance of Language*, pp. 51–71.

[24] Barfield, 'Poetic Diction and Legal Fiction', p. 55.

[25] Barfield, 'Poetic Diction and Legal Fiction', p. 64.

[26] Ricoeur, 'Metaphor and Symbol', p. 47 and p. 49.

interpretation.'[27] Metaphors are close to what Gilbert Ryle called a category mistake, that is, an unexpected or odd pairing of words from different semantic domains. Much of this becomes more acute in symbol. Symbols also involve extension of meaning, and often draw on multiple contexts. Again, they show 'an interplay of similarity and dissimilarity'.[28] He added that symbols cannot be exhaustively treated by conceptual language, and 'give rise to endless exegesis'.[29] Ricoeur concluded his work on metaphors, first by endorsing Max Black's observation, 'A memorable metaphor has the power to bring two separate domains into cognitive and emotional relation by using language directly appropriate for the one as a lens for seeing the other.'[30] He finally observed, 'Metaphor implies a tensive use of language in order to uphold a tensive concept of reality.'[31]

In the light of all this, it is clear that the situation of metaphors and symbols even surpasses the ambiguity of pictures. *Whether or not they are primarily visual, metaphors have to be interpreted if their meaning is to become beyond doubt.*

Negative theories of metaphor: Nietzsche and Derrida

Friedrich W. Nietzsche (1844–1900), atheistic existentialist and quasi-nihilist, was sceptical about *all* language. He insisted, 'All that exists consists of *interpretation.*'[32] If this is so, Nietzsche concluded, 'We shall never be rid of God, so long as we still believe in grammar.'[33] Hence he must 'philosophize with the hammer'. In *The Antichrist* Nietzsche pressed what today we should call an anti-theistic 'ideological critique' of language in religion. He writes, 'A priest or a pope not only errs, but actually lies with every word that he utters.'[34] In his *Notebooks* of 1873, he asked, 'What is truth?' and replied: 'A mobile army of metaphors, metonyms, and anthropomorphisms.'[35] In *The Will to Power* he wrote, '*Truth is that*

---

27 Ricoeur, 'Metaphor and Symbol', p. 50 (my italics).

28 Ricoeur, 'Metaphor and Symbol', p. 56.

29 Ricoeur, 'Metaphor and Symbol', p. 57.

30 Ricoeur, 'Metaphor and Symbol', p. 67; from Max Black, *Models and Metaphors* (Ithaca: Cornell University Press, 1962), p. 236.

31 Ricoeur, 'Metaphor and Symbol', p. 68.

32 Friedrich Nietzsche, *The Will to Power*, vol. 2, aphorism 493 (Nietzsche's italics), in *The Complete Works* (18 vols, London: Allen & Unwin, 1909–13, vol. 15).

33 Friedrich Nietzsche, *The Twilight of the Idols* (London: Penguin Classics, 1990), p. 22, aphorism 5.

34 Friedrich Nietzsche, *The Antichrist* (London: Penguin Classics, 1990), p. 177, aphorism 38.

35 Friedrich Nietzsche, in W. Kaufman (ed.), *The Portable Nietzsche* (New York: Viking Press, 1968), p. 46.

kind of error without which a certain species of being cannot live.'[36] He has in mind religious believers who cannot live without 'illusions that we have forgotten are illusions'.[37] Such people, he said, draw comfort from 'the salvation of the soul', failing to realize that this really means only: 'The world revolves round me'.[38] Nietzsche concluded that metaphor serves as a tool for manipulation and illusion. Many writers have attacked Nietzsche's negative view of metaphor. The Barthian theologian, Eberhard Jüngel, argues that Nietzsche simultaneously seeks to honour metaphor and to discredit truth. He tries, he said, to stress 'deception, lying, deluding, talking behind the back, putting up a false front, living in borrowed splendour, wearing a mask, hiding behind convention', as if all this was simply to preserve the self.[39] By contrast, Jüngel regards metaphors as 'the articulation of discoveries' beyond actuality.[40]

Nietzsche's relativism leads on to the negative verdicts on metaphor by such thinkers as Jacques Derrida (1930–2004), French postmodernist philosopher. Indeed Derrida attacks not only many uses of metaphor, especially in philosophy, but also many kinds of visual and aural communication. He has many affinities with Nietzsche, including his scepticism about truth and much language. In his essay 'Structure, Sign, and Play in the Discourse of the Human Sciences' in his book *Writing and Difference*, Derrida writes, 'The Nietzschean affirmation . . . is the joyous affirmation of the play of the world, and the innocence of becoming; the affirmation of a world of signs without fault, without truth.'[41] This reflected Nietzsche's early and consistent stance concerning tragedy, and the contrast between Pentheus and Dionysius. He placed himself alongside the raw energy and driving force of life-affirming Dionysian joy and exuberance, in contrast to the Apollonian principle of restraint, moderation and sobriety. This contrast is dramatically played out in Euripides' tragedy *The Bacchae*, with the contrast between the responsible sobriety of Pentheus and Dionysian frenzy. Nietzsche devalued truth and language, which his other work implies, and increasingly looked towards nihilism (see above). Derrida shares much of his scepticism about representational language and truth, in which he attacks 'logocentrism'. His major influences were

[36] Nietzsche, *The Will to Power*, vol. 2, aphorism 481.

[37] Friedrich Nietzsche, *Notebooks* (Cambridge: CUP, 2003), p. 46.

[38] Nietzsche, *The Antichrist*, p. 186, aphorism 43.

[39] Eberhard Jüngel, *Theological Essays* (2 vols, Edinburgh: T&T Clark, 1989), vol. 1, p. 28.

[40] Jüngel, *Theological Essays*, p. 51.

[41] Jacques Derrida, *Writing and Difference* (Chicago: University of Chicago Press, 1978; Fr., 1967), p. 292; cf. pp. 278–94.

Nietzsche, Freud, Husserl and Heidegger. He regarded language as yielding a virtually limitless 'deferral' of meaning. With Roland Barthes, he was one of the most influential founders of deconstructionism, in which language loses many of its anchors in the extra-linguistic world.

Derrida has particular problems with metaphor. His seminal essay 'White Mythology: Metaphor in the Text of Philosophy', published in his book *Margins of Philosophy*, expressed his concern.[42] His main targets included Plato, Aristotle, Descartes and Hegel.[43] Metaphors, he said, are 'the dream at the heart of philosophy'.[44] He cited such examples as 'God', 'soul', 'absolute', 'Being' and so on. He regarded these as being *symbols* rather than *signs*, and commented, 'Metaphysical metaphor has turned everything upside down, and although it also has erased piles of physical discourses, one always should be able to reactivate the primitive inscription and restore the palimpsest.'[45] He then added, 'Metaphysics – white mythology which reassembles and reflects the culture of the West . . . he [humankind] must still wish to call Reason.'[46]

With one particular point, few would disagree. Derrida constantly considered 'dead metaphors', and the possibility or otherwise of their re-activation. Some metaphors, he wrote, are like coins 'which have been worn away [Fr., *usé*], defaced, and polished in the circulation of the philosophical concept'.[47] These have entirely lost their power, and yet are sometimes reintroduced with seductive effects. Their original meaning was probably sensory and material, but the problem is that the metaphor is no longer noticed, and has 'a double effacement . . . carried away in and of itself'.[48] Metaphor can become much worn and thinned down, losing its picturesque nature and original brilliance. He wrote, 'The value of *usure* [French for metaphor that has deteriorated through usage] has to be subjected to interpretation. It seems to have a systematic tie to the metaphorical perspective.'[49] Derrida wrote that the metaphorical element in the use of formerly creative words disappears and by custom the word changes from a metaphorical to a literal expression.[50] He attacked

[42] Jacques Derrida, 'White Mythology', in Derrida, *Margins of Philosophy* (Eng., New York: Harvester Wheatsheaf, 1982; Fr., 1972) pp. 207–72.
[43] Derrida, 'White Mythology', p. 266.
[44] Derrida, 'White Mythology', p. 268.
[45] Derrida, 'White Mythology', p. 212.
[46] Derrida, 'White Mythology', p. 213.
[47] Derrida, 'White Mythology', p. 211.
[48] Derrida, 'White Mythology', p. 211.
[49] Derrida, 'White Mythology', p. 215.
[50] Derrida, 'White Mythology', p. 225.

especially spatial metaphors, which, he noted, fell especially under the suspicion of Henri Bergson.

Rhetorical metaphors fall less immediately under suspicion than others. But even then, Derrida wrote:

> Each time that a rhetoric defines metaphor, not only is a philosophy implied, but also a conceptual network in which philosophy itself has been constituted. Moreover each thread in this network forms a *turn*, or one might say metaphor, if that notion were not too derivative here.[51]

In two respects two of the most influential philosophers of the twentieth century (rightly or wrongly), Wittgenstein and Derrida, make common cause. Wittgenstein, like our previous quotation from Derrida, speaks of 'a whole cloud of philosophy [being] condensed into a drop of grammar'.[52] Both also speak of metaphors or ostensive definitions as needing interpretation.[53] A sub-system of metaphors, Derrida remarked, 'seems to belong to the great mobile chain of Aristotelian ontology, with its theory of the analogy of Being, its logic, its epistemology, and . . . its poetics and its rhetoric'.[54] He commented on metaphor, 'Little by little, I slowly attempted to pry the mind loose from its attachment to privileged images.'[55] Together with Aristotle, he targeted Plato, Descartes and Hegel. He concluded,

> Metaphor is determined by philosophy as a provisional loss of meaning . . . The philosophical evaluation of metaphor has always been ambiguous: metaphor is *dangerous* and foreign as it concerns *intuition* (vision or contact), *concept* (the grasping or proper presence of the signified), and *consciousness* (proximity or self-presence).[56]

The cognitive power and extra-linguistic reference of metaphors: Ricoeur and Soskice

In addition to his book *The Rule of Metaphor* and other works on the subject, Ricoeur's article of 1975 in volume 4 of *Semeia* is particularly useful in making the points at present under consideration.[57] He began his article

[51] Derrida, 'White Mythology', p. 230 (his italics).
[52] Wittgenstein, *Philosophical Investigations*, 2, xi, p. 222.
[53] Wittgenstein, *Philosophical Investigations*, sect. 28.
[54] Derrida, 'White Mythology', p. 236.
[55] Derrida, 'White Mythology', p. 260.
[56] Derrida, 'White Mythology', p. 270 (first italics mine; subsequent italics Derrida's).
[57] Paul Ricoeur, 'Biblical Hermeneutics', in *Semeia: An Experimental Journal for Biblical Criticism* (1975), pp. 29–145, especially 'The Metaphorical Process', pp. 75–106.

on metaphor by making two crucial points, which precisely confirm our present argument. He stated that he was making two particular claims for metaphor in biblical discourse. He first argued, 'Metaphor is more than a figure of style, but contains *semantic innovations*'; further, 'metaphor includes a keynote in native or referential dimension, i.e., the power of *redefining reality*'.[58] Metaphor conveys reality and not merely ideas. To support this, he pointed out that metaphor relates to sentences or propositions rather than words. On his first argument he conceded that metaphor is a trope, or 'an extension of naming by a deviation from the literal'.[59] He observed, 'Metaphor is only meaningful in a statement; it is a phenomenon of predication.'[60] This is not to deny that there is usually a tension between the vehicle and the tenor of metaphor, to use Richards' terminology. By operating at the metaphorical level, he said, 'Metaphorical interpretation consists in transforming a self-defeating, sudden contradiction into a meaningful contradiction. It is the transformation which imposes on the word a sort of "twist".'[61]

Ricoeur acknowledged that in literary theory and too often in poetic discourse this view is too readily misunderstood, and that metaphor is treated as closed in upon itself or as a purely *intra-linguistic* phenomenon. Perhaps this should invite caution about those biblical scholars who are experts in literary criticism rather than philosophy or linguistics. Ricoeur utilized Gottlob Frege on sense and reference, or *Sinn* and *Bedeutung*. He explained:

> Meaning is *what* a statement says, reference is *that about which* it says it. What a statement says is immanent within it – it is its internal arrangement. That with which it deals is extra-linguistic . . . It is what is said about the world.[62]

Ricoeur was equally critical of structuralism, where language, he said, functions purely internally or immanently. To see everything in terms of the interplay of differences (as Derrida usually does) is not enough. Even Northrop Frye sees language as 'self-contained'. Further, he argued, poetic language 'does not mean the abolition of all reference'.[63]

To support this claim, Ricoeur cited Jakobson, and his work on

---

[58] Ricoeur, *Semeia* 4 (1975), p. 75 (his italics).

[59] Ricoeur, *Semeia* 4 (1975), p. 76.

[60] Ricoeur, *Semeia* 4 (1975), p. 77.

[61] Ricoeur, *Semeia* 4 (1975), p. 78.

[62] Ricoeur, *Semeia* 4 (1975), p. 81 (Ricoeur's italics).

[63] Ricoeur, *Semeia* 4 (1975), p. 83.

'split-reference'. Jakobson argued, 'The supremacy of the poetic function over the referential function does not obliterate the reference (the denotational), but renders it ambiguous', that is, 'reference split in two.'[64] The upshot is that 'A new vision of reality springs up'.[65] Ricoeur sought further support from the work of Max Black, *Models and Metaphors*, and Mary Hesse, *Models and Analogies in Science*. Scientific language uses models as a heuristic device to break up inadequate interpretation, and to blaze a trail towards more adequate interpretation. Mary Hesse called this an **instrument of redescription**. Black distinguished between three types of models: scale models (e.g. a model boat); diagrams; and theoretical models, which construct an imaginary object to be transposed into a more complex reality. Ricoeur regarded all three as heuristic models. He endorsed Black's dictum, 'A memorable metaphor has the power of cognitively and affectively relating two separate domains by using language appropriate to the one as a lens for seeing the other.'[66] Thus Black urged the interactive function of metaphor. Both Ricoeur and Black endorse Nelson Goodman's claim that the language of poetry and art is not unrelated to the more supposedly 'objective' language of the sciences. In both cases, pictorial language organizes reality. Ricoeur concluded, 'Poetic language also [like science and theology] speaks of reality.'[67] Ian Paul observes that Ricoeur moved metaphor 'from the perceptual to the cognitive'.[68]

Much of the remainder of this essay (i.e. the one in *Semeia*) simply repeated the themes which we have introduced. He said again that metaphor describes reality by 'redescription'. He also considered the history of parable interpretation, which we do in Chapter 6, criticizing Jülicher for devaluing metaphor. He argued that Jülicher retained an inadequate 'substitution' theory of metaphor (when literal meaning can be substituted for the metaphor without change of meaning), in contrast to Eberhard Jüngel, who took account of the creative power of metaphor. Jüngel accepts the tension or 'twist' of metaphor, in contrast to Jülicher (see Chapter 6, below).[69] Further, if the appreciation or interpretation of metaphorical tension is instantaneous, this coheres with the notion of the parable as an 'event' of revelation. Tradition allows some metaphors to become 'dead'

---

64 Ricoeur, *Semeia* 4 (1975), p. 84.

65 Ricoeur, *Semeia* 4 (1975), p. 84.

66 Ricoeur, *Semeia* 4 (1975), p. 85; and Black, *Models and Metaphors*, p. 237.

67 Ricoeur, *Semeia* 4 (1975), p. 87.

68 Ian Paul, 'Metaphor', in Kevin J. Vanhoozer (ed.), *Dictionary for Theological Interpretation of the Bible* (London: SPCK, and Grand Rapids: Baker Academic, 2007), p. 507; cf. pp. 507–10.

69 Ricoeur, *Semeia* 4 (1975), pp. 91–3.

metaphors, but 'sustaining' metaphors may give them new life. This especially applies to the 'root' metaphors of the Old Testament, in which God is King, Father, Husband, Judge, Rock, Fortress and Redeemer. These have 'potential interpretations at a more conceptual level'.[70] Fictional narrative may perform a heuristic function, and Ricoeur agreed with much in John Dominic Crossan's *In Parables*, considered in Chapter 6. He rightly stressed participation in the narrative's referent. He also considered the work of Dan Otto Via on metaphor and plot, also considered in Chapter 6.[71] Wider referents in the Gospels, Ricoeur concluded, are 'not only "parables of Jesus", but of the "Crucified"'.[72]

After Ricoeur, Janet Martin Soskice has also explored the *cognitive* power of metaphors, their extra-linguistic reference, and the parallels between religious and scientific metaphors.[73] On the latter, she especially drew upon Mary Hesse and Ron Harré.[74] They speak of 'theory-constitutive metaphors' as metaphors which propose a model.[75] Ian Ramsey also drew on models in science (e.g. 'wave' in physics), which he applied to theology. Models can be used to describe the unobservable. Soskice concluded:

> The Christian theist typically has not taken models like 'God is father' or 'Kingdom of God' as merely evaluative re-descriptions of human experience, but as speaking, albeit obliquely, about states and relations which he knows himself not fully to understand.[76]

She argued that the traditional contrast between models of science as explanatory, and those of religion as affective or emotive, are grossly overdrawn. She detected hints of this in Sallie Teselle's work and in the work of Thomas Fawcett, even if Fawcett attempted a middle position.[77] In the end Soskice concluded, 'The models of science are dispensable, whereas those of religion are not'.[78] She spells this out in her chapter 'Metaphor,

[70] Ricoeur, *Semeia* 4 (1975), p. 94.

[71] Ricoeur, *Semeia* 4 (1975), pp. 96–9.

[72] Ricoeur, *Semeia* 4 (1975), p. 105.

[73] Soskice, *Metaphor*, especially pp. 97–161.

[74] Mary B. Hesse, *Models and Analogies in Science* (Notre Dame, IN: Notre Dame University Press, 1966); and Ron Harré, *The Principles of Scientific Thinking* (London: Macmillan, 1970).

[75] Soskice, *Metaphor*, p. 102.

[76] Soskice, *Metaphor*, p. 102.

[77] Soskice, *Metaphor*, p. 110; Sallie McFague Teselle, *Speaking in Parables: A Study of Metaphor and Theology* (London: SCM, 1975), pp. 43–89; and Thomas Fawcett, *The Symbolic Language of Religion* (London: SCM, 1970).

[78] Soskice, *Metaphor*, p. 112.

Reference, and Realism'. Here she cites Ronald Hepburn, 'The . . . greatest concern to the theologian is . . . whether or not the circle of myth, metaphor, and symbol is a closed [i.e. non-referential] one, and, if closed, then in what way propositions about God manage to refer.'[79]

Most of this chapter is devoted to attacking the inadequacy of 'naïve realism'. Even with metaphor, Soskice pointed out, such expressions as 'God gets angry' or 'the "King of heaven"' lack sufficient qualification. Harré, she added, even made this kind of comment about metaphors and models in the sciences. By contrast, the 'theory-constitutive metaphor . . . is useful because it provides a network of partially denoting terms', and Soskice welcomed 'just that vagueness' in new metaphors.[80] In this respect she even expressed reservations about Max Black's theory of metaphor. In naïve realism 'The theist can *only* claim to refer to God at the cost of making God finite, of making Him a thing amongst the things whose qualities we delimit and describe.'[81] She also attacked Don Cupitt, on one side, for using utterly non-objective words about God, and A. J. Ayer and other positivists, on the other side, for an imperializing empiricism. In her closing pages she agreed with Ricoeur about 'useful fictions' for exploring concepts of God, but with one proviso.[82] She wrote, 'Community is essential because each speaker is a member of a particular community of interest, which provides the context for his referential claims.'[83] She then added, 'Corresponding to the scientific communities of interest there are religious communities of interest (Christians, for example) which are bound by shared assumptions, interests, and traditions of interpretation, and share a descriptive vocabulary.'[84] In a later sentence, which is crucial for the argument of this chapter, Soskice comments, 'In implying that revelation exists as a body of free-floating truths that can be picked up anywhere indifferently, they (people) misunderstand the sense in which Christianity is "a religion of the book".'[85] She then concludes her chapter with such metaphors as are well established from the Gospel of John (e.g. running water), the book of Revelation (e.g. the river of the water of life) and the devotional writer John Newton (e.g. the smitten Rock), to

[79] Soskice, *Metaphor*, p. 118; Ronald Hepburn, 'Demythologizing and the Problem of Validity', in Antony Flew and Alasdair MacIntyre (eds), *New Essays in Philosophical Theology* (London: SCM, 1955), p. 237 and pp. 227–42.

[80] Soskice, *Metaphor*, p. 133.

[81] Soskice, *Metaphor*, p. 141.

[82] Soskice, *Metaphor*, p. 147.

[83] Soskice, *Metaphor*, p. 149.

[84] Soskice, *Metaphor*, p. 150.

[85] Soskice, *Metaphor*, p. 154.

conclude that such metaphors as God's being a fountain of living water, or a rock or a fortress, are well established in Christian tradition with clear meaning. I find myself fully agreeing with her work.

To sum up our positive view of metaphor, metaphors do not only make positive truth-claims, they also open new horizons, constitute an antidote against the limits of 'my' world and narcissism or self-centredness, avoid dead over-familiarization (or familiarity with the already known and limited), and open the door to what has as yet been unknown, or at least, insufficiently understood. Our examples of the visual imagery of the book of Revelation will confirm this, alongside the teaching of Jesus and Paul.

4

Interpreting pictures and visual images

System as an interpretative frame

Janet Martin Soskice has taken us to exactly the point at which this chapter begins. She has pointed out that there is all the difference in the world between regarding pictures or visual images as 'free-floating', and regarding them as embedded in a system, tradition or community, or even in a few cases in an established convention. Admittedly some conventions can be wrong, as, for example, when some popular misunderstanding of a parable or theological metaphor becomes firmly grounded among the majority. But this does not invalidate Soskice's main point about authentic systems, traditions and communities.

We begin with Donald Evans on 'onlooks', to which we referred briefly in Chapter 1, in the context of Wittgenstein on the dawning of an aspect. Evans wrote, '"Looking on *x* as *y*" involves placing *x within a structure*, organization or scheme.'[1] The matter in question can be viewed from within two different systems, or in terms of two points of view. In this respect it builds on Chladenius' notion of 'points of view' in hermeneutics. As I also commented, I have applied this principle to justification by grace through faith, where humankind receives the verdict 'sinful' within the framework (or system) of history and law, but also receives the verdict 'righteous' or 'put right' within the framework (or system) of eschatology or being-in-Christ.[2] These are emphatically *not contradictions*, as the older Catholic writer F. Prat, followed by F. Amiot, claimed that they were.[3] This is not only because they refer to two different *systems*; but mainly because they constitute two divine *verdicts*, not *two flat statements* or *propositions*. John L. Austin (1911–60) would have called them 'verdictives'. Wittgenstein considered the phenomenon of 'seeing

[1] Donald Evans, *The Logic of Self-Involvement* (London: SCM, 1963), p. 127 (my italics).

[2] Anthony C. Thiselton, *The Two Horizons: New Testament Hermeneutics and Philosophical Description* (Grand Rapids. Eerdmans, 1980), pp. 417–22.

[3] F. Prat, *The Theology of St. Paul* (Eng., 2 vols, London: Burns & Oates, 1945), vol. 2, p. 247; similarly F. Amiot, *The Key Concepts of St. Paul* (Eng., Freiburg: Herder, 1962), pp. 120–5.

. . . as' further. He cited the example of seeing a radio circuitry diagram now as a jumble of meaningless lines; now as a description or direction about how a given type of radio might be constructed, depending on one's training.[4] Even in art, he observed, one glance may dismiss a picture as jumbled and meaningless lines; but a second glance or second observer may see it as a picture of a landscape.[5] Elsewhere Wittgenstein observed, 'The same thing can come before our minds when we hear the word, and the application still be different.'[6] This is because we insert the metaphor or picture into a different system or set of expectations. Sometimes, he said, 'It represents a kind of object I am very familiar with.'[7] In the same section he compared 16 types of situation (or system) which would influence how one viewed and interpreted a representation. Wittgenstein compared many kinds of example. Suppose, he said, that someone sees visually the face of a clock, but is unfamiliar with the conventions of how a clock can tell us the time. Can he come to see the hands as pointers? He responds, 'It all depends on the *system* to which the sign belongs.'[8]

The notion of 'system' derives from situations in life. Wittgenstein observed, 'Only in the stream of thought and life do words have meaning.'[9] This applies all the more to visual representations and pictures. He said, 'Understanding is effected by explanation; but also by training.'[10] Once we have been trained in a given area, we know how to slot the picture into this repertoire. But this also explains how misinterpretation can occur. One of my negative experiences as a theological teacher occurred when some students began not with a good theological dictionary, but with a general English dictionary which entirely missed the *theological* meaning of a concept. The problem which is worse than no understanding in theology arises when accurate understanding is eclipsed by popular conceptions of a given concept or picture. Some popular pictures of heaven portray heavenly existence as static 'perfection', rather than that which characterizes the ever-new nature of the Holy Spirit, who also characterizes the resurrection life (1 Cor. 15.44). Worse, some popular images portray God as 'high' in the sense of 'up there'. As Ian Ramsey showed,

---

4 Ludwig Wittgenstein, *Zettel* (Oxford: Blackwell, 1967), sect. 201.

5 Wittgenstein, *Zettel*, sect. 195.

6 Ludwig Wittgenstein, *Philosophical Investigations* (Eng. and Ger., Oxford: Blackwell, 1958), sect. 140.

7 Wittgenstein, *Philosophical Investigations*, sect. 197.

8 Wittgenstein, *Zettel*, sect. 228 (his italics).

9 Wittgenstein, *Zettel*, sect. 173.

10 Wittgenstein, *Zettel*, sect. 186.

these models of God have been carefully qualified by complementary models, so that God's being 'high' is qualified by his being 'beyond', 'within', 'infinite' and other characteristics.[11]

When we look at human faces, Wittgenstein observed, it makes all the difference if the face belongs to a circle of friends.[12] Often we have to 'delimit the concept of "visual impression"', when we cannot fit it into a prior system.[13] Once you see a figure in this way, he said, it is difficult to see it otherwise. He remarked, 'We don't understand Chinese gestures any more than Chinese sentences.'[14] At one point Wittgenstein considered the conventions of map-reading. The conventions of map-reading are ambiguous until the reader has been trained in the rules. He suggested that imagination is not enough. He commented, 'That one can "imagine" something does not mean that it makes sense.'[15] He even drew a four-dimensional cube in several versions. Often expressions of faces are 'surprisingly ambiguous'. If we share understanding of the appropriate system, we can enjoy a film in a darkened cinema. But, he noted, 'Now the lights are turned on . . . Suddenly we are outside it [the film] and see it as movements of light and dark patches on a screen.'[16] It is like waking up after a dream. He explains: '*A picture*, whatever it may be, *can be variously interpreted* . . . the picture . . . *by itself* . . . *is dead*.'[17]

'System' does not here imply a rigid logical frame. In daily life it means a set of expectations, assumptions and beliefs which form 'the surroundings' in the light of which we can make sense of a picture, whether as it was intended or otherwise. An utterly isolated picture remains dead, unless we bring to it some appropriate or inappropriate frame. Wittgenstein observed in *On Certainty*: 'When we first begin to believe anything, what we believe is not a single proposition; it is a whole system of propositions.'[18]

[11] Ian T. Ramsey, *Religious Language: An Empirical Placing of Religious Belief* (London: SCM, 1957), pp. 49–89; cf. Ian Ramsey, *Models and Mystery* (Oxford: OUP, 1964); Ian Ramsey, *Christian Discourse* (Oxford: OUP, 1965); and Ian Ramsey, *Models for Divine Activity* (London: SCM, 1973).

[12] Wittgenstein, *Zettel*, sect. 198.

[13] Wittgenstein, *Zettel*, sect. 205.

[14] Wittgenstein, *Zettel*, sect. 219.

[15] Wittgenstein, *Zettel*, sect. 250.

[16] Wittgenstein, *Zettel*, sect. 233.

[17] Wittgenstein, *Zettel*, sect. 236 (my italics).

[18] Ludwig Wittgenstein, *On Certainty* (Eng. and Ger., Oxford: Blackwell, 1969), sect. 141.

Tradition and texts as interpretative frames

As Soskice reminded us, in the case of metaphor, tradition or community can provide a frame which guarantees historical continuity for the consistent interpretation of a metaphor. Soskice wrote, 'The descriptive vocabulary which any individual uses is, in turn, dependent on the community of interest . . . embedded in particular traditions of investigation and conviction'.[19] She cited the application of this principle to such scientific communities of interest as geneticists and biochemists, and most especially to Christians and churches. A reference to 'established beliefs' and 'shared assumptions and traditions' is relevant to science and religion, and Soskice referred to serious debates about Christians and scientists in the thought and work of Thomas Aquinas, Giambattista Vico and Thomas Kuhn. Even 'the abstractions of natural theology' remain relevant.[20] Metaphor, she argued, could perform a catechetical function, when St John of the Cross could speak of the 'dark night of the soul'; and others of the 'beatific vision', or the descent of the Cloud of Divine Presence of the exodus. Even the language of mystics, she argued, needed to be anchored in the mystical tradition.[21] We shall examine this theme in Part 3.

Soskice added several more points of relevance to our argument. The first is that extra-linguistic reference or 'realism' involves the possibility of error.[22] This is why we stress that however powerful they might be, pictures or metaphors can *also seduce us* if we misinterpret them. Second, metaphors must be understood 'within traditions of conviction and practice . . . Models must be understood contextually', as Ian Ramsey demonstrated concerning 'spirit'.[23] Third, models reflect an accumulation of favoured concepts confirmed by generations. The smitten rock, the riven side and the fountain of life reflect generations of reflection on biblical texts. Often this relates to a typological reading of Scripture.

This coheres with Wittgenstein's work in *On Certainty*. He wrote, 'What I hold fast to is not *one* proposition but a nest of propositions.'[24] Some concepts, he said, 'belonged to the *scaffolding* of our thoughts. (Every human being has parents.)' Wittgenstein then looked at the proposition

---

19 Janet Martin Soskice, *Metaphor and Religious Language* (Oxford: Clarendon Press, 1985), p. 149.

20 Soskice, *Metaphor*, p. 150.

21 Soskice, *Metaphor*, p. 152.

22 Soskice, *Metaphor*, p. 152 (also).

23 Soskice, *Metaphor*, p. 153; and Ramsey, *Models for Divine Activity*, pp. 1–14.

24 Wittgenstein, *On Certainty*, sect. 225 (his italics).

'It is written'.[25] Hence he considered such propositions as 'The earth exists'. These become 'hinges' on which further or secondary debates may turn.[26]

There are, of course, different types of tradition. To distinguish between such types was the purpose of Richard Hanson's book, *Tradition in the Early Church*.[27] The mainstream tradition in the early Church, he argued, was rooted in Christian Scripture, and might have continued until at most about AD 170.[28] Initially the Greek *paradosis* was used both by Paul of the common apostolic, pre-Pauline tradition, and the Jewish 'tradition of the elders', which Jesus rejected. Hanson, Oscar Cullman, and in effect Yves Congar make this point.[29] Congar's most distinctive point was to declare, 'Tradition is not just a conservative force, but rather a principle that ensures *the continuity and identity* of the same attitude through successive generations.'[30] Tradition, he said, always implies learning from others. The older controversy, 'Scripture versus Tradition', reflects a serious misunderstanding of both Scripture (which contains and transmits tradition) and Tradition (which includes Scripture as its foundation). Whether we begin with the Greek, *paradosis*, or the Latin, *traditio*, the word means *handing on*, or *handing over*. Paul wrote:

> I handed on to you as of first importance what I in turn received: that Christ died for our sins in accordance with the scriptures, and that he was buried, and that he was raised on the third day in accordance with the scriptures.
> (1 Cor. 15.3–4)

The Greek for the repeated English 'that' was probably an example of '*hoti* recitative', which was equivalent to using quotation marks for describing the received tradition. Paul used the identical terms 'handed on' and 'received' again of the Lord's Supper (1 Cor. 11.23). As Cullmann argued, Paul also used this formula when he quoted words of Jesus (1 Thess. 4.15; 1 Cor. 7.10; 9.14).[31]

Hanson added, 'The Fourth Gospel distinguishes emphatically between the continuation of Christ's work through the apostles and its

[25] Wittgenstein, *On Certainty*, sects 211 and 216 (his italics).
[26] Wittgenstein, *On Certainty*, sect. 343 and sect. 655.
[27] R. P. C. Hanson, *Tradition in the Early Church* (London: SCM, 1962), p. 7.
[28] Hanson, *Tradition in the Early Church*, p. 9.
[29] Hanson, *Tradition in the Early Church*, p. 11; Oscar Cullmann, 'The Tradition', in *The Early Church* (Eng., London: SCM, 1956), pp. 62–4; cf. 55–99; and Yves Congar, *The Meaning of Tradition* (San Francisco: Ignatius Press, 1964,) pp. 9–46.
[30] Congar, *The Meaning of Tradition*, p. 2.
[31] Cullmann, *Early Church*, pp. 64–5; Hanson, *Tradition in the Early Church*, p. 11.

continuation in the post-apostolic Church.'[32] He also explored 'laws of tradition' which transmitted words of Jesus, in contrast to the sceptical work of some form critics. Today the work of Richard Bauckham has superseded the earlier work of B. Gerhardsson.[33] Cullmann and Hanson agree with each other about the uniqueness of the apostolate. Congar and J. P. Mackey, as Catholics, take a different view. However, Irenaeus (*c.*130–*c.*200) and Tertullian (*c.*150–*c.*225) also have many positive things to say about tradition, especially public tradition. Irenaeus spoke of 'the rule of faith' as rooted in apostolic tradition. He advocated public apostolic tradition in contrast to the private oral traditions of the Gnostics, whom he called heretics.[34] He included an embryonic creed in the apostolic tradition. Tertullian insisted on the biblical foundation of the Christian tradition, calling it, in Latin, *regula fidei,* in contrast to Marcionite and some Gnostic claims.[35] Hanson expounded the creed as part of the New Testament tradition, through Ignatius and Polycarp, to the *Didaché* and Church Fathers.[36] In his chapter on 'The Rule of Faith', Hanson asserted, 'Origen never despaired of refuting the heretics from Scripture'.[37] Cyprian, he said, likewise 'confined [i.e. restricted] doctrinal tradition entirely to the Bible'.[38] Early apostolic preaching and custom were included in the tradition.

The interpretation of visual art or pictures thus has a context in which accuracy of understanding is assured. The further comments of Irenaeus, Tertullian, Origen and Cyprian do not suggest that other traditions would provide a safe context for interpretation. In the case of three-dimensional artefacts this becomes even more urgent. Wolfgang Iser drew his theory of reader-response largely from Roman Ingarden, who was a disciple of Husserl. Objects of perception, he argued, are interpreted in terms of how they are presented. The subject 'fills in' what he or she cannot see. For example, when the subject perceives a table, one of the table legs must be hidden from view; but since we have always hitherto found that tables have four legs, we 'fill in the blank' which cannot actually be seen.[39] Our

32 Hanson, *Tradition in the Early Church,* p. 13.

33 Richard Bauckham, *Jesus and the Eyewitnesses: The Gospels as Eyewitness Testimony* (Grand Rapids: Eerdmans, 2006), throughout.

34 Irenaeus, *Against Heresies,* 1, 9, 1–2 and 1, 10, 1–4 (Eng., ANF, vol. 1, pp. 329–32); and 3, 12, 1–15 (Eng., ANF, vol. 1, pp. 429–36.

35 Tertullian, *Prescription against Heretics,* 37–8 and 42 (Eng., ANF, vol. 3, pp. 62–4).

36 Hanson, *Tradition in the Early Church,* pp. 52–74.

37 Hanson, *Tradition in the Early Church,* p. 98.

38 Hanson, *Tradition in the Early Church,* p. 99.

39 Wolfgang Iser, *The Act of Reading: A Theory of Aesthetic Response* (Baltimore: Johns

minds 'actualize' what strictly we cannot see. While Iser applied this approach to reading written texts, we can readily see how this might apply to viewing three-dimensional objects. Much depends on the activity of the mind to recognize appropriate 'systems' or expectations. If these are inappropriate, vision, interpretation and understanding will become seriously flawed. This entire section confirms what we have so far concluded about visual interpretation, or the perception of pictures. These require an appropriate system, tradition or expectation.

Convention as an interpretative frame: popular notions

Community is part of 'tradition', for tradition is simply the beliefs, conduct and expectations of a given community. When community roots become less conscious and distinctive, the continuity guarded by generations of communities may become transformed into a convention which is merely taken for granted. We offer five concrete examples of such pictures, images or symbols.

(1) Our first major example is **the symbol of the cross.** In origin in Christian tradition, as Martin Hengel and Jürgen Moltmann point out, it was perceived as a mark of horror, which deserved disgust. It could not be mentioned in polite Roman society. Paul described it as a scandal, cause of stumbling, or cause of shame and offence (Gk, *skandalon*, 1 Cor. 1.18). Hengel wrote:

> The course of execution . . . included flogging beforehand, and the victim often carried the beam to the place of crucifixion, where he was nailed to it with outstretched arms raised up, and seated on a small wooden peg . . . The form of execution could vary considerably: crucifixion was a punishment in which the caprice and sadism of the executioners were given full rein. All attempts to give a perfect description of the crucifixion in archaeological terms are therefore in vain; there were too many different possibilities for the executioner.[40]

Hengel continues:

> By the public display of a naked victim at a prominent place – at a crossroads, in the theatre, on high ground, at the place of his crime – crucifixion

---

Hopkins University Press, 1978 and 1980), p. 21 and pp. 182–3; also Iser, 'Indeterminacy and the Reader's Response in Prose Fiction' in J. Hillis Miller (ed.), *Aspects of Narrative* (New York: Columbia University Press, 1971), pp. 1–45; and Wolfgang Iser, *The Implied Reader* (Baltimore: Johns Hopkins University Press, 1974).

[40] Martin Hengel, *The Cross of the Son of God* (Eng., London: SCM, 1986), p. 117.

> also represented his uttermost humiliation . . . The Jew in particular was very aware of this.[41]

This is precisely why Paul uses the word 'curse' of the crucified One (Gal. 3.13, also reflecting Deut. 21.23), and describes the message of a Christ crucified as 'folly' (Gk, *mōria*, 1 Cor. 1.18). The writer to the Hebrews called it 'a sign of shame (*aischuné*, Heb. 12.2)'.[42] The early Christian writer Justin (*c.*100–*c.*165) commented that the ancient world regarded the proclamation of a crucified Christ as 'madness' (*mania*).[43]

Nevertheless Hengel's meticulous historical research remains strikingly at variance with the popular tradition today of the cross. Jürgen Moltmann quotes H. J. Iwand as having written, 'We had become far too used to it [the cross]. We have surrounded the scandal of the cross with roses.'[44] 'In Israelite understanding,' he wrote, 'someone executed in this way was rejected by his people, cursed among the people of God by the God of the law, and excluded from the covenant of life.'[45] Moltmann added, 'Jesus himself set out for Jerusalem, and actively took the expected suffering upon himself.'[46] However, in the largely unthinking West, crosses are often worn as decorative jewellery, or even become symbols of decoration in churches. Clearly two totally different and incompatible conventions have emerged in interpretations and understandings of the cross. Kierkegaard might have called one a Christian view, and the other, one of secularism or even 'Churchianity'. This example of the cross of Christ shows how visual representation in and of itself offers no guarantee of appropriate interpretation and understanding.

(2) Our second closely related picture or image is that of **the crucifix**. This has retained an entirely different tradition within Roman Catholicism and Protestantism, even if sometimes these two traditions overlap. This visual representation of the crucified Christ has appeared since the fifth century in Christian devotion, and was frequent from the mediaeval period onwards. However, many Protestants reject the validity and relevance of this image. The protest can be illustrated from the philosopher

---

41 Hengel, *The Cross of the Son of God*, p. 179.

42 Hengel, *The Cross of the Son of God*, p. 99.

43 Hengel, *The Cross of the Son of God*, p. 93.

44 Jürgen Moltmann, *The Crucified God: The Cross of Christ as the Foundation and Criticism of Christian Theology* (Eng., London: SCM, 1974), p. 36.

45 Moltmann, *The Crucified God*, p. 33.

46 Moltmann, *The Crucified God*, p. 51.

Georg Wilhelm Friedrich Hegel (1779–1831). He protested that the crucifix represents only a picture of the dead Christ, and frozen or stultified tradition, in which Catholicism does not allow for the living presence of Jesus Christ through the Holy Spirit.[47] He wrote, 'The Idea unfolds itself in . . . divine history [through] the process of self-differentiation [i.e. God as Father, Son, and Holy Spirit].'[48] In other words, God unfolds himself, first, by creation; second, in his 'death' in the crucifixion of the Son; and third, in the exhortation of the Son and the gift of the Spirit, who raises the Church. He argued therefore that Roman Catholicism remained at the second stage, with a static crucifix, rather than becoming a religion of the Spirit. The Holy Spirit gives 'the formation of the Spiritual Community'.[49] Not all Protestants adopt this view, since it harmonizes with Hegel's particular approach to history and to the Holy Trinity. Yet the majority of Protestants probably have suspicions about the crucifix, whereas in the tradition of Roman Catholicism it is venerated and regarded as a positive symbol of the crucifixion of Christ. This second example illustrates how broad traditions may interpret a visual phenomenon in their own way, each in accordance with a sub-tradition.

(3) The shamrock provides a third example of a variously interpreted visual representation. It is the name of a variety of three-leafed clovers in Ireland. The word is an anglicized version of the Irish *seamrog*. In Christian tradition it is said to have been important to Patrick in fifth-century Ireland. Allegedly Patrick found it difficult to explain the Holy Trinity to the Celts. He is said to have held up a shamrock, and said, 'Look! Three leaves, and yet, united on one stalk, and only one plant: the same with the Trinity, Father, Son, and the Holy Spirit; and yet one God.' Ever since, the shamrock has been an important symbol or picture in Ireland.

This raises several problems which arise from different traditions. First, some point to a pre-Christian tradition in Ireland, in which the number *three* was sacred and almost magical. *Three* might be taken to represent sky, earth and underworld; or past, present and future. The shamrock was also supposed to have healing properties. More important, however, is the contrary teaching of Gregory of Nyssa (*c*.330–95) and Gregory of Nazianzus (*c*.330–90). They emphatically *rejected the notion that numerals* had anything to do with the Trinity. To speak of the Trinity in

---

[47] Cf. G. W. F. Hegel, *Lectures on the Philosophy of Religion* (3 vols, London: Kegan Paul, Trench, Trübner, 1895), vol. 3, pp. 103–8).

[48] Hegel, *Philosophy of Religion*, vol. 3, pp. 2–3.

[49] Hegel, *Philosophy of Religion*, vol. 3, p. 108.

such a way grossly distorts this Christian doctrine. In his creative work, 'On Not Three Gods', Gregory of Nyssa insisted that numerals (including 'three') could be applied only to finite entities. We can speak of 'three Johns', 'three Peters' or 'three tables', but not three Divine Beings. To do this, he argued, would be to demean and reduce the otherness of God. Gregory of Nazianzus similarly argued that a 'swarm' of biblical texts support the deity of the Holy Spirit. Hence he also distances himself from using numerals to explain, or speak of, the Holy Trinity.[50]

Today a more favoured approach to the Trinity is through biblical narrative, as exemplified by Jürgen Moltmann, Wolfhart Pannenberg and Eugene F. Rogers.[51] In this particular case, it has become clear that the shamrock is not as useful a Christian picture as was traditionally supposed. Popular imagery seems seductive especially when it has 'Christian' exponents, and as we have regularly argued, it is possible that they can recur. Pictures of the Holy Trinity seem generally less useful than biblical narrative, in which *one* God performs his gracious acts, while the Father, the Son, and the Holy Spirit are present and distinctively involved. The classic example is the baptism of Jesus, when the Father expresses his delight in his Son; the Son submits to baptism; and the Holy Spirit descends upon the Son to empower him for his ministry.

(4) As a fourth example, we may consider an early paradigmatic biblical visual symbol, namely **the rainbow**. In Genesis 9, after the promised flood had subsided, God established a **covenant** with Noah that he would never again send such a deluge upon the earth. In token of this, the rainbow in the cloud was to be a continuing reminder of God's promise (Gen. 9.8–17). Clearly the rainbow did not appear at this point for the first time; it was a natural phenomenon before that. From that moment, however, it was to be seen as a reminder of God's mercy and covenant promise. The rainbow receives attention in the Jewish Talmud. It is a strikingly beautiful atmospheric phenomenon, caused by reflection, refraction and dispersion of light in water droplets resulting in a spectrum of light appearing in the sky.

In a primary or normal rainbow, the arc shows red on the outer part and violet on the inner side. This rainbow is caused by light being refracted when entering a droplet of water, then reflected inside on the back

---

[50] Gregory of Nyssa, 'On Not Three Gods' (Eng., NPNF, ser. 2, vol. 5, pp. 331–6, especially p. 334; and Gregory of Nazianzus, *Fifth Theological Oration: On the Holy Spirit*, 2–8, 12 and 19 (Eng., NPNF, ser. 2, vol. 7, pp. 318–23).

[51] For example, Eugene F. Rogers, *After the Spirit* (London: SCM, 2006), pp. 98–199.

of the droplet and refracted again when leaving it. A spectrum obtained using a glass prism and a point source is a continuum of wavelengths without bands. The number of colours is numerous, although the human eye is able only to distinguish them as a spectrum. The division into the 'main' perceived colours is somewhat artificial. In conventional terms the colours of the spectrum are red, orange, yellow, green, blue, indigo and violet. In a double rainbow, a second arc is seen outside the primary arc, and has the order of its colours reversed, with red on the inner side of the arc. As a natural phenomenon, but with a divinely revealed meaning, it fits all the criteria for becoming a biblical symbol.

The rainbow became a powerful symbol in the Old Testament. After the waters receded, and Noah and his family once again stood on solid ground, God reaffirmed his covenant relationship with them. In Genesis, God said of the rainbow: 'This is the sign [Heb., *ōth;* KJV/AV, token] of the covenant [Heb., *berith*] between me and the earth' (Gen. 9.12). The Hebrew word for *rainbow* (*qeshet*) also means *bow*, as in archery, which could be used as a military weapon. Some argue, therefore, that God had taken one of his weapons of judgement, and made it a sign or token that 'the waters would never again become a flood to destroy all flesh' (Gen. 9.15). The most frequent use of the Hebrew *qeshet* is to denote a bow as a weapon of war (Gen. 27.3; Isa. 7.24; Job 20.24; etc.), but it is used one further time to denote a rainbow in Ezekiel 1.28.

In Christian tradition the rainbow is used in accordance with the biblical foundation. Hugh Latimer (1483–1555), Bishop of Worcester, Chaplain to Edward VI, and martyr, took as the primary application that 'God is true to his promise'. This is of the utmost importance, for a promise is a commitment in which one is committed to act only as one has promised. Promise was vital to Luther and William Tyndale. This is the basis of Christians' assurance of salvation. But Latimer also made secondary applications. For example, he cited its fiery colour as symbolizing divine judgement. This was not the main meaning in Genesis.[52] By contrast, Henry Vaughan (1621–95), Welsh metaphysical poet, wrote that the rainbow is a 'Bright pledge of peace and Sun-shine, the surety of Thy Lord's hand'.[53] John Milton also understood the symbol in the context of a covenant promise, in *Paradise Lost*.[54]

It is clear that a community or tradition versed in the Bible will know

[52] Hugh Latimer, *Sermons* (New York: Dutton, 1906), 14, 2.

[53] Henry Vaughan, 'The Rainbow', in H. C. Beeching (ed.), *Lyra Sacra: A Book of Religious Verse* (London: Methuen, 1903), now online since 2011.

[54] John Milton, *Paradise Lost* (London: Simmons, 2017), Bk 11, lines 883–97.

exactly how this symbol or sign is to be interpreted and understood. In secular society, however, it has simply become a symbol of general hope and optimism, which was not its biblical purpose. The popular phrase 'at the end of the rainbow', on the contrary, denotes something which is much sought after, but which is impossible to attain. 'To chase rainbows' is to pursue an illusory goal. In politics or sociology a rainbow coalition denotes an alliance of different groups, or of different races or colours. All these popular uses of the term have nothing to do with the biblical symbol.

(5) The New Jerusalem is another potent symbol in Christian tradition. The imagery of Jerusalem plays a profound part throughout both Testaments, and has been central to the consciousness of believers in every age. In the book of Revelation the term is a synonym for the holy city of God at the end time. John, the Seer, writes, 'I saw the holy city, the new Jerusalem, coming down out of heaven from God, prepared as a bride for her husband' (Rev. 21.2; cf. 21.1—22.5). Clearly this is part of the symbolism of Revelation, in which Jerusalem embraces unheard-of dimensions, has gates which each consist of a single pearl, and has streets paved with gold. Robert Gundry insists, 'John is not describing the eternal dwelling place of the saints. He is describing *them* [the holy people] and them *alone*.'[55] Although Jerusalem is a dwelling place, Gundry argues, it is *God's* dwelling place. We already know that the bride adorned for her husband represents the saints (Rev. 19.7–8). The New Jerusalem is holy, for the cowardly, unbelieving, abominable, sorcerers and murderers will not be part of it.

The city of God is likewise symbolic in Ezekiel: 'The circumference of the city shall be eighteen thousand cubits. And the name of the city . . . shall be "The Lord is There"' (Ezek. 48.35). Revelation 21.22 adds, 'I saw no temple in the city for its temple is the Lord God the Almighty and the Lamb.' Revelation also declares that the city contains

> the river of the water of life, bright [or clear] as crystal, flowing from the throne of God and of the Lamb through the middle of the street of the city. On either side of the river is the tree of life with its twelve kinds of fruit, producing its fruit each month; and the leaves of the tree are for the healing of the nations. (Rev. 22.1–2)

[55] Robert H. Gundry, 'The New Jerusalem: People as Place, Not Place for People', in Robert H. Gundry, *The Old Is Better: New Testament Essays in Support of Traditional Interpretations* (WUNT 17; Tübingen: Mohr, 2005), p. 400; cf. pp. 399–411 (his italics).

Jerusalem was also a symbol of Jewish nationalistic or imperial hopes. The site of the city was called 'Jebus' before King David conquered it (2 Sam. 5.6–10; 1 Chron. 11.4–9). It was also identified as Mount Moriah, where Abraham offered the sacrifice of Isaac. David established it as the capital of Israel (2 Sam. 5.6–10; 1 Chron. 11.4–9). David brought the Ark of the Covenant to Jerusalem (2 Sam. 6.17), and brought the Ark of the Covenant there. Hence in both Jewish and Christian traditions, the 'city' is associated with the presence of God. Otherwise strong differences of understanding emerge. Jesus proclaimed the restoration of the people of God from captivity (Luke 4.18–19), but the Jewish and Christian concepts of restoration were very different. The earliest Christians still thought of the New Jerusalem as the 'throne of his father, David' (Acts 2.29–36). The Epistle to the Hebrews looks forward to the city to come: 'But you have come to Mount Zion and to the city of the living God, the heavenly Jerusalem, and to innumerable angels in festal gathering' (12.22); and 'Here we have no lasting city, but we are looking for the city which is to come' (Heb. 13.14).

The Christian longing for the New Jerusalem, therefore, is not the result of military conquest, but brings unhindered worship of *God*. The peace, wealth and security involved are not so much of value in themselves, but are a consequence of the unhindered presence of God.

Augustine spoke of the new heaven and the new earth in *The City of God*. He quoted Revelation 21.1–5 and 15.2. The 'sea of glass' is not a literal sea, because John said it appeared 'as it were' sea. He explained,

> Prophetic diction delights in mingling figurative and real language, and thus in some sort veiling the sense, so the words, 'And there was no more sea' may be taken in the same sense as the previous phrase, 'And the sea presented the dead which were in it.' For then there will be no more of this world, no more of the surgings and restlessness of human life, and it is this which is symbolized by the *sea*.[56]

By contrast, Ambrose considered 'the foundations of the Heavenly City' in minute detail, and these he called 'the foundation of faith'.[57] His exposition was not incompatible with biblical and received doctrine, but was not exactly true to an exegetical understanding of the New Jerusalem in the New Testament.

John Bunyan was not the first to depict the journey from the city of

[56] Augustine, *The City of God*, Bk 20, ch. 16 (Eng., NPNF, ser. 1, vol. 2, p. 436).

[57] Ambrose, *Of the Christian Faith*, Bk 2, Prologue, 5 (Eng., NPNF, ser. 2, vol. 10, p. 224).

destruction to the celestial Jerusalem. Geoffrey Chaucer (1343–1400) had depicted a journey from 'Babylon' to 'Jerusalem celestial' in the *Canterbury Tales.* The heavenly city represented 'the endelees blisse of hevene'. He wrote, (in modern English),

> Where joy has no contrary of woe or grievance; where all harms of this present life are passed; there is the safety from the pain of hell; there is the blissful company that rejoice themselves ever more, everyone of others' joy.[58]

This well grasped the point of the symbolism.

During the Crusades, however, the more Jewish notion of military arms came to the fore. These are difficult to date, because after the first Crusade initiated by Pope Urban (1095), three of perhaps five Crusades occurred between the twelfth century and the sixteenth. Sir Walter Raleigh's *History of the World* (1614), by contrast, regarded the descent of New Jerusalem as the culmination of history. John Cotton (1585–1652) gave a new turn to 'Jerusalem'. He was a Puritan preacher, initially educated in Trinity College, Cambridge. But owing largely to his Presbyterian principles, he emigrated to the Massachusetts Bay Colony in America, and strongly influenced Boston. He called his fellow Americans to 'Awake, put on thy strength, O New English Zion, and put on thy Beautiful Garments, O American Jerusalem'. The concept of the New Jerusalem as America gave a new turn to the symbol, which has remained influential since then.

More faithful to the biblical tradition was Jeremy Taylor (1613–67). Taylor was a protégé of Archbishop Laud. He was educated at Gonville and Caius College, Cambridge, was ordained as an Anglican, and later became Fellow of All Souls, Oxford. He wrote a number of literary works and poems. In *The Golden Grove,* he offered meditations on the four Last Things: Death, Judgement, Heaven and Hell. In the 'Meditation of Heaven' he wrote, 'The great King's transparent throne is of an entire jasper stone . . . And above all thy holy face makes an eternal clarity.'[59] This broadly captures the eschatological context of Revelation 21. Richard Baxter (1615–91), Puritan, poet and hymn-writer, saw the New Jerusalem as the culmination of a journey prompted by grace. In outlook his attitude to the New Jerusalem was similar to that of his younger near contemporary John

[58] In Chaucer's English: 'There joye hath no contrarioustee of wo, ne grevaunce; ther alle harmes been passed of this present lyf, ther as is the sikenesse fro the peyne on helle, ther as is the blissful compaignye that rejoysen hem everemo everich of others joye' (Chaucer, *Canterbury Tales,* 10, line 1076).

[59] Jeremy Taylor, *The Golden Grove* (London: Royston, 1665), 'A Meditation of Heaven'.

Bunyan (1628–88), Puritan and author of *The Pilgrim's Progress*. Bunyan portrayed 'Christian' as travelling from the City of Destruction to the Celestial City, passing through trials, conflicts and temptations. The closing lines are well worth repeating:

> I saw in my dream that these two men went in at the gate; and lo! as they entered, they were transformed; and they had raiment put on that shone like gold. There was also that met them men with harps and crowns, and gave them to them; the harps to praise withall, and the crowns in token of honour. Then I heard in my dream that all the bells in the City rang again for joy, and that it was said to them, Enter into the joy of our Lord. I also heard the men themselves say that they sang with a loud voice, saying, Blessing, honour, glory, and power be unto him that sits upon the throne, and to the Lamb forever and ever.[60]

This fully accords with the New Jerusalem in the book of Revelation.

Tragically, for most people in secular society Jerusalem is regarded as a centre of irresolvable conflict, where Jews and Palestinians utterly believe in the rightness of their cause, and no solution seems to be in sight. It has become almost a symbol of incommensurability. Most people outside the Abrahamic faiths see it as a purely socio-political entity. The gap between at least three traditions on the New Jerusalem is far apart. The symbol remains ambiguous without a Jewish, Christian or Islamic tradition of interpretation. Even then, the traditions of the three faiths are far apart. At best, to secular society, it means a city that is sacred to the three Abrahamic faiths. The New Jerusalem would come about in three radically different ways, and be entirely different in content. The picture or symbol means anything or nothing until it is interpreted by the appropriate system, tradition or community.

60 John Bunyan, *The Pilgrim's Progress* (London: The Religious Tract Society, no date given), p. 169.

Part 2

BIBLICAL PICTURES, SYMBOLS AND IMAGES

5

Visual pictures and symbolic acts in the Old Testament

The Old Testament not only draws on symbols and metaphors, but includes a number of symbolic acts, which are usually public and physical, and can be represented visually. One example is that of prophetic symbolism, which frequently entails physical, public action. Symbolic actions may constitute covenantal signs or public testimonies to God's acts of promise. We select the following from these many symbolic acts and symbols.

The development of symbols and symbolic acts in the Old Testament

Two of the most fundamental themes in the relationship between God and humankind in the Old Testament are those of **promise** and **covenant**. As Eichrodt has observed, in the covenant *people know 'exactly where they stand' with God; 'an atmosphere of trust and security* is created' in a defined and assured or explicit relationship.[1] The covenant entails pledges or promises both on God's part and on the part of humankind. *Promises* constitute vital speech-acts, which both *limit the available options* that the speaker of the promise would potentially otherwise have, and constitute *commitments* to fulfil that which has been promised. To use a homely illustration, if I promise to take my grandson to a football match, but am then given tickets to go to an exceptional concert, I should not be free to go to the concert. If I promise to preach at a mission hall, but am then invited to preach at Westminster Abbey, I am not free to accept the latter. It is not surprising, then, that *words and acts of solemn promise* are usually witnessed by *symbolic physical or public actions*, which underline their importance and *irrevocable* nature.

In the making of God's covenant with Abraham, an animal was killed

[1] Walther Eichrodt, *Theology of the Old Testament*, vol. 1 (London: SCM, 1961), p. 38 (first italics mine; second, his).

and divided into two pieces, and the parties walked between them, to show that they invoked a similar doom of destruction upon themselves if they proved unfaithful to their oath. Genesis 15.8–19 recounts this foundational covenant between *God and Abraham.* Abraham asked, 'O Lord God, how am I to know that I shall possess it [the land]?' (v. 8). By way of reply God commands Abraham to take a heifer, a turtledove and a young pigeon, and 'cut them in two, laying each half against the other' (vv. 9–10). Wenham comments, 'Were this a sacrifice, the pieces would now be placed on the altar and burned. Instead, they are put in two rows.'[2] After other events, including that of a flaming torch passing between the pieces, the narrator concludes, 'On that day the LORD made a *covenant* with Abram, saying, "To your descendants I give this land, from the river of Egypt to the great river, the river Euphrates"' (v. 18). He then lists nine tribes or nations, concluding with the Jebusites (v. 19).

The Brown-Driver-Briggs Hebrew Lexicon (BDB) associates the covenant with Abraham with a number of other passages. In Genesis 17.9–21 **circumcision** constitutes a second covenant sign; in Exodus 2.24 God delivered Israel because he recalled the covenant with Abraham, repeated in Exodus 6.4–5, Leviticus 26.42 and 2 Kings 13.23.[3] Jeremiah 34.18–19 looks forward to a renewed covenant, in which 'the calf is cut . . . in two'.

Sometimes the person who took the oath would place a hand under the 'thigh' (NRSV) of the one to whom the promise was made, for example in Genesis 24.2 (the aged Abraham and his servant, Eliezer, who was charged with finding a wife for Isaac); and Genesis 47.29 (Jacob and Joseph). The Hebrew word *yārēk*, according to BDB, means 'thigh, loin, side, base', but here is a euphemism for genitals, as the 'seat of procreative power'.[4] This is clearly an alternative for the symbolic act of 'cutting' between two animal parts. It likewise provides a physical act, adding solemnity and seriousness to an important promise. It is something more than writing.

'Drawing off the shoes in transferring a possession' constituted another symbolic act in business transactions.[5] Thus in Ruth 4.7–10 the narrator declared:

> Now this was the custom in former times in Israel concerning redeeming and exchanging: to confirm a transaction, one party took off a sandal and

[2] Gordon Wenham, *Genesis 1–15* (WBC 1; Texas: Word, 1987), p. 331.

[3] Francis Brown, S. R. Driver, and Charles A. Briggs, *The New Hebrew and English Lexicon* (Lafayette, IN: Associated Publishers, 1980), p. 136.

[4] Brown, Driver and Briggs, *The New Hebrew-English Lexicon*, pp. 437–8.

[5] Maurice H. Farbridge, *Studies in Biblical and Semitic Symbolism* (London: Kegan Paul, Trench, Trübner, 1923), p. 9.

> gave it to the other; this was the manner of attesting in Israel. So when the next-of-kin said to Boaz, 'Acquire it for yourself', he took off his sandal. Then Boaz said to the elders and all the people, 'Today you are witnesses that I have acquired from the hand of Naomi all that belonged to Elimelech . . . I have also acquired Ruth the Moabite, the wife of Mahlon, to be my wife, to maintain the dead man's name on his inheritance.

We shall now consider prophetic symbolism, and prophetic symbolic acts.

(1) An early example of what turned out to constitute a prophetic symbolic act comes in a pronouncement from Samuel to Saul.[6] 1 Samuel 15.27–28 reads:

> As Samuel turned to go away [from rebuking Saul], Saul caught hold of the hem of his robe, and it tore. And Samuel said to him, 'The LORD has torn the kingdom of Israel from you this very day, and has given it to a neighbour of yours.

This accidental action became a symbolic act, in which the prophet Samuel understood it as indicating that Saul's kingdom would be torn away from him.

(2) In 1 Kings 14.2 Abijah is described as a prophet. Jeroboam had been appointed to high office by Solomon, but he was ambitious and rebelled. Being 'very able' (1 Kings 11.28), Jeroboam came virtually to reign as king. In 1 Kings 11.29–33 Abijah, clothed in a new robe, found Jeroboam on the road, and 'laid hold of the new garment he was wearing, and tore it into twelve pieces'. He then said to Jeroboam, 'Take for yourself ten pieces; for thus says the LORD, the God of Israel, "See, I am about to tear the kingdom from the hand of Solomon, and will give you ten tribes"' (vv. 30–31). The two tribes of Judah then became the subjects of Rehoboam, King of Judah. In 1 Kings 14 Jeroboam sent his wife in disguise to Abijah, with gifts of loaves, but Abijah recognized her (in spite of his blindness) by her footsteps (v. 6). Abijah repeated his prophecy about the 'tearing apart' of Israel (vv. 8–9), affirming his prophetic symbolic act of tearing his garment.

(3) In the reigns of King Jehoshaphat of Judah and King Ahab of Israel, political intrigue reached a high temperature. The two kings conspired to capture Ramoth-gilead from Syria. Jehoshaphat demanded that they seek God's guidance (1 Kings 22.1–8). Ahab's four hundred 'tame' prophets all claimed

[6] For a brief summary cf. Farbridge, *Studies in Biblical and Semitic Symbolism*, p. 10.

that God approved the venture (v. 6). Reluctantly Ahab consulted Micaiah, the genuine prophet, who advised against it. Then Zedekiah, another false prophet, *imitated an act of prophetic symbolism.* He 'made for himself horns of iron, and he said, "Thus says the LORD: With these you shall gore the Arameans until they are destroyed"' (v. 11). Micaiah prophesied to the contrary: 'I saw Israel scattered on the mountains, like sheep that have no shepherd' (v. 17). He also warned Ahab and Jehoshaphat that false prophets were trying to seduce the kings, with 'a lying spirit' (v. 22). Zedekiah then brazenly assaulted Micaiah, saying, 'Which way did the spirit of the LORD pass from me to speak to you?' (v. 24). The kings wore disguise in the battle, but in the end were utterly defeated, as Micaiah had prophesied.

(**4**) In Zechariah 11 the prophet is rebuking the 'shepherds' of Israel for their unfaithful service: 'their own shepherds have no pity on them' (v. 5). Then Zechariah took two staffs, called 'Favour' and 'Unity'. In due course he broke 'Favour' to symbolize the annulling of the covenant (v. 10). Then he broke the staff 'Unity', 'annulling the family ties between Judah and Israel', the two Israelite kingdoms (v. 14).

(**5**) In Isaiah 20.2–5 Sargon, King of Assyria, is expanding his empire by conquest. God commanded Isaiah to walk about naked and barefoot. The Lord then said:

> Just as my servant Isaiah has walked naked and barefoot for three years as a sign and a portent against Egypt and Ethiopia, so shall the king of Assyria lead away the Egyptians as captives and the Ethiopians as exiles.

Chapters 21—24 are then oracles of doom, which include the line: 'Let us eat and drink, for tomorrow we die' (22.13). The prophet traces the successive conquests of Assyria.

(**6**) Such symbolical prophetic actions are particularly common in Jeremiah and Ezekiel. In Jeremiah 19.1–13 God commanded Jeremiah to buy a potter's earthenware jug (19.1). In sight of the elders and senior priests, he was to proclaim:

> Hear the word of the LORD, O kings of Judah and inhabitants of Jerusalem. Thus says the LORD of hosts, the God of Israel: I am going to bring such disaster upon this place that the ears of everyone who hears it will tingle. Because the people have forsaken me, and have profaned this place by making offerings in it to other gods . . . and because they have filled this place with the blood of the innocent. (vv. 3–4)

After more words of rebuke, and the description of more disasters, Jeremiah receives the Lord's command: 'Then you shall break the jug in the sight of those who go with you, and shall say to them: "Thus says the LORD of hosts . . . I break this people and this city, as one breaks a potter's vessel, so that it can never be mended"' (Jer. 19.10–11).

(7) On another occasion, in Jeremiah 27.2, the Lord said to Jeremiah,

> Make yourself a yoke of straps and bars, and put them on your neck. Send word to the king of Edom, the king of Moab, the king of the Ammonites, the king of Tyre, and the king of Sidon by the hand of the envoys . . . Thus says the LORD of hosts, the God of Israel: This is what you shall say to your masters: It is I who by my great power and my outstretched arm have made the earth, with the people and animals that are on the earth, and I give it to whomsoever I please. Now I have given all these lands into the hand of King Nebuchadnezzar of Babylon, my servant. (Jer. 27.2–6).

Jeremiah repeated the oracle to Zedekiah (v. 12). In Jeremiah 28.10 the yoke was broken by the false prophet, Hananiah.

(8) Eichrodt provided a detailed discussion of 'Symbolic actions and their meaning' with special reference to Ezekiel 4 and 5.[7] He commented:

> A symbolic action on the part of a prophet is more than a mere accompaniment to his discourse . . . As the anticipatory representation and actualization of a real event, it guarantees, establishes, or serves to indicate the fact that God acts. It involves the spectator and makes him become an actor.[8]

In Ezekiel 4.1–3 Ezekiel sketches the siege-plan of a city on a brick of soft, sunbaked clay. The siege-plan includes a siege-wall, ramp and battering ram (v. 2). The action does not specify the identity of the city. Most suggest that the city is Jerusalem, as the Hebrew and NRSV indicate; Eichrodt prefers to think of it as Babylon. The narrator commented: 'This is a sign for the house of Israel' (v. 4).

(9) In Ezekiel 4.4–8 the Lord commanded Ezekiel to lie on his left side, and 'place the punishment of the house of Israel upon it; you shall bear their punishment for the number of the days that you lie there' (v. 4). He

[7] Walther Eichrodt, *Ezekiel: A Commentary* (London: SCM, 1970), pp. 78–91.
[8] Eichrodt, *Ezekiel*, pp. 81 and 82.

supposedly lay absolutely still for 190 days in order to give a sign. According to Eichrodt this represents a sick man under a diagnosis of catalepsy. Thus it represents 'the immobilization or "paralysing" of the besieged'.[9] Ezekiel 4.9–15 represents the hardships of the besieged.

(**10**) In Ezekiel 5.1–4 God commanded Ezekiel to take a sharp sword, and declared:

> Use it as a barber's razor, and run it over your head and your beard; then take balances for weighing, and divide the hair. One-third of the hair you shall burn . . . when the days of the siege are completed; one-third you shall take and strike with the sword all around the city; one-third you shall scatter to the wind. (v. 2)

These acts serve to illustrate the fate in store for the nation. One third signifies the liquidation of the nation by starvation and pestilence; while another third signifies those who fall in battle; the third thrown to the wind stands for those who escape, but are carried into exile.

Symbols for God: God's character and actions, and the covenant

We have not restricted the main argument of this book to public actions. Many Old Testament symbols simply provide visual representations or pictures which require interpretation along established lines. We first consider symbols for God, which communicate what would otherwise be more abstract truths. Symbols for God belong to a different order of things from the acted-out symbols in prophetic symbolism. Some symbols for God are word-symbols, or potential pictures or visual representations.

(**1**) The symbol of God as **Shepherd** (Heb., *rā'ah*) resonated most vividly for ancient Israel, because sheep-farming was a fundamental activity in society. Yet even today 'The Lord is my Shepherd' (Ps. 23.1) remains a potent symbol of God. Similarly 'He will feed his flock like a shepherd' (Isa. 40.11) remains a potent symbol, not least because of Handel's *Messiah*. In the Old Testament, however, the contrast between God as a faithful shepherd of his people, and the false shepherds who scatter God's people, resonates through both Testaments (Jer. 23.1–4; Ezek. 34.1–22; John 10.11).

[9] Eichrodt, *Ezekiel*, p. 84.

(**2**) At least equal to this is the symbol of God as **Father** (Heb., *'āb*). One example comes from Psalm 103.13, 'As a father has compassion for his children, so the LORD has compassion for those who fear him.' Another comes from Hosea 11.3, 'I . . . taught Ephraim to walk', which is paralleled in the New Testament by Matthew 6.9, 'Our Father in heaven'. This symbol speaks of love, care and discipline. Pannenberg observes:

> On the lips of Jesus . . . 'Father' . . . became a proper name for God. It ceased to be simply one designation among others . . . The words 'God' and 'Father' are not just time-bound concepts from which we can detach the true content of the message.[10]

(**3**) Probably the third most prominent symbol for God is that of **King** (Heb., *melek*). For example, 'The LORD is king for ever and ever' (Ps. 10.16); 'Who is this King of glory? The LORD of hosts, he is the King of glory' (Ps. 24.10); 'The LORD is our king; he will save us' (Isa. 33.22b). In the light of Pannenberg's observation about 'Father', some post-colonialist interpreters who want to reject the term might like to think again. Jesus' proclamation of the kingdom of God is central to the first three Gospels. The qualities of kingship on which the psalmist and prophets reflect are not only majesty and omnipotence, but care, statesmanship and defence of the poor, the widows and orphans.

(**4**) In addition to these three symbols, many are used which together constitute an important but varied collection of symbols. We shall select five.

(**a**) **Cloud and a pillar of fire** (Heb., *anān* and *ēsh*) represent a familiar symbol of God's guidance of Israel through the wilderness after their deliverance from Egypt. Exodus 13.21–22 reads:

> The LORD went in front of them in a pillar of cloud by day . . . and in a pillar of fire by night . . . so that they might travel by day and by night. Neither the pillar of cloud by day nor the pillar of fire by night left its place in front of the people.

In his commentary Brevard Childs points out that Exodus 13.17–19 explains why God's guidance is important. Israel's journey from Egypt to the Promised Land explicitly involved 'a roundabout way' (v. 18). God purposed this because Israel might be disheartened if they had immediately to

[10] Wolfhart Pannenberg, *Systematic Theology*, vol. 1 (Eng., Edinburgh: T&T Clark, 1991), pp. 262–3.

face hostility from the Philistines. Thus Childs calls this explanation of guidance 'the divine revelation . . . God's plan from the divine perspective'.[11] In addition to Exodus 13.17–18, the narrator refers to the phenomenon again in Exodus 14.19; and 14.24, where Israel faces the Egyptian army, and Numbers 14.14, when previous events are recalled. Childs sums up the episode, commenting, 'God's miraculous rescue of Israel at the sea was remembered as the event by which God brought into being his people.'[12]

(b) The blast of **trumpets and thunder** (Heb., *shōphar* and *ra'am*) constitute a symbol of God's speaking. One classic example occurs in Exodus 19.19: 'As the blast of the trumpet grew louder and louder, Moses would speak and God would answer him in thunder.' The psalmist declares, 'The voice of the LORD is over the waters; the God of glory thunders . . . The voice of the LORD is powerful; the voice of the LORD is full of majesty' (Ps. 29.3, 4). In the New Testament the Seer takes up the symbol of the trumpet in Revelation 8.6–13. Thunder, like the rainbow, is already a natural phenomenon, but now has added meaning.

(c) A **throne** (Heb., *kissē'*) becomes a symbol of God's glory. This is notable in Isaiah's commissioning vision, when he recalls: 'I saw the Lord sitting on the throne, high and lofty; and the hem of his robe filled the Temple' (Isa. 6.1). Ezekiel uses the same symbol: 'There was something like a throne, in appearance like sapphire; and seated above the likeness of a throne . . . I saw something like gleaming amber . . . This was the appearance of the likeness of the glory of the LORD' (Ezek. 1.26–28). Ezekiel recognizes that to describe God lies beyond the limits of human language ('above' is symbolic), and he therefore uses the phrase 'something like' to indicate transcendent otherness. He recognizes that the visual representations are not to be understood literally. Eichrodt comments, 'The world-ruler has no dwelling within the world, but is enthroned in otherworldly glory above the dome of heaven.'[13]

(d) A **rock** (Heb., *sela'*) becomes a symbol of God's faithfulness and stability. In Psalm 18.2 we read, 'The LORD is my rock, my fortress and my deliverer, my God, my rock in whom I take refuge, my shield and the Horn of my salvation, my stronghold.' Peter Craigie distinguishes two categories of symbols. One is the category of rocks, stronghold and cliff; the other

---

[11] Brevard Childs, *Exodus: A Commentary* (Eng., London: SCM, 1974), p. 224.

[12] Childs, *Exodus*, p. 237.

[13] Eichrodt, *Ezekiel*, p. 58.

is the military metaphor of shield, safe retreat and deliverer.[14] Psalm 40.2 speaks of being delivered from a miry bog, to stand secure upon a rock.

(e) God's sovereignty is not surprisingly symbolized by **his sceptre** (Heb., *shēbet*, sceptre or rod). Psalm 45.6–7, which is quoted in Hebrews, applying it to Christ, declares, 'Your throne, O God, endures for ever and ever. Your royal sceptre is a sceptre of equity; you love righteousness and hate wickedness' (cf. Heb. 1.8–9). Shepherds, fathers, kings, clouds, fire, trumpets, thunder, thrones, rocks and sceptres can all be represented visually or aurally.

(f) Among cultic symbols, the use of the **rainbow** (Heb., *qeset*) as a symbol to ratify the covenant with Noah (Gen. 9.12) has already been explained in Chapter 4. This does not imply that the rainbow came into being at that point, but that from henceforth it served as a reminder to Noah that God would keep his covenant promise not to flood the earth again.

(g) Circumcision (Hebrew, *mûlāh*) constitutes another symbol of the covenant. In Genesis 17.11 God said to Abraham, 'You shall circumcise the flesh . . . and it shall be a sign of the covenant between me and you.' This is to be 'throughout your generations' (v. 12). It is explicitly physical, involving action, but Jeremiah appealed for a 'circumcision' of the heart (Jer. 4.4).

(7) '**Bread of the Presence**' (Heb., *lechem pānîm*) also constitutes a covenantal sign. This time it is a physical symbol, not a merely conceptual one. Exodus 25.30 reads, 'You shall set the bread of the Presence on the table before me always', that is in the tabernacle. More detailed instructions can be found in Leviticus 24.5–9. These convey the Lord's instructions to Moses: 'You shall bring the sheaf of the first fruits of your harvest to the priest. He shall raise the sheaf before the Lord, so that you may find acceptance . . .' Twelve loaves were baked of fine flour, and put on the table that stood in front of the Most Holy Place. This served as a symbol of an everlasting covenant. William Tyndale translated this as *shewbread*. Brevard Childs underlined 'the symbolic approach to the tabernacle'.[15] Wenham comments, 'The bread was placed on a fairly small low table covered in gold plate . . . Along with the bread, various small dishes had to be placed on the table.'[16]

---

[14] Peter Craigie, *Psalms 1–50* (Waco: Word, 1983), p. 173.

[15] Childs, *Exodus*, p. 539.

[16] Gordon Wenham, *The Book of Leviticus* (Grand Rapids: Eerdmans, 1979), p. 310.

(8) The institution of **the Sabbath** (Heb., *shabbāt*) provides another example. In Exodus 20.8–10 and 23.12–17 this becomes a covenant symbol (v. 16) although in other biblical references it sometimes has a humanitarian motivation (Deut. 5.15), and is also related to God's 'resting' on the seventh day of creation. Childs has devoted a bibliography to critical opinion on the Sabbath.[17]

(9) This does not exhaust the symbols used in the Old Testament. (a) A **signet ring** (Heb., *chōthām*) is used in Haggai 2.23 as a sign of authority, as when God declares, 'I will take you, O Zerubbabel . . . and make you like a signet ring; for I have chosen you.' (b) A more controversial symbol or picture is that of **Jacob's ladder** (Gen. 28.12). Mediaeval mystics sometimes interpreted this as a ladder up to heaven, but others argue that the ladder portrays only mediation or access between earth and heaven. Luther attacked the notion of an 'upward' path to God, independently of God's 'downward' grace. (c) Sometimes **arrows** can denote the judgement of God. In Psalm 38.2 the speaker says, 'Your arrows have sunk into me.'

(10) Symbols of God's character and actions include **anointing** as a symbol of God's empowerment or commission. In 1 Samuel 16.13, 'Samuel took the horn of oil, and anointed him [David] in the presence of his brothers; and the spirit of the Lord came mightily upon David from that day forward.' In Isaiah 61.1, 'The spirit of . . . the Lord has anointed me [the Servant of the Lord]; he has sent me to bring good news to the oppressed, to bind up the broken-hearted, to proclaim liberty . . .' Anointing installs kings, prophets and priests into office, and seems to be a rough anticipation of coronations, ordinations or any formal God-given tasks. In the New Testament Jesus appropriates Isaiah's words in Luke 4.18.

(11) God's face (Heb., *'aph, pānîm*) seems to become a symbol of his presence. In Numbers 6.25–26 God's priest declares, 'The Lord bless you and keep you; the Lord make his face to shine upon you; the Lord lift up his countenance upon you, and give you peace.' *Face* is used as metonymy for *person*, or for a person's *presence*. Thus 2 Chronicles 30.9 declares, 'The Lord your God is gracious and merciful, and will not turn away his face from you.' Conversely Isaiah 59.2 warns the readers, 'Your sins have hidden his face from you'. Similarly the psalmist prays, 'Hide your face from my sins' (51.9), in other words, please ignore them. Yet Psalm 11.7

---

[17] Childs, *Exodus*, pp. 412–13.

declares, 'The upright shall behold his [God's] face.' David Ford has written on the significance of face in his *Self and Salvation*. He writes:

> The face of someone important to us . . . conjures up past events, stories and associations, a world of meaning . . . The face as relating, welcoming, incorporating others is fundamental to social life. It is possible to have a glimpse of the fact that individuality and sociality need not be in competition with each other, when we think of the way in which faces can interanimate each other and at the same time each seem to become more fully and distinctively itself.[18]

Symbolic visual representation and symbolic animals and plants

Sometimes visual representation (usually by analogy or metaphor) may also involve a traditional symbolism of animals.

(1) **The eagle** is synonymous with speed and strength, as in Isaiah 40.31: 'Those who wait for the LORD shall renew their strength, they shall mount up with wings like eagles, they shall run and not be weary.' Jeremiah 49.22 reads, 'He [the LORD] shall mount up and swoop down like an eagle . . . against Bozrah . . .' In Ezekiel 17.3 and 7, the prophet is commanded to speak an allegory (v. 2) in which 'A great eagle . . . came to the Lebanon. He took the top of the cedar, broke off its topmost shoot; he carried it to a land of trade'. Eichrodt observes, 'As the eagle is the embodiment of strength and swiftness, it makes a very suitable symbol for a conqueror, and is thus used in Deutero-Isaiah as well (Isa. 46:11).'[19] In Ezekiel 17, above, the cedar of Lebanon appropriates the house of David in the allegory.

(2) **The lion** is similarly a symbol of 'strength, sovereignty, and courage'.[20] Genesis 49.9 applies 'lion' to Judah. Lions, with oxen and cherubim, adorn the bases of the brazen sea in 1 Kings 7.29. Joel 1.6 uses the metaphor of the lion for strength. Hosea 13.8 reads: 'I will devour them like a lion'. The same metaphor was used in Egypt, for example by Tukulti Nihib I (1275 BC) and Amenhoteb III. Lions are also represented on seal cylinders in Gilgamesh episodes in Babylonia.

---

[18] David Ford, *Self and Salvation: Being Transformed* (Cambridge: CUP, 1999), pp. 18–19.
[19] Eichrodt, *Ezekiel*, p. 224.
[20] Farbridge, *Studies in Biblical and Semitic Symbolism*, p. 69.

(**3**) At the opposite end of the spectrum **snakes** are ambiguous in what they represent. Farbridge comments, 'In Egypt every house has a serpent which is regarded as its protector.'[21] Egyptians did not regard snakes as hostile to humankind, and Moses' brazen serpent brought healing. Often Arabs also regarded them as sacred; and Babylonian mythology had similar attitudes. In Phoenicia and Oriental Greece the snake becomes associated with healing. Hebrew attitudes varied. The most familiar account occurs in the Genesis narrative of the fall of humankind (Gen. 3.1–15), when the first humans, despite God's warning, were tempted to eat some of the fruit of the 'tree of the knowledge of good and evil'. In Genesis 3.4, 'The serpent said to the woman, "You will not die; for God knows that when you eat of it your eyes will be opened, and you will be like God."' In verses 14–15, 'God said to the serpent . . . "Cursed are you . . . I will put enmity between . . . your offspring and hers."' Farbridge sees some Hebrew traditions as viewing the serpent 'as a symbol of renewed energy and vigour'.[22] He even speculates controversially that this attitude lies behind the narrative of Moses and the brazen serpent in Numbers 21.6–9.

(**4**) **The horse** is universally regarded as a symbol of war. Typically Job 39.19–25 asks:

> Do you give the horse its might? Did you clothe its neck with mane? Do you make it leap like the locust? Its majestic snorting is terrible. It paws violently, exults mightily; it goes out to meet the weapons. It laughs at fear, and is not dismayed . . . With fierceness and rage it swallows the ground; it cannot stand still at the sound of the trumpet. When the trumpet sounds, it says 'Aha!' From a distance it smells the battle, the thunder of the captains, and the shouting.

Horses and chariots are regular metaphors used in the Bible. Famously the psalmist declares, 'Some take pride in chariots, and some in horses, but our pride is in the name of the LORD our God' (Ps. 20.7). Nahum 3.1–3 reflects on the bloodshed of battle, declaring, 'The crack of whip and rumble of wheel, galloping horse and bounding chariot! Horsemen charging, flashing sword and glittering spear, piles of dead, heaps of corpses, dead bodies without end – they stumble over the bodies!' By contrast, the donkey, ox and camel are creatures of commerce and peace.

---

[21] Farbridge, *Studies in Biblical and Semitic Symbolism*, p. 71.

[22] Farbridge, *Studies in Biblical and Semitic Symbolism*, p. 76.

(**5**) In the realm of birds, **the dove**, in contrast to the raven, seems to be 'a symbol of purity and innocence'.[23] Farbridge comments that doves and pigeons hold the same symbolic place among birds as sheep and lambs hold among animals. In the Talmud, doves are mild, true and loving; ravens are cunning and deceptive. Doves and turtledoves were the only birds admitted as sacrifices. Leviticus 5.8 sanctions them as sacrifices for those who could not afford a sheep or goat (as offered by Mary and Joseph in Luke 2.24). The ordinance is repeated in Leviticus 12.6–8 and 14.22.

(**6**) In the realm of trees, plants and flowers, a variety of symbolism is used, and many phrases become metaphors. Such phrases as 'lily of the valley, the lily among thorns, the orchard of pomegranates, myrrh and camphor, spikenard and cinnamon' are often used.[24] Often the transient character of plants and vegetation features, as when 'grass' is symbolic of human frailty: 'All people are grass, their constancy is like the flower of the field. The grass withers, the flower fades . . . but the word of our God will stand for ever' (Isa. 40.6–8). By contrast, Ezekiel 47.12 speaks of trees whose 'leaves will not wither nor their fruit fail, but they will bear fresh fruit every month'. The trees, plants and flowers of the Bible represent a various range of realities.

(a) **Olive trees** have a positive meaning. Jeremiah 11.16 states, 'The Lord once called you, "A green olive tree, fair with goodly fruit"; but with the roar of a great tempest he will set fire to it, and its branches will be consumed.' Hosea 14.6 declares, 'His shoots shall spread out; his beauty shall be like the olive tree, and his fragrance like that of Lebanon.' Farbridge comments:

> The evergreen freshness of the tree, the enormous quantity of oil it produces, the fact that it was so necessary for lighting and medicinal purposes, as well as for food, caused it to be regarded as one of the main necessities of life. Its timber is also of a rich amber colour. This explains why the prophets spoke of the olive tree as a symbol of beauty and strength.[25]

1 Kings 6 tells us that the door and post of Solomon's Temple, and the cherubim, were all made of olive wood (vv. 23, 31–33).

---

23 Farbridge, *Studies in Biblical and Semitic Symbolism*, p. 80.
24 Farbridge, *Studies in Biblical and Semitic Symbolism*, p. 28.
25 Farbridge, *Studies in Biblical and Semitic Symbolism*, p. 41.

(b) The vine became the emblem of the nation of Israel. In Isaiah 5.1–2, God planted a vineyard on a fertile hill, cleared it of stones, built a watch-tower over it, and expected it to yield grapes. But the indictment begins: 'But it yielded wild grapes'. Nevertheless it would be wrong to assume that this negative picture always refers to Israel. More generally, it can be a symbol of beauty, wealth and prosperity. To dwell under one's vine and fig tree is emblematic of peace and prosperity (Mic. 4.4; and Zech. 3.10). It can also be a symbol or metaphor of domestic bliss: 'Your wife will be like a fruitful vine within your house' (Ps. 128.3). The picture is not free-floating, but depends on a contextual frame for correct interpretation.

(c) The cedar tree constitutes a symbol of height and exalted, vigorous growth. Ezekiel 31.3–5 considers the cedar

> with fair branches and forest shade, and of great height, its top among the clouds. . . So it towered high above all the trees of the field; its boughs grew large and its branches long, from abundant waters in its shoots.

Farbridge observes:

> It is sound to its very core, the roots of the tree are expansive, and being firmly fixed in the soil, it is enabled to withstand the violence of storms. Like a palm tree, it loves water, and is an evergreen. It is always covered with leaves, and its bark and leaves are highly aromatic, and the 'smell of Lebanon' has become a proverb for fragrance.[26]

Psalm 92.12 notes, 'The righteous flourish like the palm tree, and grow like a cedar of Lebanon.' These are strictly similes rather than metaphors. Numbers 24.6 agrees that they are 'like cedar trees beside the waters'. Babylonian and Assyrian literature often alludes to palaces and temples built of cedar wood. Shalmaneser II of Assyria provides an example in the temple of Anu.

(d) Oak trees could be places of revelation in the early writings. God appeared to Abraham at the oak of Shechem, where he built an altar (Gen. 12.6). Later, angels appeared to Abraham beside the oaks of Mamre, as he sat by the entrance to his tent (Gen. 18.1). An angel appeared to Gideon as he was sitting under the oak at Ophrah (Judg. 6.11). Then Amos notes the strength of oaks (Amos 2.9). Zechariah 11.2 says, 'Wail, oaks of Bashan'. Isaiah 2.13 declares that God is 'against all the oaks of Bashan', as symbols

---

[26] Farbridge, *Studies in Biblical and Semitic Symbolism*, p. 63.

of pride and haughtiness. Clearly oaks are valued for their strength and beauty. Whereas many symbols vary in meaning, Farbridge says, 'The oak is unvarying in its meaning – strength, protection, fidelity . . . dependability, honour, and courage.'[27] Thus Joshua set up a stone to commemorate the covenant 'under the oak in the sanctuary of the LORD' (Josh. 24.26).

(e) **Figs** often indicate the peace and prosperity of a nation. Micah 4.4 captures the mood when it declares, 'They shall all sit under their own vines and under their own fig trees, and no one shall make them afraid.' Figs were common in Israel. Sometimes the failure and destruction of figs indicate God's judgement. Isaiah prophesies: 'The skies roll up like a scroll . . . [They] shall wither like . . . fruit withering on a fig tree' (34.4). Figs are part of the mulberry family. They have a unique, sweet taste, and a soft and chewy texture. Fresh figs are delicate and perishable, so are often dried to preserve them. There are multiple different varieties of fig, all of which vary widely in colour and texture. One of the world's oldest trees, the fig tree can be traced back to the earliest historical documents, and features prominently in the Bible. Figs are native to the Middle East and Mediterranean and were held in high regard by the Greeks.

(f) **The lily** has symbolic significance. Hosea says of Israel, 'He shall blossom like the lily; he shall strike root like the forests of Lebanon' (14.5). In the Song of Solomon, 'His lips are lilies, distilling liquid myrrh' (5.13). In the gardens [the] beloved . . . gather[s] lilies' (Song of Sol. 6.2). In a famous analogy, 'As a lily among brambles, so is my love among maidens' (2.2), that is, the beloved stands out as precious among what threatens to obscure her. In later Jewish thought Israel is compared to lilies.

(g) **Almonds** are well known especially from the call of Jeremiah. The Hebrew for almond (*shaked*) is also the word for 'wake'. Hence when Jeremiah says, 'I see a branch of an almond tree' (Jer. 1.11), the Lord replies, 'You have seen well, for I am watching over my word to perform it.' The meaning would be clearer if we were to render this: 'I see a wake-tree.' The almond was the first tree to wake to life after winter. In the detailed instructions about the Ark of the Covenant and the tabernacle, 'Three cups shaped like almond blossoms' feature (Exod. 37.19; repeated in 37.20). In Numbers 17.8, when Moses went into the tent of the covenant, the staff of Aaron 'bore ripe almonds'.

---

[27] Farbridge, *Studies in Biblical and Semitic Symbolism*, p. 44.

(h) The myrtle is regarded as a symbol of joy, peace and happiness. Thus in Isaiah 41.19 the reversal of wilderness barrenness is 'the cedar, the acacia, the myrtle, and the olive'. In Isaiah 55.13, 'Instead of the brier shall come up the myrtle.' In Zechariah 1.8–10 the man with the red horse stood among the myrtle trees. Many refer to their rich colouring and dark-green, shining leaves. Similarly the Greeks wore garlands of myrtle on festal occasions.

What may we infer from this relatively detailed look at symbols, images and pictures in the Old Testament? First, we may note how prodigious is the resort to the use of visual imagery in virtually every book of the Old Testament. This achieves its most striking example in prophetic symbolism, which usually involves action as well as visual content. At bare minimum, it provides a precedent for the importance of pictures, symbols or images for various types of communication. It provides examples of the power and memorable nature of such pictures. It therefore suggests that modern communication by teachers and preachers should draw heavily upon pictures and symbols in the same way.

Second, it also demonstrates the second theme of this book, namely that usually pictures, symbols and images require informed interpretation rather than simply being regarded as free-floating pictures, the meaning of which may be constructed by the reader. Most are firmly embedded in particular traditions of interpretation. But this does not apply to every picture or symbol. In these cases a regard for context and for the aim of the author remains indispensable. Sometimes popular understandings of images or symbols may not match their meaning in context. Hence this first biblical example of the use of pictures and symbols coheres with the double purpose of this book. On the one hand, it illustrates the power of pictures and the need to draw on them. On the other hand, it suggests that a cursory interpretation of symbols might in some cases be misleading and even seductive.

6

Pictures and images in the teaching of Jesus

Everyday rural Galilean life: the power of Jesus' vivid visual imagery

A classic quotation from Charles H. Dodd sums up both the positive and negative aspect of what we want to say. Dodd declared:

> At its simplest, the parable is a metaphor or simile drawn from nature or common life, arresting the hearer by its vividness or strangeness, and leaving the mind in sufficient doubt to its precise application to tease the mind into active thought.[1]

This sums up well our positive point about the power of pictures, for the parables are vivid, even if they are often strange. But on the other side they also leave the mind in sufficient doubt as to their precise application to require serious and prolonged thought. A mistaken interpretation can seduce us and mislead us.

Dodd is also right in stating that the reservoir from which Jesus draws his pictures and images is the 'common world' of the hearers. In the words of Ernst Fuchs:

> Without a doubt Jesus speaks in this sphere of provincial and family life as it takes place in peaceful or normal times. It is from this life that he takes the examples of his parables. One observes the people walking along the street and knocking on the window; one hears the loud voice of their festivities. The farmer goes to his field, sows and harvests. The wife plants the small plot of land adjoining her house. There are the rich and the poor, the honest and the frauds; there is happiness and need, sadness and thankfulness. But all that is not only . . . 'source material' . . . not only a kind of 'point of contact'; instead he has in mind precisely this 'world'.[2]

1 Charles H. Dodd, *The Parables of the Kingdom* (London: Nisbet, 1953), p. 16.

2 Ernst Fuchs, 'The New Testament and the Hermeneutical Problem', in James M. Robinson and John B. Cobb (eds), *New Frontiers in Theology, vol. 2, The New Hermeneutic* (New York: Harper & Row, 1964), p. 126; cf. pp. 111–45.

Jesus was seeking to reach what Fuchs calls 'mutual understanding' (*Einverständnis)* by fully entering the world of the hearers, rather than expecting that they would enter into his theological world directly. Here, Fuchs asserts, 'he calls for faith – that is, for decision. The decision places him who enters in upon it on the side of God and the miracle of divine action'.[3] Thus the picture or image has more than an illustrative function. It provides a way of meeting, understanding and obeying God. But Dodd is not alone in stressing that the application of a parable is left imprecise. Robert Funk declared that it is 'left imprecise in order to tease the hearer into making his own application'.[4] This is broadly correct, but raises the problem of 'right' interpretation.

This problem is compounded by comments which Joachim Jeremias has made about the nature of the parables. He declared that to draw distinctions 'between metaphor, simile, parable, similitude, allegory, illustration, and so forth' was

> a fruitless labour in the end, since the Hebrew *māshāl* and the Aramaic *mathla* embraced all these categories and many more without distinction. The word may mean . . . parable, similitude, allegory, fable, proverb, apocalyptic revelation, symbol, pseudonym, fictitious person, example, theme, argument, apology, refutation, jest. Similarly παραβολή in the New Testament has not only one meaning, 'parable', but also 'comparison' . . . and 'symbol'.[5]

The word means *comparison* in Luke 5.36; Mark 3.23; *symbol* in Hebrews 9.9; 11.19; *proverb* or *commonplace* in Luke 4.23; and *riddle* in Luke 14.7. Many others, of course, will disagree about the exact translation, but the general principle is clear. In Amos Wilder's words, 'Jesus uses figures of speech in an immense number of ways.'[6] Certain features, however, are common: all are told in order to evoke a practical response. Hence Jesus says, 'He who has ears to hear, let him hear.' The parables are also examples of 'indirect communication', which avoids undue confrontation and premature decision.

In the end, however, certain general characteristics apply to most parables, even if they cannot be applied rigidly or mechanically. For example, whereas allegory often contains several distinct points, parables generally serve to make one key point, as Adolf Jülicher and Eta Linnemann have rightly insisted. An allegory often offers a string of relatively independent

---

3 Fuchs, 'The Hermeneutical Problem', p. 129.

4 Robert Funk, *Language, Hermeneutic and Word of God* (New York: Harper, 1966), p. 133.

5 Joachim Jeremias, *The Parables of Jesus* (Eng., London: SCM, rev. edn, 1963), p. 20.

6 Amos N. Wilder, *Early Christian Rhetoric* (London: SCM, 1964), p. 81.

evaluations, such as we have, for example, in the allegory of *The Pilgrim's Progress* by John Bunyan. Further, the allegory, as Linnemann argues, is usually addressed to the initiated or to insiders; it 'presupposes an understanding'; whereas parable prepares for understanding, and is often used to reconcile opposition. Linnemann remarks, 'For the uninitiated the allegory is a riddle, which needs to be interpreted.'[7] The fine distinctions within the word 'parable' (*māshāl* or *parabolē*) do not undermine the distinction between parable and allegory. Nevertheless the distinction is not so rigid as to suggest that Jesus would never have uttered an allegory. The allegory of the Royal Wedding (Matt. 22.1–14) and the 'Interpretation' of the Parable of the Sower (Mark 4.3–9) cannot be excluded from authentic words of Jesus simply because elsewhere he usually preferred parable over allegories. On the other hand, parables are usually understood as having one main point, and to be addressed mainly to opponents or outsiders.

The concrete imagery of parables stands in contrast to abstract ideas or principles. For example, Jesus said, 'Whenever you give alms, do not sound a trumpet before you' (Matt. 6.2). To say 'Beneficence should not be ostentatious' would be abstract and without punch. A second example that Dodd cites is the memorable saying, 'It is easier for a camel to go through the eye of a needle than for someone who is rich to enter the kingdom of God' (Matt. 19.24). The sheer power of such images is beyond question.

Many of the so-called conventions of storytelling enhance the power of the imagery which Jesus used. He often used the convention of **three characters** (discounting the man himself) to build up the story towards making a climax. This occurs in the Parable of the Good Samaritan, which involved a Jewish priest, a Levite and a Samaritan (Luke 10.29–37). The use of **contrast** exemplified in the Parable of the Rich Man and Lazarus (Luke 16.19–31), the elder and younger sons in the Parable of the Prodigal Son (Luke 15.11–32), and the wise and foolish maidens (Matt. 25.1–13) provide vivid and memorable antitheses. Most parables tell of events which occurred once; but Jesus also used 'similitudes', which depict events which happen regularly, and often represent regularities of nature. These include the parable about the mustard seed which gives a large yield (Mark 4.30–32). On the other hand, while it tells of a regular event the Parable of the Sower places the stress not upon the difference in size of yield from various sowings, but on encouragement to go on sowing, whatever

7 Eta Linnemann, *Parables of Jesus: Introduction and Exposition* (Eng., London: SPCK, 1966), p. 7.

the temporary obstacles or difficulties (Mark 4.3–8/Matt. 13.3–8/Luke 8.5–8).[8] Writers often speak of the artistry of Jesus. The usual economy and brevity of the narrative allows many of the devices to be used which make the parables memorable and powerful in their uses of common imagery. The parables of the Unscrupulous but Judicious Manager (Luke 16.1–9), of the Barren Fig Tree (Luke 13.6–9), of the Weeds among the Wheat (Matt. 13.24–30), and of the Lost Sheep (Luke 15.6), all make good use of direct speech and soliloquy. These touches are not merely for decorative artistry, but to give power and memorability to the parables. The principle of interpretation which is normally correct is that each of this kind of parables makes one substantial point which is drawn from each story.

In his list of parables Jeremias counts 39 or 40, including those which he conflates from the *three* Synoptic Gospels.[9] He includes the Parable of the Sower (Mark 4.3–8; Matt. 13.3–8; and Luke 8.5–8); the Patient Husbandman (Mark 4.26–29); the Mustard Seed (Mark 4.30–32; Matt. 13.31; and Luke 13.18–19); the Wicked Husbandmen (Mark 12.1–11; Matt. 21.33–44; Luke 20.9–18); the Budding Fig-tree (Mark 13.28–29; Matt. 24.32–33; Luke 21.29–31); and the Doorkeeper (Mark 13.33–37; Luke 12.35–38). Of these six, five are from the triple tradition; all come from Mark, and three come early in his Gospel. We have used Jeremias' titles of the parables. Jeremias argued that the Parable of the Sower clearly belongs to Mark's earliest, foundational, tradition. As we earlier noted, it placed the emphasis on the word of God. He regarded the popular view of it as a parable of the different soils as a derivative interpretation verging on allegory. In his view, the traditional interpretation 'misses the eschatological point of the parable', and turns it into a psychology of the hearers; its real meaning is *encouragement to go on sowing the word, as Jesus did in the face of opposition*, for this can produce *fantastic results out of all proportion to expectations.*[10] This picture is unforgettable.

The Parable which Jeremias calls the Patient Husbandman is better known as the Seed Growing Secretly. He called it a parable of contrast:

> The inactivity of the farmer after sowing is vividly depicted: his life follows its ordered round of sleeping and waking, night and day: without his taking anxious thought . . . or any active steps, the seed grows from stalk to ear, and from ear to ripened corn – the naming of each stage of the process

[8] Jeremias, *The Parables of Jesus*, pp. 149–51.
[9] Jeremias, *The Parables of Jesus*, pp. 247–8.
[10] Jeremias, *The Parables of Jesus*, pp. 78–9.

> describes the unceasing process of growth. Then suddenly the moment arrives which rewards the patient waiting. The corn is ripe, the sickle is thrust in, the joyful cry rings out, 'harvest has come'. Thus it is with the kingdom of God; thus with the same certainty as the harvest comes for the husbandman after his long waiting, does God when his hour has come.[11]

Jeremias conveys the vividness and power of the pictures which Jesus produced.

A third Markan parable is the Parable of the Wicked Husbandmen, with parallels in Matthew and Luke. In view of sharp distinctions between parable and allegory, it is refreshing to note Jeremias' comment, 'It exhibits an allegorical character which is unique among the parables of Jesus.'[12] The sending of the servants in an ascending order in Mark, which ends in a climax, follows the popular love of climax, and anticipates the fate which the Son was to suffer. Jeremias adds that there is here a reference to the prophets and their fate. At all events, the meaning is memorable and clear.

Nineteen of the parables cited by Jeremias are from Matthew, of which nine are also found in Luke. Five are from Matthew's special source in Matthew 13. (Jeremias also cites parallels in the *Gospel of Thomas.*) Matthew includes the Tares among the Wheat (Matt. 13.24–30); the Leaven (Matt. 13.33; Luke 13.20–21); the Treasure (Matt. 13.44); the Pearl (13.45); and the Seine-net (13.47–48). All (or perhaps all but one) of these reflect Matthew's characteristic interest in the Church. In 13.24–30 Jesus told how an enemy came by night to sow weeds among the good crop. When the servants ask whether they are to root out the weeds now, they are told to wait until the harvest. Most interpreters understand this as a vivid picture of the mixed, visible Church. The Parable of the Seine-net makes the same point by means of different pictures or images. The net 'caught fish of every kind', but only 'at the end of the world' shall angels 'separate the evil from the righteous'. The Pearl of Great Price paints a picture of wholehearted discipleship. A merchant will give anything to acquire the precious pearl. The Treasure that is buried and hidden requires patient labour to discover it. This may apply to believers within the Church, or to those who seek to enter it and find Christ.

Jesus' use of pictures, images, symbols and analogies is by no means restricted to what we formally call 'the parables'. Some of the more pithy, brief and succinct pictures come from material shared by Matthew and

---

[11] Jeremias, *The Parables of Jesus*, p. 151.

[12] Jeremias, *The Parables of Jesus*, p. 70.

Luke, which many assign to a shared source, traditionally called the 'Q' source; even this has remained a controversial speculation. Luke's 'Sermon on the Plain' in Luke 6.17–49, for example, contains numerous such pictures. Jesus appealed to the picture of the blind leading blind people, when both 'fall into a pit' (Luke 6.39; Matt. 15.14). He imagined someone offering to take a speck out of someone's eye, while he does 'not notice the log in [his] own eye' (Matt. 7.3–4; Luke 6.41). He appealed to the absurdity of brambles bearing grapes, and thorns bearing figs, to illustrate that good comes from good character, not from isolated actions (Matt. 7.16; Luke 6.43–45). He compared superficial goodness with a person building a house without foundations (Luke 6.48–49; Matt. 7.24–27).

However, Jesus used pictures, images and analogies from the very beginning of his public ministry. At this point it is convenient to follow Luke's outline in the first place, since sometimes Luke seems to offer marginally more of these snapshot pictures than Matthew. Further, some claim that when Matthew and Luke draw on 'Q', generally Luke retains a more accurate chronological sequence.[13] In Luke 4.23, Jesus said, 'Doubtless you will quote to me this proverb, "Doctor, cure yourself."' In 4.23–28, Jesus pointed out that God does not restrict his work to homes in Israel by using the analogy:

> There were many widows in Israel in the time of Elijah . . . yet Elijah was sent to none of them except to a widow at Zarephath in Sidon. There were also many lepers in Israel in the time of the prophet Elisha, and none of them was cleansed except Naaman the Syrian.

In Luke 5.10 and Matthew 4.19, Jesus coined a word-play or pun on the disciples' catching not fish, but people. In Luke 5.31/Mark 2.17/Matthew 9.12, he repeated the analogy: 'Those who are well have no need of a physician, but those who are sick.' In Luke 5.36/Mark 2.21/Matthew 9.16, he used the analogy of sowing a patch on to an old or new garment. Sometimes, as in the Old Testament prophets, he used action (or strictly a speech-act, i.e. when the speech performs an act), as when he said to the paralysed man, 'Stand up . . . and go to your home', or 'Stand up and walk' (Mark 2.11; Luke 5.23; Matt. 9.6).

---

[13] Vincent Taylor, 'The Original Order of Q', in A. J. B. Higgins (ed.), *New Testament Essays* (Manchester: Manchester University Press, 1959) pp. 246–69; and Mark Goodacre, *The Case Against Q* (London: Continuum, 2002); John S. Kloppenborg, *The Formation of Q Transcripts in Ancient Wisdom Collections* (Philadelphia: Fortress, 1987); James M. Robinson, John S. Kloppenborg and Paul Hoffmann (eds), *The Critical Edition of Q* (Hermeneia; Minneapolis: Fortress, 2000).

After the Sermon on the Plain, Jesus used many other analogies and pictures. In the context of the crowds' motive in seeking John the Baptist he asked, 'What did you go out into the wilderness to look at? A reed shaken by the wind? . . . Someone dressed in soft robes? Look, those who put on fine clothing and live in luxury are in royal palaces' (Luke 7.24–25). In 7.31 he compared his generation to

> children sitting in the market-place and calling to one another, 'We played the flute for you, and you did not dance; we wailed, and you did not weep.' For John the Baptist has come eating no bread and drinking no wine, and you say, 'He has a demon'; the Son of Man has come eating and drinking, and you say, 'Look, a glutton and a drunkard, a friend of tax collectors and sinners!'

In 7.41–48, he expounded the Parable of the Two Debtors. In 8.5–15, Jesus expounded and explained the Parable of the Sower. In Luke 8.16 and Matthew 5.15 he used the analogy of the lamp which people hide under a jar or under the bed. When he had healed the Gergesene demoniac, he followed his miracle by a public action: to allow the herd of swine to run down the steep bank into a lake, where they drowned. In Luke 9.47 and Matthew 8.28–32, Jesus used the visual aid of taking a little child and saying, 'Whoever welcomes this child in my name welcomes me, and whoever welcomes me welcomes the one who sent me: for the least among all of you is the greatest.'

On the need for perseverance, Jesus used the analogy 'No one who puts a hand to the plough and looks back is fit for the kingdom of God' (Luke 9.62); he continues to seek his goal. In Luke 10.3 and Matthew 10.16, Jesus used the analogy of sending the disciples 'like lambs into the midst of wolves', which stresses their courage and persistence. In Luke 11.5–8, he urged persistence by citing the friend who makes his request at midnight; and, in 11.9–13, showed how God's generosity exceeds that of an ordinary father. In 11.29–32, he condemned ingratitude by comparing his generation with the Queen of Sheba and the people of Nineveh. In 11.33 he repeated the analogy of the lamp hidden in a cellar. He compared hypocrisy with washing only the outside of a cup (11.39), and to defiling tombs which are unmarked (11.44–48).

The teaching of Jesus continued to use analogies in Luke 12, 13 and 14. Jesus explained God's care for his people by noting his concern for the smallest detail, for example, for sparrows, which are so cheap that 'Five sparrows [are] sold for two pennies' (12.6; Matt. 6.26). Further, Jesus said, 'Consider the ravens . . . Consider the lilies' (12.24, 27; Matt. 6.28).

He also told his followers, 'Make purses for yourselves that do not wear out' (12.33). Jesus warned his hearers about the suddenness of his future coming by using the analogy of the thief who broke in at night (12.39–46). He also applied the analogy of predicting weather (12.54–55). In 13.1–9 he told the brief parable of the fig tree which had to be cut down. On Sabbath observance, Jesus exclaimed, 'You hypocrites! Does not each of you on the sabbath untie his ox or his donkey from the manger, and lead it away to give it water?' After citing an analogy from everyday life, Jesus concluded: 'Ought not this woman, a daughter of Abraham . . . be set free from this bondage on the sabbath day?' (13.15–16). He expounded the analogy between the kingdom of God and the mustard seed, which 'grew and became a tree, and the birds of the air made nests in its branches' (13.19). In the next verse Jesus compared the kingdom with a housewife who took three measures of flour until it was leavened, again, to stress its growth. In 13.34, he compared his own yearning and care for Jerusalem with the yearning of a hen who 'gathers her brood under her wings'.

Jesus used further analogies in the following chapters. He compared his concern for the needy with someone whose child or ox has fallen into a well, commenting, 'Will you not immediately pull it out on a sabbath day?' (14.5). Luke 14.7–24 used two examples from life concerning counting the cost of discipleship: first, the cost of building a tower (v. 28); the second, that of calculating the force of an enemy army (v. 31). Luke 15, as is well known, contains throughout the three parables of the Lost Sheep, of the Lost Coin and of the Lost Son and his brother. Chapter 16 contains further parables of the Dishonest Manager (16.1–9), and of the Rich Man and Lazarus (vv. 19–31). Parables continue in chapter 17, although it includes the analogy of a lightning flash lighting up the sky, which illustrates the unmistakable public manifestation of the future coming of Jesus Christ. Chapter 18 resumes with the parables of the Unjust Judge, and of the Pharisee and Tax Collector. It includes the analogy of the rich man, for whom entering the kingdom of God is as difficult as 'for a camel to go through the eye of a needle' (v. 25). Chapters 19—21 begin the more intense activity of the final week before the Passion, although 20.9–19 also contains the Parable of the Wicked Tenants.

Truth-claims of the parables of Jesus and their varied interpretations

Although parables use powerful pictures, we should not hesitate to regard them as *reflecting* step by step on the clarity and character of Jesus' message, and as Jeremias concludes, 'The parables are a fragment of the original rock of tradition.'[14] Their kerygmatic function adds support to the view of Ricoeur and Soskice that pictures and images can have external reference in the world, and can make cognitive truth-claims. The use of parables also featured regularly in rabbinic Judaism. Nevertheless A. M. Hunter declared, 'Great parables are evidently so difficult to create that it is hard to name another person in history with more than one or two good ones to his credit.'[15] Indeed some of the parables, it is agreed, were probably based on genuine incidents in life, of which people were aware.

The parables of Jesus reflect human experience at all levels. Geraint Vaughan Jones has pursued an existentialist interpretation of some parables. He cited, for example, the Parable of the Prodigal Son. This embodied all the existential themes of estrangement, longing and nostalgia, and how people are shaped by their decisions and subsequent events. The Prodigal Son's situation of destitution, estrangement and abandonment was utterly different from the expectations of the confident, defiant self at the moment of departure.[16]

Needless to say, Jones did not interpret all of the parables in existential terms. He discussed metaphor, similitude, parable and allegory, as well as rabbinic parables. He eventually concluded (as Hunter did): 'The main difference between the parables of Jesus and those of the rabbis is that the former are the work of one with a superbly creative imagination providing profound insights without parallel.'[17] He also advised caution in following the over-rigid rules of interpretation associated with Jülicher and the eschatological interpretation of Dodd.[18] He drew strong inferences for Christology.

Hearers and readers from the Church Fathers until the beginning of the twentieth century offer ample examples of the misinterpretation of many of the parables. The turning point was perhaps between Archbishop Trench and Adolf Jülicher. Irenaeus (*c.*130–*c.*200 AD) advised that we should read the parables of Jesus 'with attention', so that we find Christ who is the 'treasure which is hid in the field'. Uncharacteristically, however, he interprets the 'wedding garment' in the parable as the Holy Spirit resting upon us. Those who have been called to God's Supper, but

---

[14] Jeremias, *The Parables of Jesus*, p. 11.

[15] A. M. Hunter, *Interpreting the Parables* (Philadelphia: Westminster Press, 1960), p. 18.

[16] Geraint Vaughan Jones, *The Art and Truth of the Parables: A Study in Their Literary Form and Modern Interpretation* (London: SPCK, 1964), pp. 135–205.

[17] Jones, *The Art and Truth of the Parables*, pp. 64–79.

[18] Jones, *The Art and Truth of the Parables*, pp. 206–22.

have not received the Holy Spirit because of their wicked conduct, shall be 'cast into outer darkness'.[19] He also took liberties with the Parable of the Labourers in the Vineyard (Matt. 20.1–16). He regarded the labourers who were hired at the beginning of the day as those who began to serve God at the creation of humankind. A day's wage, he suggested, was supposedly a coin bearing both the royal image and 'knowledge of the son of God, which is immortality'.[20] Tertullian (*c.*150–*c.*225) took this process further. Although he also suggested principles of interpretation which, if he had observed them, would guard against errors, he emphasized the need for self-examination, citing, 'He that has ears to hear let him hear.'[21] Similarly in the Parable of the Prodigal Son, the interpretation is reversed by Tertullian: he questioned the interpretation of those who compare the elder brother with Jews, and the younger brother with Christians. He argued that the basic fallacy of 'these heretics' is that they have used the parables to buttress their doctrines, and have made their doctrines conform to their own private interpretations of the parables. In the case of the Prodigal Son, the interpretation is reversed. Jews cannot be represented by the elder brother; nor Christians by the younger son. On the details or stage-setting of the parable, he compared the citizen who employed the younger son to feed the pigs as the devil or 'the Prince of this age', and understood the ring given by the father as symbolizing baptism. The banquet and the fatted calf become the Eucharist.

The most notorious 'interpreter' of the parables, however, was Augustine of Hippo (354–430), especially in his interpretation of the Parable of the Good Samaritan (Luke 10.29–37). The man who travelled from Jerusalem to Jericho represented Adam, who, in turn, symbolized the human race. Jericho represented our mortality. The wounds made to the traveller were sins in need of forgiveness. The thieves were the devil and his angels. The priest and the Levite represented the Old Testament, which was powerless to help. The Samaritan represented Christ. He poured on oil (good hope) and wine (exhortation to a fervent spirit). The inn became the Church. The two coins which the Samaritan gave to the innkeeper represented the charity of the apostles and the Holy Spirit, or the promise of present and future life.[22] This notorious example of allegorizing the details of this parable did not typify Augustine's

---

[19] Irenaeus, *Against Heresies*, 4, 36, 6.

[20] Irenaeus, *Against Heresies*, 4, 20, 7.

[21] Tertullian, *Against Marcion*, Bk 4, ch. 19.

[22] Augustine, *Sermons on Selected Lessons of the New Testament*, 81, 6 and 7; (Eng., NPNF, ser. 1, vol. 6, p. 503).

interpretation of every other parable. He had a keen biblical, theological and philosophical mind, and was generally more careful to interpret Scripture in accordance with well-established principles.

We must resist the conclusion that all the Church Fathers uniformly adopted allegorical interpretation of details of every parable. John Chrysostom, for example, asked, 'Why was this parable composed?' and answered: 'It is not right to inquire curiously into all things in parables word by word, but when we have learned the object for which it was composed, to reap this, and not to busy oneself about anything further.'[23]

Thomas Aquinas (1225–74) was a responsible biblical exegete, who wrote numerous commentaries. But on the parables, he often resorted to allegorical interpretation and exposition of independent details. In the Parable of the Sower, he attempted to expound the three crops of thirtyfold, sixtyfold and a hundredfold. These, for most readers, respectively represented average spiritual growth, better-than-usual spiritual growth and exceptional spiritual growth. In the Parable of the Ten Maidens, the lamps represented illumination by faith, while the oil represented good works.

At the Reformation Martin Luther (1483–1546) and especially John Calvin (1509–64) were much more sober in their exegesis of the parables of Jesus. Indeed Calvin insisted, 'Allegories ought to be carried no further than Scripture expressly sanctions: so far are they from forming a sufficient basis to found doctrines upon.'[24] Richard C. Trench (1807–86), Dean of Westminster, and Archbishop of Dublin, was a philologist and prodigious writer, who first published *Notes of the Parables of Our Lord* in 1841 and 1848.[25] He was learned in languages, but sought to provide a middle way between those who interpreted parables in terms of one main point and those who interpreted minute details. He rejected the notion of applying a single rule of interpretation to all parables. Some have insisted that in spite of his learning he brings us back to the Middle Ages and ignores Calvin. On the Parable of the Good Samaritan, for example, he still favoured the patristic notion of regarding the inn as representing the Church. On the Prodigal Son, he regarded the gift of the robe as representing the imputation of the righteousness of Christ. This volume was widely popular with many churchpeople at the time.

---

[23] John Chrysostom, *Homilies on the Gospel of Matthew*, Homily 64, sect. 3 (Eng., NPNF, ser. 1, vol. 10, p. 394).

[24] John Calvin, *Institutes of the Christian Religion*, Bk 2, ch. 5, sect. 19 (Eng., 2 vols, London: James Clarke, 1957), vol. 1, p. 291.

[25] Richard C. Trench, *Notes on the Parables of Our Lord* (Westwood, NJ: Revell, 1953).

It is therefore not surprising that Alexander B. Bruce (1831–99), Professor at Glasgow, and especially Adolf Jülicher (1857–1938), Professor at Marburg, initiated a new era in New Testament criticism, in which they focused on the context and the main point of a parable. Bruce wrote *The Parabolic Teaching of Christ* in 1882, and Jülicher wrote *Die Gleichnisreden Jesu* in 1886.[26] Bruce regarded Jesus as master or rabbi, evangelist and prophet, and divided the parables into these three sections respectively. The first group taught the truth of the kingdom of God. In this group he included the Sower, the Tares, the Hidden Treasure, the Costly Pearl and the Mustard Seed. The evangelistic parables included the Lost Coin, the Lost Sheep and the Prodigal Son. In the 'prophetic' examples Bruce included the Two Sons, the Ten Virgins and the Servant in Authority, as evidencing God's righteousness and ethical demands. Bruce repudiated allegorical interpretation. He ascribed to Jesus kindly humour, profound yet homely thought, and clear insight.

In this new era of New Testament criticism, Jülicher distinguished similitudes, which tell a recurrent situation, from parables, which narrate a particular event which happened on a particular location. On the parable itself he commented, 'The listeners are not shown what everyone does . . . But what someone did once, whether or not other people would do it in the same way.'[27] 'The similitude', he said,

> appeals to what is universally valid, the parable proper to what has happened once . . . The similitude guards against any opposition since it only speaks of established facts. The parable hopes to avoid all opposition by telling its story so attractively, so warmly and freshly, that the listener simply does not think of objections.[28]

He next, and more significantly, categorically distinguished sharply between parables and allegories. In general he assigns parables to Jesus, and allegories to the tradition of the early Church. He calls both metaphor and allegory a non-natural or *indirect* form of speech (Ger., *uneigentliche Rede*), and parable, simile or *direct* speech a literal form of speech (*eigentliche Rede*). The metaphor may be *puzzling, and needs interpretation.* The parable, Jülicher maintained, was clear, and needed no interpretation. It was perhaps unfortunate that *uneigentliche* could

---

[26] A. B. Bruce, *The Parabolic Teaching of Christ* (London: Hodder & Stoughton, 1882); Adolf Jülicher, *Die Gleichnisreden Jesu* (2 vols, Freiburg: Mohr, 1888 and 1899).

[27] Jülicher, *Die Gleichnisreden Jesu*, vol. 1, p. 93.

[28] Jülicher, *Die Gleichnisreden Jesu*, vol. 1, p. 97.

mean both indirect and inauthentic. An allegory, he argued, was merely a succession of metaphors, often created by the early Church.[29]

Today many writers believe that, while he laid a useful new beginning, Jülicher had gravely gone too far. One of the most notable is Eberhard Jüngel (b.1934), formerly Professor at Tübingen, and Director at Tübingen and Heidelberg. He has written extensively of the *creative power* of metaphor in several works.[30] He was strongly influenced in some respects by Fuchs. Madeleine Boucher, in *The Mysterious Parable* (1977), is a second notable writer. In effect two groups have expressed concern. Both groups draw on literary theory and the power of metaphor. In one group Boucher represents Roman Catholic writers; Jüngel represents Protestant or Lutheran theologians; and Robert Stein and Craig Blomberg write as broadly conservative and semi-popular Protestants. A second main group is mostly American, and often more liberal. They include Wilder, Perrin, Crossan, Funk and Dan Otto Via. They are among the many who have sought to reinstate the importance of metaphor and literary theory. We shall consider this 'American' school of interpreters below. Meanwhile, we may note that Madeleine Boucher emphasizes the place of irony and paradox in Mark's Gospel, even citing the physicist Niels Bohr for the view that in paradox the opposite of a true statement is not necessarily a falsehood. In the light of her interests in literary criticism she insists, against Jülicher, that many of the parables proper are not clear and obvious, but draw often on puzzling phenomena and allegories. One of her chapters concerns the relationship between concealment and revelation.[31] Similarly, Robert H. Stein insists that parables are 'not always self-evident'.[32] These reactions generally date from the late 1970s to the 1990s.

Our main purpose in this chapter, however, has been to show that *vivid, creative, and powerful narrative pictures and visual images can seduce*, and *in fact have seduced*, generations of readers, and have became *profoundly misinterpreted*. On the other hand, they do have *extra-linguistic referents in real life*, and convey *cognitive truth*, as well as *emotions* and the need

---

[29] Jülicher, *Die Gleichnisreden Jesu*, vol. 1, pp. 52–8.

[30] Eberhard Jüngel, *Theological Essays*, especially the first essay (London: Continuum, 1994); and in Jüngel, *Collected Works* (London: Bloomsbury/Clark, 2014); cf. Roland D. Zimany, *Vehicle for God: The Metaphorical Theology of Eberhard Jüngel* (Atlanta: Mercer University Press, 1994).

[31] Madeleine Boucher, *The Mysterious Parable: A Literary Study* (Washington, DC: Catholic Biblical Association of America, 1977), pp. 28–44 and throughout.

[32] Robert H. Stein, *An Introduction to the Parables of Jesus* (Philadelphia: Westminster John Knox Press, 1981), p. 27; cf. Craig L. Blomberg, *Interpreting Parables* (Leicester: Apollos, 1990), especially pp. 36–49 and 309–28.

for *decision and action*. The critical interpretations of Jülicher, Dodd and others remain understandable in the light of mistakes in the historic tradition from the Church Fathers onwards. These mistakes needed to be corrected. In Geraint Jones, Amos Wilder, Norman Perrin, Robert Funk, and the earlier work of John Dominic Crossan and Dan Otto Via, the interpretation of the parables rightly became less doctrinaire and rigid, although many excesses, often of a different kind, still remained. The less rational aspects of postmodernism invaded the later work of Crossan, Via and other authors.

The parables as poetic metaphor: Wilder, Funk, Crossan, Via and others

These scholars, sometimes known as 'the American School', share a common concern about literary theory. Wilder and Perrin stress the importance of *tensive* metaphor. Amos Wilder (1895–1993) distinguished between a variety of parables. The word *parable*, he wrote, 'included a wide variety of metaphors, similitudes, riddles, mysteries and illustrations. Many of these were brief tropes' (e.g. salt of the earth), 'but many of the Jewish parables reflect a narrative character, as do many of those in the Gospels' (e.g. the Good Samaritan, the Rich Fool, and the Pharisee and the Publican). 'Here we have "example-stories", not symbolic narrative.' But, he wrote, 'In the parable of the Lost Sheep, on the other hand . . . [we] have rather an extended image – the shepherd's retrieval of the lost sheep, and his joy.'[33] He adds, 'Jesus uses figures of speech in an immense number of ways.'[34] On the vividness, everydayness and power of the imagery, he quotes at length the work of Ernst Fuchs. He is especially impressed by the power of metaphor, which was far from serving as homiletic illustrations. He regards them as being especially *creative*, including 'the power of the image-maker the poet'.[35]

Norman Perrin (1920–76) of Chicago was a close admirer of Wilder. He was also influenced by Jeremias, Fuchs, Ricoeur, Funk and Via. Among many other works, the one that most clearly demonstrated his attitude to the language of the parables was his book *Jesus and the Language of the Kingdom: Symbol and Metaphor in New Testament Interpretation* (1976).[36]

---

[33] Amos N. Wilder, *Early Christian Rhetoric*, p. 80.

[34] Wilder, *Early Christian Rhetoric*, p. 81.

[35] Wilder, *Early Christian Rhetoric*, p. 95.

[36] Norman Perrin, *Jesus and the Language of the Kingdom: Symbol and Metaphor in New Testament Interpretation* (London: SCM, 1976).

He took up Dodd's view of the parable as 'leaving the mind in sufficient doubt about its precise application to tease it into active thought'.[37] He also considered Robert Funk's work on the parable as metaphor. Metaphor, Funk said, transforms the listener into a participant: 'It confronts the hearer with a new vision of reality by its power as metaphor ... raises the potential for new meaning ... [and] redirects attention ... by means of imaginative shock.'[38] Jülicher, Perrin wrote, was too exclusively ideational. He wrote, 'The "world" of the parable is the everyday world of man's ordinary creaturely existence, but the parables [also] unfold in such a way as to turn that everydayness inside out or upside down.'[39] Perrin also considered the work of Wilder, Via and Crossan, whom he regarded as the leading contemporary interpreters of the parables. He drew on literary theory to explain major detentions between symbol, allegory, and metaphor or parable. In the light of Goethe, Coleridge, Yates and Elliott, he argues:

> Allegory transforms the phenomenon into an abstract concept, the concept into an image, but in such a way that the concept can still be expressed and be held in an image. Symbolism, on the other hand, transforms the phenomenon into an idea, the idea into an image ... in such a way that the idea remains for ever infinitely active and unreachable in the image and is still inexpressible ... [metaphor however can provide] a right knowledge ... [and] participation in the referent.[40]

Sometimes Perrin uses the word *myth* in place of metaphor or parable. I have argued elsewhere, however, that the term *myth* is ambiguous and highly misleading, and that it should seldom be used unless it is strictly necessary, and then precisely defined.

John Dominic Crossan (b.1934) is an Irish-American New Testament scholar, who founded the Jesus Seminar of the Society of Biblical Literature with Robert Funk. Its conclusions have been highly controversial, and have been opposed by, among others, Tom Wright. Crossan's early work on parables is particularly valuable, especially his exposition of 'parables of reversal'. In the book *In Parables* (1973) Crossan first made the customary distinctions between allegory and parable, parable and metaphor, and so on.[41] Probably the most distinctive and insightful chapter of the book,

---

37 Perrin, *Jesus*, p. 133.
38 Perrin, *Jesus*, p. 136.
39 Perrin, *Jesus*, p. 138.
40 Perrin, *Jesus*, pp. 156–7.
41 John Dominic Crossan, *In Parables: The Challenge of the Historical Jesus* (New York: Harper

however, concerns his 'Parables of Reversal'.[42] One major example of his approach is the parable of the Good Samaritan (Luke 10.30–37). He rejects the notion that this could be merely an example story, for 'Jews have no dealings with Samaritans' (John 4.9). The parable, he writes, 'challenges the hearer to put together two impossible and contradictory words for the same person: "Samaritan" (10.33) and "neighbour" (10:36)'. The whole thrust of the story demands 'that one says what cannot be said, what is a contradiction in terms: Good + Samaritan'.[43] If the purpose of Jesus had simply been to feature an example of neighbourliness,

> For such a purpose it would have been far better to have made the wounded man a Samaritan and the helper a Jewish man outside clerical circles. But when good (clerics) and bad (Samaritans) become respectively bad and good, the world is being challenged and we are faced with polar reversal.[44]

Below the literal level lies a metaphorical level. The metaphor challenges the reader to transform his or her 'world'. The literal point suggests an impossibility; in the metaphor the world is turned upside down.

Other Parables of Reversal include (1) the Rich Man and Lazarus (Luke 16.19–31), in which the culminating event of reversal is the resurrection. Crossan writes, 'Its metaphorical point was reversal of expectation and situation, or value and judgment, which is the concomitant of the Kingdom's advent.'[45] Another (2) is the Parable of the Pharisee and Publican (Luke 18.10–14). This has echoes in Paul's comment in 2 Corinthians 1.9, 'that was to make us rely not on ourselves'. Crossan writes,

> The metaphorical challenge is again clear: the complete, radical, polar reversal of accepted human judgment, especially of religious judgment, whereby the kingdom forced its way into human awareness. What, in other words, if God does not play the game by our rules?[46]

(3) Crossan's third example is the Parable of the Wedding Guest (Luke 14.1–24), his fourth, Proper Guests (Luke 14.12–14), and the fifth, the Great Supper (Matt. 22.1–10 and Luke 14.16–24).

Crossan includes other sections, of which most are useful, although some will find his judgement about authentic sayings of Jesus controversial.

& Row, 1973), pp. 7–23.

[42] Crossan, *In Parables*, pp. 53–78.

[43] Crossan, *In Parables*, p. 64.

[44] Crossan, *In Parables*, p. 64.

[45] Crossan, *In Parables*, p. 68.

[46] Crossan, *In Parables*, p. 69.

But the 'Parables of Reversal' make a distinctive and lasting contribution. A series of further books, however, will appeal mainly to those who have sympathies with postmodern approaches to the parables. In 1976 Crossan published *Raid on the Articulate*: *Comic Eschatology in Jesus and Borges.*[47] His theme of laughter and 'play' fits well with the postmodern approach to literature of Roland Barthes and Jacques Derrida. Indeed at the beginning he quotes Barthes as 'living to the full the contradiction of my time' and as using 'the power of surprise', and later cites Derrida.[48] Derrida wrote of 'the joyous affirmation of the play of the world'.[49] Crossan writes, 'The Whole Truth which comedy whispers to our frightened or startled imaginations is that all is play'.[50] He considers the words of Jesus,

> If anyone strikes you on the right cheek, turn to him the other also, and if anyone would sue you and take your coat, let him have your cloak as well; and if anyone forces you to go one mile, go with him two miles.
>
> (Luke 6.29)

Crossan comments, 'My own theory is that Jesus' three situations represent a case parity, a deliberate comic subversion of the wise and prudent necessity of case law.'[51] He also explores what he calls paradox, in such sayings as 'To him who has will be given; and from him who has not will be taken away'.[52]

Crossan's whole approach is reminiscent of Richard Rorty. On truth and 'reality', Rorty writes that concerning 'The task of getting reality right', 'There is no such task, because there is no Way the World Is.'[53] He states, 'The true is the name of whatever proves to be good in the way of belief'.[54] The title of Rorty's related volume, *Contingency, Irony, and Solidarity* (1989) also conveys the approach of his thought. He is an American postmodernist, equivalent in his own way to the French postmodernity of

[47] John Dominic Crossan, *Raid on the Articulate: Comic Eschatology in Jesus and Borges* (New York: Harper & Row, 1976).

[48] Crossan, *Raid on the Articulate*, p. 3 and p. 34.

[49] Jacques Derrida, *Writing and Difference* (Chicago: University of Chicago Press, 1978; Fr., 1967), p. 292; cf. Roland Barthes, *The Pleasure of the Text* (Eng., New York: Hill & Wang, 1975).

[50] Crossan, *Raid on the Articulate*, p. 23.

[51] Crossan, *Raid on the Articulate*, p. 65 and p. 67.

[52] Crossan, *Raid on the Articulate*, p. 70.

[53] Richard Rorty, *Truth and Progress: Philosophical Papers*, vol. 3 (Cambridge: CUP, 1998), p. 25.

[54] Rorty, *Truth and Progress*, p. 21.

Roland Barthes and Jacques Derrida. Crossan joins all three in seeking to dethrone the classic Western tradition of thought.

In 1979 Crossan wrote *Finding Is the First Act: Trove Folktales and Jesus' Treasure Parable.*[55] Here Crossan writes, 'Jesus' treasure story is thus a mess of parable, a paradoxical artefact which succeeds precisely to the extent it fails.'[56] Such a sentence may seem typically postmodern, which indeed it is, but Crossan's aim is also to say that the kingdom of God is beyond words and incapable of conceptual discussion. But this progress towards the postmodern during the 1970s is as nothing compared with Crossan's work as editor of the so-called experimental journal, *Semeia.* The articles under his editorship move increasingly in a postmodern direction. The articles by Susan Wittig, Mary Tolbert and Dan Otto Via all seem to fall within this category.[57] Tolbert argues that the Parable of the Prodigal Son 'reflects a wish-fulfilment dream', in which two sons represent 'elements of a complex unity'. The elder son reflects rigid morality like Freud's superego; the father represents a unifying centre; the younger son seeks unity and wholeness.[58] Tolbert and Wittig both insist on multiple meanings for a parable. In her article in the same volume Wittig relies on a complex system of semiotics, while in another volume Via considers an approach to interpretation based on the work of the psychologist Carl Jung.[59]

More positive work came from American scholars before the fashion of postmodernism and deconstruction invaded much of their work. Robert Funk (1926–2005) had many positive insights in his book *Language, Hermeneutic, and Word of God.*[60] He rightly emphasized the power of metaphor over literal speech. He wrote, 'Metaphor shatters the conventions of predication in the interests of a new vision . . . The metaphor is a means of modifying the tradition.'[61] He showed the participatory and transformative effect of metaphor. For example, in the Parable of the Prodigal Son, the pharisaic critics retain the impression that they

---

[55] John Dominic Crossan, *Finding Is the First Act: Trove Folktales and Jesus' Treasure Parable* (Philadelphia: Fortress, and Missoula: Scholars Press, 1979).

[56] Crossan, *Finding Is the First Act*, p. 120.

[57] Mary Ann Tolbert, 'The Prodigal Son: An Essay in Literary Criticism from a Psycho-Analytical Perspective', *Semeia* 9 (1977) pp. 1–20; cf. her *Perspectives on the Parables* (Philadelphia: Fortress, 1979).

[58] Tolbert, 'The Prodigal Son', *Semeia* 9, pp. 7–8.

[59] Dan Otto Via, 'The Parable of the Unjust Judge: A Metaphor of the Unrealized Self', in *Semiology and the Parables* (Pittsburgh: Pickwick, 1976) pp. 1–32.

[60] Robert Funk, *Language, Hermeneutic and Word of God* (New York: Harper & Row, 1966).

[61] Funk, *Language, Hermeneutic and Word of God*, p. 139; cf. pp. 133–62.

are sitting in judgement on Jesus; but in fact the parable turns the hermeneutical dynamic on its head and it is they who are judged by the word of God.[62] The flow from subject to object is reversed. In the first part of his book, Funk discussed Heidegger, Bultmann, Fuchs and Ebeling; in Part 2 the parables and metaphor; and in Part 3 further issues about language, including analogy in Paul. He stressed that many applications of the parables were not simply to be dismissed as later creations by the Church, for they became part of the biblical canon. The problem with Jülicher and Dodd, he said, was to treat the parables as conveyers of ideas, rather than narratives, pictures or images from which readers are called to action. He corroborated this in his article 'Saying and Seeing'.[63] He also reviewed Jülicher's contrast between metaphors and similes, and sought to refine this. In effect, a simile, he argued, is illustrative; metaphor is creative of meaning.[64] Most especially, he said, 'The metaphor, like the parable, is incomplete until the hearer is drawn into it as participant.'[65] This is what Ricoeur and others have regularly been saying.

Just before we conclude this chapter, we may recall that our material primarily concerns the parables of Jesus and the teaching of Jesus in the Synoptic Gospels. We may add, therefore, a brief note on similar ideas in the Fourth Gospel. According to Moulton and Geden's *Concordance to the Greek Testament*, John uses the verb 'to see' (Gk, *horaō*) some 30 times in his Gospel.[66] Some of the more important examples include 'I saw the Spirit descending from heaven like a dove, and it remained on him' (John 1.32), and 'He on whom you see the Spirit descend and remain is the one who baptizes with the Holy Spirit' (1.33); 'You will see heaven opened and the angels of God ascending and descending upon the Son of Man' (1.51); 'It may be clearly seen that their deeds have been done in God' (2.21); and 'Come and see a man who told me everything I have ever done!' (4.29).

Further, all seven of the 'I am' sayings of Jesus offer expressions of at least potential visual representation, if only by imagination. They are: 'I am the bread of life' (John 6.35); 'I am the light of the world' (8.12); 'I am the gate for the sheep' (10.7); 'I am the good shepherd' (10.11); 'I am the resurrection and the life' (11.25); ' I am the way, and the truth, and

62 Funk, *Language, Hermeneutic and Word of God*, pp. 16–17.

63 Robert Funk, 'Saying and Seeing: Phenomenology of Language and the New Testament', *Journal of Bible and Religion* 34 (1966), pp. 197–213.

64 Funk, *Language, Hermeneutic and Word of God*, pp. 136–7.

65 Funk, *Language, Hermeneutic and Word of God*, p. 143.

66 W. F. Moulton and A. S. Geden, *A Concordance to the Greek Testament* (Edinburgh: T&T Clark, 1899), p. 702.

the life' (14.6); and 'I am the true vine' (15.1). In accordance with John's style, many of these are illustrated and interpreted by the actions which surround them. For example, 'I am the resurrection and the life' is illustrated by the narrative of the raising to life of Lazarus in John 11. 'I am the true vine' becomes amply explained by the exposition that 'the branch cannot bear fruit by itself unless it abides in the vine . . . neither can you unless you abide in me' (v. 4), and few Jewish (and later Gentile) readers would fail to know that in the Old Testament the vine is a regular symbol of Israel. Similarly, 'I am the bread of life' follows the Feeding of the Five Thousand (6.5–14). Whereas the Synoptic writers interdisperse words and deeds of Jesus, John usually follows an acted 'sign' with a lengthier discourse to expound it.

To conclude: this chapter on the teaching of Jesus has shown both the power and vividness of concrete images, which far surpass that of abstract or prose discourse, and how readily such imagery can seduce us, and become misinterpreted if it is torn out of its purpose and aim or intention. The history of interpretation and concrete examples have made this abundantly clear, whether we cite allegorizing in the early Church, Jülicher and Dodd's single point, or the excesses of plurivocal postmodernity and deconstruction. The power of pictures is unforgettable and unsurpassed provided that they are informatively interpreted.

7

Pictures and analogies in the earlier letters of Paul: 1 Thessalonians, Galatians and 1 Corinthians

The pictures and analogies used regularly by Paul differ greatly from the images and parables found in the teaching of Jesus. Jesus used pictures which reflected rural life in Galilee, including allusions to farming, housekeeping and the countryside. Paul, by contrast, was a dweller in towns, a traveller to far-off places, familiar with docks, ships and buildings, and the colourful life of busy places of commerce. Their differences are only those of style and expression; their spiritual vision was similar.

Nevertheless the notion that the teaching of Jesus was full of pictures, while Paul engaged in abstract discourse and debate, is far from correct. One of the standard works on this subject is Herbert Gale, *The Use of Analogy in the Letters of Paul*.[1] He treats Paul's uses of analogy chronologically, and cites 34 major examples in the epistles which are generally undisputed as Pauline. He also argues that most pictures serve to make a single point, and that often they contain other elements that are inapplicable to understanding Paul's theology and cannot be used out of their context.[2] Gale frequently uses the word 'pictures'. So also does Walter Butcher in his essay, 'The Metaphors of St. Paul', which concerns the later writings in the Pastoral Epistles.[3] Butcher includes many examples, which he categorizes under several headings: metaphors of imperial warfare, of classical architecture, of ancient agriculture, of Greek games, of Roman law, of medical science, of seafaring life and of the fowler's craft. Thus he makes nine subsections, with a number of examples within each heading. To my reckoning, there are, in fact, even more than Gale's 34 analogies or metaphors in Paul.

1 Herbert M. Gale, *The Use of Analogy in the Letters of Paul* (Philadelphia: Westminster Press, 1964).

2 Gale, *The Use of Analogy*, pp. 223–8; cf. p. 81 and elsewhere.

3 Walter A. Butcher, 'The Metaphors of St. Paul', *Baptist Quarterly* 9 (1939), pp. 484–7.

Victor Pfitzner has devoted an entire book to a single picture in Paul, *Paul and the Agon Motif* (i.e. contest or struggle).[4] He discussed Greek athletic images and Paul's letters, especially 1 Corinthians 9.24–27.[5] A further source is an older work, which is still well worth consulting, not least for its wealth of detail. Werner Straub (1937) found a sixfold classification of Paul's 'picture' uses.[6] These include image-words or picture-words (*Bildwörter*), pictorial expressions or graphic phrases (*bildhafte Redewendungen*), comparisons (*Vergleiche*), metaphors (*Metaphern*), 'somewhat distorted reflection', which nevertheless describes the resulting image as puzzling sayings or verdicts (*Bildsprühe*), and parables, similes or figures of speech (*Gleichnisse*).[7] Under each category Straub included very many examples. For example, he included over 100 examples under the first heading. Gale's main examples include only Straub's eighteenth example, sleeping and waking (1 Thess. 5.6); his thirty-second, building (1 Cor. 8.1, 10); his thirty-eighth, running (Gal. 5.7); and his forty-first, leading in triumph (2 Cor. 2.14). Straub included 15 graphic phrases, such as removing mountains (1 Cor. 13.2), even 'tearing out your eyes' (Gal. 4.15), and placarding (Gk, κατ' ὀφθαλμοὺς προεγράφη; NRSV 'publicly exhibiting') Jesus Christ (Gal. 3.1). He suggested many pictorial sayings or verdicts, for example blameless children in a wicked and perverse generation (Phil. 2.15), and 32 metaphors, which include light and darkness (2 Cor. 6.14) and milk and solid food (1 Cor. 3.2). Finally he listed 28 parables or comparisons, including planting and watering (1 Cor. 3.5–9), and the body and limbs (Rom. 12.4–5; 1 Cor. 12.12–27).

It is well known that Paul made much of communication with his Gentile churches. His use of figures and pictures well known to his Gentile readers is part of his pastoral strategy. We must make one important disclaimer and proviso: not all of Paul's analogies constitute pictures, even of the imaginative kind. We shall not classify Paul's well-known analogy in 1 Corinthians 2.11 ('No one comprehends what is truly God's except the Spirit of God', i.e. the analogy between the thought of humankind and the thoughts of God) as not exemplifying a picture, although it does imply a warning against trivializing 'pictures' of the Holy Spirit.

---

4 Victor Pfitzner, *Paul and the Agon Motif: Traditional Athletic Imagery in the Pauline Literature* (NovTSup 16; Leiden: Brill, 1967).

5 Pfitzner, *Paul and the Agon Motif*, respectively pp. 16–38 and 82–109.

6 Werner Straub, *Die Bildersprache des Apostels Paulus* (Tübingen: Mohr, 1937).

7 Straub, *Die Bildersprache des Apostels Paulus*, pp. 20–97.

Paul's earliest epistle: 1 Thessalonians

(**1**) One of Paul's best-known pictorial analogies comes in **1 Thessalonians 2.7**: 'But we were gentle [Gk, *ēpioi*] among you, **like a nurse** tenderly caring for her own children [Gk, *nēpioi*]'. 1 Thessalonians 2.1–12 is concerned with Paul's relationship with the church, both as pastor and friend. Donfried calls it both speech-act and example of a 'friendship letter', because after his unexpected departure from Thessalonica Paul wants to assure the members of the church of how much he cares for them with genuine affection.[8] His abrupt, enforced departure, in effect, left the new converts as 'orphans'. Abraham Malherbe argues that Paul's analogy reflects the Cynic philosophers' stress on sincerity and integrity as against the Sophists' double-talk.[9] Otto Merk also understands this as an expression of Paul's pastoral affection and concern for follow-up.[10]

Clement of Alexandria (*c.*150–215) noted the play on *ēpioi* (gentle) and *nēpioi* (babes), calling the nurse or preacher gentle or quiet, rather than childish, and comments on Paul's strategy of preaching.[11] He also quoted Paul to similar effect on 2 Corinthians 6.4, 10, 11.[12] Paul, he commented, avoided flattering words, as Pogoloff and Clarke note today.[13] Origen (*c.*185–*c.*254) commented that apostles or bishops should similarly be humble and 'little', like a child.[14] John Chrysostom (*c.*347–407), comments on this verse, 'We exhibited nothing that was offensive or troublesome . . . Does a nurse flatter, that she may obtain glory? Does she ask money of little children? Is she offensive or burdensome for them?'[15] He adds, 'Nothing can be sweeter than such [Paul's] love.' Augustine (354–430) noted the analogy, and compares Paul's words, 'The love of Christ constrains us . . .' (2 Cor. 5.13–14).[16] Bede (673–735) noted that Paul spoke of 'her own' children,

[8] Karl R. Donfried and Johannes Beutler (eds), *The Thessalonians Debate: Methodological Discord or Methodological Synthesis?* (Grand Rapids: Eerdmans, 2002), p. 5.

[9] Abraham Malherbe, 'Gentle as a Nurse: The Cynic Background of 1 Thess. 2:2', *NovT* 12 (1970), pp. 203–17; Malherbe, *The Letters to the Thessalonians* (Anchor Bible; New Haven: Yale University Press, 2000), pp. 140–53; and Malherbe, *Paul and the Thessalonians: The Philosophic Tradition of Pastoral Care* (Philadelphia: Fortress, 1987), pp. 9 and 18–33.

[10] Otto Merk, '1 Thessalonians 2:1–12: An Exegetical-Theological Study', in Donfried and Beutler (eds), *The Thessalonians Debate*, pp. 89–113.

[11] Clement of Alexandria, *The Instructor*, 5 (Eng., ANF, vol. 2, p. 214).

[12] Clement, *Stromata*, 1, 1 (Eng., ANF, vol. 2, p. 300).

[13] Stephen Pogoloff, *Logos and Sophia: The Rhetorical Situation of 1 Corinthians* (SBLDS 134; Atlanta: Scholars Press, 1992) pp 71–172; Andrew D. Clarke, *Secular and Christian Leadership in Corinth* (Leiden: Brill, 1993), pp. 9–58 and 109–28.

[14] Origen, *Commentary on Matthew*, sect. 29 (Eng., ANF, vol. 4, p. 492).

[15] John Chrysostom, *Homilies on Thessalonians*, Homily 2 (Eng., NPNF, vol. 13, p. 330).

[16] Augustine, *On the Catechizing of the Uninstructed*, 10, 15 (Eng., NPNF, ser. 1, vol. 3, pp. 293–4).

because he had borne them in Christ.[17] Thomas Aquinas (1225–74) added that acting like a nurse 'gives evidence of Paul's humility'.[18]

Up to this point in the history of the Church, most expositions of the nurse analogy emphasized its main point: Paul's friendship, care and tenderness. John Wycliffe (*c.*1333–84), however, tended to dwell on the pastoral office, especially the primacy of preaching.[19] On the other hand, the earlier works were commentaries, whereas Wycliffe was writing to a theological agenda. Martin Luther (1483–1546) also addresses a wider agenda. But John Calvin (1509–64) focused on Paul's 'not pleasing men' and avoiding flattery.[20] With William Law (1686–1761), John Wesley (1707–88) and Søren Kierkegaard (1813–55) the agenda becomes wider again. But from the later nineteenth century writers observe exegetical discipline more seriously. Benjamin Jowett (1817–93) adheres to the main point of the analogy, as do most twentieth-century commentators. Gale commented, 'Paul is quite capable of comparing himself to an infant and nursing mother in the same sentence – he calls himself a father a few lines further down (v.11), and an orphan in the same chapter (v.17).' He also states that the purpose of the picture is 'the absence of an authoritarian attitude' and 'a humble, unassuming disposition'.[21]

In the modern period, it is unnecessary to quote commentators one by one. They generally focus on the main point of the analogy. Straub classified the picture under 'comparisons', his third group, and speaks of Paul's readers or hearers as newborn babies.[22] Ernest Best speaks of Paul's accommodating himself to the level of his hearers as children in the faith.[23] Malherbe stresses the language of nurture, pointing out that the Old Testament used the analogy of birds warming their eggs and caring for their young (Deut. 32.6 and Job 19.14).[24] We have already noted his allusion to the Cynic philosophical tradition of pastoral care. Thus a rapid survey of historical remarks confirms that accurate interpretations of Paul's picture may follow from the appropriate tradition, but

---

17 Bede, *Excerpts from the Works of St. Augustine*, ed. David Hurst (Cistercian Publications, 1999), p. 285.

18 Aquinas, *Commentary on St Paul's First Letter to the Thessalonians and Letter to the Philippians* (Albany: Magi Books, 1969), p. 15.

19 John Wycliffe, 'On the Pastoral Office', in Matthew Spinka (ed.), *Advocates of Reform* (LCC 214; London: SCM, 1963), 2, 2, p. 39 and pp. 48–9.

20 John Calvin, *1 and 2 Thessalonians* (Wheaton, IL: Crossway, 1999), p. 26.

21 Gale, *The Use of Analogy*, pp. 22 and 23.

22 Straub, *Die Bildersprache des Apostels Paulus*, p. 49.

23 Ernest Best, *The First and Second Epistles to the Thessalonians* (London: Black, 1972), p. 101.

24 Malherbe, *The Letters to the Thessalonians*, p. 146.

not from independent or distracted writers or thinkers. This is our main argument.

(2) Gale's second example from Paul's earliest epistle is **1 Thessalonians 5.1–11**. In this chapter Paul uses the *picture or analogy of* **the thief** (Gk, *kleptēs*) at night (5.2). The main point of the analogy is to emphasize the suddenness or *unexpectedness* of the Parousia or final coming of Christ at the End. Gale argues that in Paul's eschatological language there is 'a strange mixture of analogical statements', for example, language about times and seasons, the Day of the Lord, labour pains, and so on. This verdict may be partly true. However, Gale is entirely correct to say that this metaphor of the thief is common to much primitive or early Christian thought, as evidenced in Matthew 24.42–44,

> Keep awake . . . for you do not know on what day your Lord is coming. But . . . if the owner of the house had known what part of the night the thief was coming, he would have stayed awake and would not have let his house be broken into. Therefore you also must be ready, for the Son of Man is coming at an unexpected hour.[25]

Almost the identical language occurs in 2 Peter 3.10, 'The day of the Lord will come like a thief', and more conditionally in Revelation 3.3, 'If you do not wake up, I will come like a thief, and you will not know at what hour I will come to you.' 2 Peter certainly refers to the final coming of Christ; whether the 'coming' in Revelation 3.3 refers to a public and final Parousia may be debated.

Also like Jesus Christ in the Gospels, in 1 Thessalonians 5.3 Paul uses the analogy of a woman in labour pains. The moment of birth may catch out pregnant women, hence, 'about that day or hour no one knows, neither the angels in heaven, nor the Son, but only the Father' (Mark 13.32). This also is a similarly derived metaphor from the Old Testament (Job 30.5; Jer. 2.26; 49.9; Joel 2.9). Malherbe comments with irony, 'What you actually know now is that you cannot know what you seek to know.'[26] Paul's reference to 'peace and security' reminds us of Amos 5.18–20, 'Alas for you who desire the day of the LORD.' Paul assures his readers, however, that as 'children of light', they have nothing to fear from these end events, even if 'the day' comes as a surprise. He will expound on the 'children of light' theme in 5.4–11. Elsewhere he says, 'The night is far gone, the day is

[25] Gale, The *Use of Analogy*, p. 27.

[26] Malherbe, The *Letters to the Thessalonians*, p. 290.

near. Let us then lay aside the works of darkness and put on the armour of light' (Rom. 13.12). Paul regularly uses the metaphors of light and darkness for the new and old life. He states that the Day of the Lord will bring the secret things of darkness to light (1 Cor. 4.5), and that 'God, who said, "Let light shine out of darkness" . . . has shone in our hearts' (2 Cor. 4.6). Paul, therefore, makes full use of the biblical symbols of light and darkness, as the Old Testament, John (John 12.36) and the community of Qumran also do (1QS 3.13—4.26).

Gale is right, that the 'thief' metaphor does not stand alone, but belongs to a complex of metaphors: women in childbirth, darkness and light, sleeping and waking, vigilance and slumber, and so on. Our only reservation concerns his use of 'strange' to describe them, since they are already embedded in Old Testament tradition. Irenaeus compared their use in Jeremiah and the Apocalypse.[27] Clement called for vigilance, appealing to the 'thief' metaphor and to sleep and wakefulness in 1 Thessalonians 5.[28] Cyprian (d.258) used Paul's analogy of the thief also.[29] Gregory of Nyssa (*c*.330–90) used the phrases 'children of light' and 'children of the day' to denote the character of Christians.[30] Ambrose (*c*.338–97) used the thief metaphor in exactly the Pauline context of our ignorance of the exact date of Christ's coming.[31] John Chrysostom (*c*.347–407) also placed Paul's pictures exactly in an appropriate context, including the thief, the day, darkness and light, and labour pains.[32] Augustine cited 1 Thessalonians. 5.5–8, emphasizing the division of light from darkness, and waking from sleep.[33]

Once again, the mediaeval period used these pictures in a variety of ways. Robert Grosseteste (*c*.1170–1253), Bishop of Lincoln, used the picture of light, but as 'knowledge of the truth', and darkness as 'disobedience of the law'. Indeed 'light' can allegorically mean 'spiritual prelates' and 'vision of the truth'. This fits less easily with 1 Thessalonians 5.[34] Admittedly Thomas Aquinas is more accurate in his commentary about the timing of the Parousia, although broader and yet exegetically sober in the *Summa Theologiae*.[35] Luther and Calvin took account of the eschato-

---

27 Irenaeus, *Against Heresies*, 5, 50, 2 (Eng., ANF, vol. 1, p. 559).

28 Tertullian, *On the Resurrection*, 24 (Eng., ANF, vol. 3, p. 563).

29 Cyprian, *Treatises*, 89 (Eng., ANF, vol. 5, p. 553).

30 Gregory of Nyssa, *Against Eunomius*, 3, 6 (Eng., NPNF, ser. 2, vol. 5, p. 148).

31 Ambrose, *Of the Christian Faith*, 5, 17, 211 (Eng., NPNF, ser. 2, vol. 10, p. 311).

32 Chrysostom, *Homily on Thessalonians*, 9 (Eng., NPNF, ser. 1, vol. 13, p. 360).

33 Augustine, *City of God*, Bk 11, ch. 7 (Eng., NPNF, ser. 1, vol. 2, p. 209) and Bk 11, ch. 33 (Eng., p. 224); and *On the Trinity* 15, 9 (Eng., NPNF, ser. 1, vol. 3, p. 207).

34 Robert Grosseteste, *On Six Days of Creation* (London: British Academy, 1996).

35 Thomas Aquinas, *Commentary on Thessalonians*, p. 41; and *Summa Theologiae*, Pt. 3

logical context in Paul. Luther was most explicit in his 'Letter to Michael Stiefel' in 1533. Stiefel had predicted the Parousia as occurring on 19 October 1533. Luther was appalled. Even Jesus, he stated, did not know of the date! Paul also quieted restless hearts.[36] John Calvin agreed that speculation about the timing of the Parousia was a 'curious and unprofitable enquiry', and 'indeed the day of the Lord comes like a thief in the night'.[37] Jeremy Taylor (1613–67) attempted broader or looser applications in his *Holy Living* (1650), and John Gill (1697–1771) quoted 1 Thessalonians 5.1–2, together with 2 Peter 3.10, 1 Corinthians 1.8; 5.5, and numerous other biblical references. From Hermann Olshausen (1796–1839) until virtually today responsible applications can be found in exegetical commentaries. The moral seems, again, to be that appropriate interpretations of Paul's pictures will be found within an informed exegetical tradition, but other interpretations can readily be found outside these traditions.

Among modern writers Straub considered 1 Thessalonians 5.2 among his third category of 'comparisons', of which it constitutes his eleventh example. Paul's 'picture' was often associated with 'the day of the Lord', as in Matthew 24.43–44, 2 Peter 3.10 and Revelation 3.3.[38] The modern commentary by Best is more illuminating. He speaks of the 'two vivid metaphors' in verses 2 (the thief) and 3 (labour pains), both of which stress 'unpredictability and yet its inevitability'.[39] Hence Paul urges his readers to be alert. Probably they feared that if the Parousia were delayed, they could not participate in it. If it is unexpected, some argue that it would not be certain that it would occur in Paul's lifetime, as some claim. The second metaphor of labour pains hammers home the dual phenomenon of unexpectedness and inevitability. In view of the use of the metaphor in the Synoptic tradition, Malherbe argues that it is 'plausible' that Paul knew of this tradition.[40] Witherington comments with insight, 'Paul is describing here a sudden intrusion into human history, catching many unaware and unprepared.'

The metaphor 'thief in the night' goes back to the Jesus tradition (cf. Matt. 24.43; Luke 12.39–40; 2 Pet. 3.10; Rev. 3.3; 16.15), and stresses 'both

(suppl.) qu. 73, arts 1–2.

36 Martin Luther, *Letters of Spiritual Counsel* (ed. T. G. Tappert; London: SCM, 1965), pp. 301–2.

37 John Calvin, *1 and 2 Thessalonians*, p. 51; and John Calvin, *Of the Institutes of the Christian Religion*, Bk 4, ch. 19, sect. 34, respectively.

38 Straub, *Die Bildersprache des Apostels Paulus*, pp. 50–1.

39 Best, *First and Second Thessalonians*, p. 203.

40 Malherbe, *The Letters to the Thessalonians*, p. 190.

the suddenness of the event, but also its unknown timing'.[41] Moore calls attention to Paul's use of the present tense for the English 'will come' to stress the vividness and possible nearness of the Parousia.[42] Finally, we may note that Beda Rigaux included all the standard biblical texts, such as Matthew 25.6, and referred to comments by Jerome, Frame and Straub, and anticipated Moore's comment about 'the prophetic present', *erchetai*.[43] Paul uses not one metaphor, but a network of interrelated metaphors.

The Epistle to the Galatians

(3) As a third example, Gale turns next to **Galatians 3.15–18**, which uses word-play on Greek *diethēkēn* to mean both '**will**' or testament and '**covenant**' or agreement. In verse 17, he said, Paul's allusion was to the covenant, although verse 15 is debatable. In verse 17 the covenant refers to promises made to Abraham and his offspring. This is not annulled by the law, which came later. This is the main point of Paul's picture.[44] Burton remarked that the picture allowed the secondary allusion to our relationship with God, as evidenced both by Hebrew *b*ᵉ*rîth* and the LXX *diathēkē*.[45] Straub included Galatians 3.15–18 in his fifth category of similes or parables, in fact as the twenty-seventh example.[46] The NSRV interprets Greek *kata anthrōpōn* as 'an example from daily life', and the NEB, 'from ordinary life'. NJB, however, translates: 'To put it in human terms'. This coheres with the use of the phrase in Romans 3.5 and 1 Corinthians 9.8, that is, to express divine truths in human terms, such as analogies or pictures. Straub seems to apply this to the legal terminology that Paul uses, and especially to his use of the singular 'offspring'.

Hans Dieter Betz asks how the primarily Hebrew or Jewish meaning, *covenant*, would be readily intelligible to Gentile readers. He replies, with Ernst Bammel, that the meaning *covenant* was more widespread than is usually assumed.[47] He confirms his conclusion by appealing to such similar legal terms as validate, ratify and confirm. Paul mainly appeals to

---

41 Ben Witherington III, *1 and 2 Thessalonians: A Socio-Rhetorical Commentary* (Grand Rapids: Eerdmans, 2006), p. 14.

42 Arthur L. Moore, *1 and 2 Thessalonians* (NCB; London: Nelson, 1969), p. 73.

43 Beda Rigaux, *Les Épitres aux Thessaloniciens* (Paris: Gabalda, 1956), p. 557.

44 Gale, *The Use of Analogy*, pp. 41–2.

45 Ernest de Witt Burton, *The Epistle to the Galatians* (ICC; Edinburgh: T&T Clark, and New York: Scribner, 1920), p. 497; cf. 'Appendix on *diathēkē*', pp. 496–505.

46 Straub, *Die Bildersprache des Apostels Paulus*, pp. 95–6.

47 Hans Dieter Betz, *Galatians* (Hermeneia; Philadelphia: Fortress, 1979), pp. 155–9.

the covenant promise (*epaggelia*) to Abraham in Genesis 15.4–6, 18–21; 17.1–14; 22.16–19; and others. The covenant with Abraham was renewed with Israel in the time of Moses (Exod. 19.5–6; 24.3–8; 34.10; Deut. 29.1). In Paul, Betz comments further, the singular 'seed' (Gk, *sperma*) focuses on Christ. His addition 'I mean this' calls for special attention. The law (the Torah) was given 430 years after the promise to Abraham. Abraham could not have become righteous, therefore, by the law.

The term 'inheritance' (Gk, *klēronomia*) becomes crucial in Paul's theology of the inheritance of salvation. F. F. Bruce suggested that God added, as it were, a codicil to the will (Gk, *epidiathēkē*), citing precedents from Roman law and Greek papyri.[48] Bruce also comments, 'There is no need to make heavy weather of Paul's insistence that the biblical text has *spermati* (i.e. singular) . . . the biblical text uses a collective singular . . . and could refer to a single descendant or to many descendants.'[49] Whether this strictly comes under the heading of 'pictures' or visual representation, the reader may determine, but Gale includes the example among analogies, and Straub includes it among comparisons.

(4) Gale's fourth example can more definitely be *visualized as a picture.* In Galatians 3.24 Paul wrote, 'The law was our **disciplinarian** [NRSV; Gk, *paidagōgos*] until Christ came.' The English versions vary: 'kind of tutor' (NEB); 'serving as a slave' (NJB); 'put in charge' (NIV); and 'schoolmaster' (KJV/AV). Danker (BDAG) explains: 'slave . . . whose duty it was to conduct a boy or youth . . . to and from school and to superintend his conduct'; he was not strictly a teacher; thus 'one who has responsibility for someone who needs guidance, a guardian, leader, or guide . . . Gal. 3:24'.[50] Danker's explanation of ancient Graeco-Roman customs well illustrates the problem. There is no exact equivalent in the modern Western world, but once we understand the background, it becomes easy to visualize what Paul intends. None of the English versions as they stand capture the Greek word exactly, but all convey something of its meaning. Gale explains it by citing five meanings: (a) it is temporary; (b) it has the aspect of a custodian or guardian; (c) it has a disciplinary function; (d) the custodian has a

---

48 F. F. Bruce, *The Epistle to the Galatians: A Commentary on the Greek Text* (Grand Rapids: Eerdmans, 1982), p. 171; and Papyrus 21 in E. P. Grenfell, *An Alexandrian Erotic Fragment and Other Greek Papyri* (Oxford: Clarendon Press, 1896), pp. 44–6.

49 Bruce, *Galatians*, p. 172.

50 Frederick W. Danker (with Walther Bauer, W. F. Arndt and F. W. Gingrich, eds), *A Greek-English Lexicon of the New Testament and Other Early Christian Literature* (Chicago: University of Chicago Press, 3rd edn, 2000), p. 748.

teaching function (though only in general); (e) the guardian has a protective function. Gale's explanation, as well as that of Danker, shows that this composite picture could not function accurately without explanatory words and socio-historical context.

Once the picture has been carefully explained, however, it may helpfully embrace the multiform aspects of what Paul says about the law. Unlike most of the parables of Jesus, it is not what Lewis calls a 'Master' metaphor to advance understanding, but a useful 'Pupil' metaphor to explain and to educate. Straub lists it only among his 'comparisons', although he lists the occurrence of *paidagōgos* in 1 Corinthians 4.15 under 'metaphors'.[51] This passage fits well with John Calvin's emphasis on the law as a restraint on wickedness, a tool of education or instruction, a device to teach our weakness and dependency, and a mirror of what God wills. But this is subject to its abrogation with the coming of Christ.[52]

F. F. Bruce stresses similarly the instructive role of the law, but even more the contrast between the restrictive discipline of the slave-attendant who accompanied the free-born boy wherever he went, and the boy's coming of age.[53] James Dunn suggests that 'baby-sitter' may be an approximate modern near-equivalent, urging its protective, rather than oppressive, nature.[54] Betz also seems to emphasize this protective aspect when he explains, 'The task of the slave was to protect the child against molesters and accidents, and also to ensure that he learned good manners.'[55] He also traces the custom of using a *paidagōgos* back to Aristotle. John Bligh attempts to ask how this picture applies to Christians today, and after admitting that there is no clear picture, stresses the interim situation of Christians who have been freed, and yet still await the End.[56] Here, however, we may begin to see divergences about interpretations of the role of the law. Even within the Reformation tradition, Luther would have urged the Christian's freedom from the law, while Calvin would have urged its continuing relevance as a protective and disciplinary representation of

51 Straub, *Die Bildersprache des Apostels Paulus*, pp. 55 and 61.

52 Calvin, *Institutes of the Christian Religion*, Bk 2, ch. 8, especially sects 3, 5, 6, 8, 11, 18, etc.

53 Bruce, *Galatians*, p. 182.

54 James D. G. Dunn, *The Theology of Paul the Apostle* (Edinburgh: T&T Clark, 1998), pp. 140–3; Dunn, *Paul and the Mosaic Law* (WUNT 89; Tübingen: Mohr, 1996); and Dunn, 'Was Paul Against the Law? The Law in Galatians and Romans: A Test Case of Text in Context', in T. Fornberg and D. Hellholm (eds), *Texts and Contexts: Biblical Texts in Their Textual and Situational Context* (Oslo: Scandinavian University Press, 1995), pp. 455–75.

55 Betz, *Galatians*, p. 177.

56 John Bligh, *Galatians: A Discussion of St Paul's Epistle* (London: St. Paul Publications, 1969), p. 319.

God's will for all. This has an important bearing on the argument of this book. Thus Gale comments, '*The significance of the picture is determined by the context of thought in which it is to be found; the thought is not to be determined by all the implications that the picture may provide.*'[57] The appropriate interpretation of the picture depends both on sound exegesis and on an accurate understanding of Paul's theology of the law. An understanding of both Galatians and Romans is required for this.

(5) In Galatians 4.19–20 Paul compares himself with **a mother who is suffering labour pains** to bring forth a child formed in the likeness of Christ. The NRSV translates: 'My little children, for whom I am again in the *pain of childbirth until Christ is formed in you*, I wish I were present with you now and could change my tone, for I am perplexed about you' (my italics). As Gale comments, the main point of the simile or picture is to emphasize the *pain* or *distress* which is an inevitable part of the process of bearing children of God, who are in the likeness of *Christ*. The purpose of this allusion to labour pains is not, as it was in 1 Thessalonians 5.3, the idea of suddenness or surprise, but to emphasize inevitable pain and suffering. The goal, as Bruce, writes, is that 'Paul longs to see Christ visibly living in the Galatians'.[58]

Paul will later refer to himself as spiritual father (1 Cor. 4.15), just as he had earlier spoken of himself as 'mother', 'nurse' or 'nursing mother' (1 Thess. 2.7). Wickenhauser observed, 'The community is born through the growth of Christ in individuals.'[59] We should not be put off the use of this picture by the anti-paternal and anti-authoritarian arguments of Antoinette Wire and Elizabeth Castelli, who one-sidedly interpret Paul's image of 'father' as authoritarian and not as one of affection and fatherly care.[60] Wire interpreted Paul's appeal to fatherhood as serving the purpose of manipulative rhetoric; Castelli understood him in the light of Michel Foucault's postmodern opposition to all authoritative people or institutions. Indeed the previous example suggests that the authoritarian agency is simply that of the law. Contrary to Wire and Castelli, Burton called verses 19–20 'language of deep affection and emo-

---

[57] Gale, *The Use of Analogy*, p. 49 (his italics).

[58] Bruce, *Galatians*, p. 212.

[59] Alfred Wickenhauser, *Pauline Mysticism* (Edinburgh: Nelson, 1960), p. 44.

[60] Antoinette Wire, *The Corinthian Women Prophets* (Minneapolis: Fortress, 1990), pp. 45–7 and elsewhere; Elizabeth A. Castelli, *Imitating Paul: A Discourse of Power* (Louisville: Westminster/John Knox, 1999), pp. 1–58 and throughout.

tion, called forth by the previous words defending his right to continue his zealous efforts to hold the affection of his readers'.[61]

Betz argues that Galatians 4.19 should be dealt with as a conglomerate of concepts, and certainly more than one metaphorical allusion is involved in these verses. The notions of 'birth', 'sons', and being born and shaped run through these verses. He accuses some commentators of indulging in what 'becomes merely guesswork'.[62] Clearly, well-informed interpretation is necessary when we encounter mixed metaphors. The controlling metaphor in verses 19–20 is *ōdinō*, which Danker renders 'to experience pain associated with giving birth, have labour-pains'.[63] It is cognate with *ōdin,* birth pains. Straub catalogues *ōdinō* as his eighteenth metaphor, placing *ōdin* among 'comparisons' in 1 Thessalonians 2.7–8.[64] He regarded both words as representing 'spiritual birth'. What Gale classified as a single picture Straub often treated as multiple metaphors. The metaphor of birth pains is used by Philo to compare an embryo which will become fully shaped, with what is confused or blurred.[65] In the background is Paul's discourse about coming to God as *Abba* (Gal. 4.4–7), the word for God used by Jesus.

(6) Galatians 4.21–31 presents the *picture or allegory of* **Hagar and Sarah**. Paul drew the historical context from the Old Testament, but in verse 24 called it an allegory (Gk, *allēgoroumena*). The interpretation of this is controversial. Leonhard Goppelt insisted that Paul's exposition of the historical narrative in Galatians 4.21–31 may be broadly called an allegory, but in fact Paul expounded it as 'entirely confined to a *typological* interpretation as we conceive it'.[66] Goppelt argued that Abraham was a type of Christ, and that the comparison between Hagar and Sarah 'becomes typology because the relationship was ordained by God (Rom. 4:11f., 23; Gal. 3:8) and was mediated through Christ (Gal. 3:17). The typological heightening flows automatically from Christ's office as mediator'.[67] As a rough-and-ready distinction, allegorical interpretation usually indicates

---

[61] Burton, *Galatians*, p. 248.

[62] Betz, *Galatians*, p. 236.

[63] BDAG, p. 1102.

[64] Straub, *Der Bildersprache des Apostels Paulus*, pp. 61 and 48.

[65] Philo, *On Mating*, 135–6.

[66] Leonhard Goppelt, *Typos: The Typological Interpretation of the Old Testament in the New* (Eng., Grand Rapids: Eerdmans, 1982), p. 139; cf. pp. 136–51; and '*tupos*' in G. Kittel and G. Friedrich, *TDNT*, vol. 8, pp. 236–60.

[67] Goppelt, *Typos*, p. 137.

a parallelism between *ideas*; typological interpretation indicates a parallel between historical *events*. One writer who supports this is Richard Hanson.[68]

Bruce, in effect, agrees with Hanson and Goppelt. Paul, he says,

> is not thinking of allegory in the Philonic sense (allegory in the Philonic sense was introduced into Christian interpretation of Origen and his successors); he has in mind that form of allegory which is commonly called *typology*: a narrative from Old Testament history is interpreted in terms of the new covenant . . . Typology presupposes that salvation-history displays a recurring pattern of *divine action* . . . The Exodus typology in particular was widespread in the New Testament period (cf. Heb. 3:7–4:6; Jude 5).[69]

Paul, he adds, presents a more elaborate example of biblical interpretation in 2 Corinthians 3.3—4.6. He concedes:

> In the present 'allegory', however, there is a forcible inversion of the analogy which is unparalleled elsewhere in Paul . . . This unique clash between type and antitype demands an explanation . . . namely that the incident of the two sons of Abraham had been adduced by Paul's opponents in Galatia in support of *their* case, and that Paul felt obliged to refute their argument by inverting it and showing that the incident, properly understood, supported the gospel of free grace, with its antithesis between flesh and spirit.[70]

Several other commentators, however, do call it an allegory. Burton, for example, wrote that Paul decided,

> apparently as an after-thought, that he [Paul] might make his thought clearer and more persuasive by an allegorical interpretation of the story of Abraham and his two sons, Ishmael and Isaac, the one born in the course of nature only, the other in fulfilment of divine promise. The two mothers he interpreted as representing the two covenants, that of law and that of promise.[71]

Burton explains further that in the antagonism between the two sons, or their descendants, he finds a parallel to the persecution to which the Gentile Christians had been subjected at the hands of Jewish Christians. Hence he explains that there are two branches of Abraham's family: our relation to Abraham is spiritual, not physical; we are the sons not of the slave but of the free.

---

[68] Richard P. C. Hanson, *Allegory and Event: A Study of the Sources and Significance of Origen's Interpretation of Scripture* (London: SCM, 1959), p. 7.

[69] Bruce, *Galatians*, p. 217 (my italics).

[70] Bruce, *Galatians*, p. 218 (his italics).

[71] Burton, *Galatians*, p. 251.

Almost every commentator supports one side or the other. Bligh, for example, wrote, 'The argument from the law is typological: in the household of Abraham there arose a crisis which prefigured the crisis that has now arisen in the Church.'[72] The solution, he said, which God authorized, was, 'Send away the slave-girl and her son!' (see Gen. 21.10, 12). Bligh then set out 'typological correspondences' in two parallel columns. In addressing more fully the question, 'Is it a type or an allegory?' Bligh rightly showed that much depends on definition. He observed,

> An allegory is an extended metaphor . . . Read as an allegory, this story looks like the composition of a prophet or churchman who disapproved of Gentile Christianity but took the view that it ought to be tolerated in order to preserve the unity among all true Jewish Christians.[73]

Bligh resumes:

> A 'type' on the other hand is a historical event which prefigures another historical event. The story of the setting up of the brazen serpent in Num. 21:8–9 is not an allegory but a type, because the author means that Moses did in reality set up a brazen serpent. In Gal. 4:25, St Paul describes the story of Sarah and Agar as allegorical. If he is using the word 'allegory' correctly, he is saying that the story of the two women does not describe events which actually took place in the past, but is a prophetic description, in an extended series of metaphors.[74]

Bligh then compares the Antiochene Fathers' interpretation with that of the Alexandrian Fathers. Chrysostom says, 'Paul has incorrectly described as allegory what is in fact a type.'[75] The Alexandrians, however, viewed it as an allegory. Thus controversy today reflects a debate which has arisen since the third century.

Gale concludes that the Old Testament account, allegorically interpreted, becomes an analogy. He also concludes, 'A single figure in the story is used at one moment to represent one thing or one idea and at the next moment to represent something quite different', while 'even single points of correspondence are not developed or carried through to their full conclusions'.[76] Thus he makes two or three points in line with the argument of this book. First, this passage presents not one picture or one

---

[72] Bligh, *Galatians*, p. 391.
[73] Bligh, *Galatians*, p. 395.
[74] Bligh, *Galatians*, p. 395.
[75] Chrysostom, *Patrologia Graeca*, vol. 61, line 662 B.
[76] Gale, *The Use of Analogy*, pp. 67 and 68.

metaphor, but a network of diverse pictures or metaphors. Second, how these pictures or metaphors are to be interpreted remains controversial and to some extent problematic. Much depends on the particular tradition of theology and exegesis which is relevant to the picture's interpretation. Gale even admits that the picture of Hagar and Sarah as representing two seemingly rival covenants would be thoroughly inappropriate.[77] Pictures may be powerful and vivid, but they may also be seductive and misleading, if they are not appropriately interpreted.

1 Corinthians: Paul's most plentiful examples

(7) Following Gale's enumeration of analogies in Paul, his first in the Corinthian correspondence is **1 Corinthians 2.11**. This features an *analogy* between the thoughts of humankind and the **thoughts of the Spirit of God**. But is this a *picture* or metaphor? Paul explains that only the Holy Spirit of God fully knows God's purposes, just as the human spirit understands human purposes. Gale asserted that the purpose of this analogy is clear: it affirms the status of God's wisdom in order to stress that 'The depths (Gk, *ta batha*) of God can be understood . . . only through divine revelation, since only God himself fully comprehends the "things" of God'.[78] But does this present any picture? Even 'spirit', when applied to human beings, does not match the use of 'Spirit' when applied to God. From Bultmann to Jewett and others it has long been recognized that the human spirit normally means simply 'person', not some reified entity of a trichotomous view of the human self. Gale recognized this, and even quoted Bultmann's corroborating words.[79] Gale even admitted, 'The analogy is one that cannot be carried through . . . completely.'[80] He called it a 'picture' of the human being, but admitted that it does generally fit with Paul's view elsewhere. He simply stated that Paul did not ascribe to humans complete self-understanding.

Paul does not imply a dualist view of spirit 'within' a human body. But the analogy constitutes a powerful argument for the need for divine revelation and the limits of human knowledge. In 2000 I commented:

> The point of analogy does not turn on human spirit within/divine spirit within, but on the possession of an *exclusive initiative to reveal*

[77] Gale, *The Use of Analogy*, p. 72.
[78] Gale, *The Use of Analogy*, p. 76.
[79] Gale, *The Use of Analogy*, p. 77; Rudolf Bultmann, *Theology of the New Testament*, vol. 1 (Eng., London: SCM, 1952) p. 206.
[80] Gale, *The Use of Analogy*, p. 77.

one's thoughts, councils, stance, attitudes, intentions, or whatever else is 'within' in the sense of hidden from the public display, not in the sense of location.[81]

To take the analogy in any other way would be to impose modern psychology on to Paul. Indeed it rescues our understanding of Paul from an uncritical indebtedness to Graeco-Roman tradition, which would be alien to Paul and his Old Testament roots. Only in the nineteenth century did the older idealist view of Paul emerge, for example in H. Lüdemann. Karl Barth well sums up the thought of this verse: 'God is known through God alone.'[82] This divine wisdom is centred on the cross. To confirm the argument Paul insists that the Spirit comes forth, proceeds or 'issues forth' (my translation) from (*ek*) God, in contrast to the immanent world-soul of the Stoics. He is transcendent; not the spirit of the world (v. 12). The Greek, *to pneuma to ek tou theou*, is exceptionally strong.[83] The Spirit of God is 'Beyond'. I also discuss the post-history of interpretation, which suggests that Athanasius, Luther and Calvin have well grasped Paul's concern about revealed truth and epistemology.[84]

In spite of these further explanations, does Paul provide here any 'picture' or visual representation? This seems at best unlikely. The example shows that not every analogy qualifies as a picture. Nevertheless, the above explanations do impinge on the question of visual art in a way which is perhaps unexpected. By stressing the transcendence and otherness of the Holy Spirit, and his intimacy with God, by implication this excludes many of the trivial and mundane pictures of the Holy Spirit which are all too frequently found in some Christian discourse. If such imagery as the shamrock or even the dove are interpreted in isolation from the biblical tradition, this may lead to an anthropomorphic reductionism of our concept of God's Holy Spirit. In other words, this provides a strongly qualifying principle to some popular images of the Holy Spirit.

(8) In **1 Corinthians 3.5–17** Paul uses several analogies which *may easily be visualized.* Initially they come from agriculture: **planting**, and **watering**, while God gives the increase (1 Cor. 3.6). Paul writes, 'I planted, Apollos watered, but God gave the growth. So neither the one who plants

[81] Anthony C. Thiselton, *The First Epistle to the Corinthians: A Commentary on the Greek Text* (NIGTC; Grand Rapids: Eerdmans, 2000), p. 258; cf. pp. 255–86 (italics original).

[82] Karl Barth, *Church Dogmatics* (Eng., 14 vols, Edinburgh: T&T Clark, 1957–75), vol. 3 (Ger., II.1), sect. 27, p. 179.

[83] Thiselton, *First Corinthians*, pp. 260–3.

[84] Thiselton, *First Corinthians*, pp. 279–86.

nor the one who waters is anything, but only God who gives the growth' (vv. 6–7). The main point of the analogy this time is to make *two* points: first, that the *agents* of gardening are ineffective, unless God and his Spirit provide the growth; second, that Paul and Apollos are *not rivals* who are in competition with each other, but fellow workers who *cooperate and complement* each other in the same task.

To these two visual pictures Paul adds several more: first, the believers at Corinth need to be fed by **baby's milk** (Gk, *gala*), **not solids** (Gk, *brōma*, v. 2); second, Paul provides the analogy of the **master-builder or architect** (Gk, *architektōn*, v. 10) and builders: *fellow workers and another person* (Gk, *allos*); third, in 3.12–15 Paul pens the analogy of a **fire burning a building** (Gk, *en puri apokaluptai*); and fourth, in 3.17 he adds the further analogy of the **holy shrine** (Gk, *naos*) **or temple.** If we add these four to Gale's primary analogy, we have *five or six* analogies which all *constitute visual representations or pictures.*

Planting and *watering* constitute suggestive and useful pictures. Paul uses a punctiliar aorist for 'I planted' (Gk, *ephuteusa*, v. 6) and 'Apollos watered' (Gk, *epotisen*), while 'God gave the growth' (NRSV) supposedly translates the Greek *continuous* imperfect (Gk, *ēuxanen*). This difference in tense underlines the principle that ministers come and go, while God's sovereign work of causing growth and life continues. Straub expounded all these six or more metaphors in 1 Corinthians 3.2, 6–9, 10–15, 26–27: milk/solids (Gk, *gala/brōma*); planting and watering (Gk, *phuteuō/potizō*); field (Gk, *geōrgion*); building/fire (Gk, *oikodomē/pur*); and temple or shrine (Gk, *naos*).[85] If 1 Corinthians 2.11 offered a non-pictorial analogy, 1 Corinthians 3.17 presents an abundance of concrete visual pictures.

The first metaphor, milk, in 1 Corinthians 3.1–2 suggests that the Corinthians are not yet mature (Gk, *teleios*) but are positively infantile, when compared with verse 1, 'I could not address you as people of the Spirit' (my translation). They could take only a milk-and-water diet. This is exemplified by their immature jealousies and support of rival factions in the church (vv. 3–4). They are not the 'spiritual people' which they fancied themselves to be in chapter 2. Paul's second metaphor of the field and its labourers shows in part that the 'workers', that is, local leaders, are not to be regarded as if they were patrons; indeed Clarke wrote, 'Paul has deliberately inverted the Graeco-Roman scale of values . . . He is describing them as *diakonoi* [servants] (1 Cor. 3:5–8).'[86] Yet he does not denigrate

[85] Straub, *Die Bildersprache des Apostels Paulus*, pp. 57–8, 72–3 and 85–8.

[86] Clarke, *Secular and Christian Leadership in Corinth*, pp. 19–20; cf. pp. 31–6.

this office. They are 'one', that is, either 'equal', or (more likely) one in task and goal. Both 'planting' and 'watering' are absolutely necessary. In modern terms, both the evangelism that founds Christian communities and the pastoral work that cares for and sustains them are necessary. Both kinds of work may involve toil (Gk, *kopos*). The notion of 'reward' is not an independent metaphor; *reward* is probably 'internal', that is, working for God brings its own reward. In verse 15, 'only as through fire' is a metaphorical idiom which means 'only just' or 'by a narrow margin'.

The Corinthians would have been used to seeing buildings (Gk, *oikodomē*) constructed with mixed materials. After the destruction of Corinth by Julius Caesar in 44 BC, the city had lain partly in ruins. When it became a Roman colony, it began to rise from its ruins, sometimes with fine buildings, but often with patched-up clay, stubble or even thatch alongside the marble wall. The possibility of fire was a genuine terror for city-dwellers at that time. All this means not, as Gale reminds us, that each of these details has a meaning, but that it demonstrates the power of pictures in that every detail would resonate with the experience of the first readers. In fact commentators agree that the six diverse materials cited (gold, silver, precious stones [possibly marble], wood, hay and straw, v. 16) divide simply into the *two* categories of combustible and non-combustible. The point of the metaphor or picture is: will your work of 'building' survive God's test? Human evaluations remain corrigible; the divine verdict is definitive. J. Shanor has suggested one further detail: inscriptions feature local trade agreements about a building 'job' (Gk, *ergon*), which include penalty clauses for damage or hindrances, with fines and losses.[87] It entirely fits Paul's extended analogy, not to press detailed applications, but, again, to underline the power and vividness of the picture. As in the case of Jesus, some of the parables reflect real life. Even 'building' has a pictorial and metaphorical dimension. Several writers insist that 'building up' constitutes a dominant theme of the epistle.[88]

Indeed one writer, Lanci, argues that 'building up' reaches its climax in the picture of the people of God as his temple or shrine.[89] In 3.16–17 Paul uses *naos* (holy shrine) three times, in contrast to *hieron* (the wider

[87] J. Shanor, 'Paul as Master Builder: Construction Terms in 1 Corinthians', *NTS* 34 (1988), p. 461; cf. pp. 461–71.

[88] Margaret M. Mitchell, *Paul and the Rhetoric of Reconciliation* (Tübingen: Mohr, and Louisville: Westminster/Knox, 1992), pp. 98–111 and elsewhere; P. Vielhauer, *Oikodomē. Aufsätze zum N.T.*, II, *Theologische Bücherei*, vol. 65 (Munich: Kaiser, 1979), pp. 1–168, esp. pp. 74–82.

[89] J. R. Lanci, *A New Temple for Corinth: Historical and Archaeological Approaches to Pauline Imagery* (New York and Bern: Lang, 1997), throughout.

area of the Temple as a whole), which takes up the previous argument. It may seem surprising that the NRSV, REB and NJB all translate *naos* by 'temple', which loses the point of the Greek.[90] Paul's phrase 'Do you not know that?' shows both the intensity of Paul's concern, and that this teaching would be familiar to the church. As Lionel Thornton sums it up, 'The Corinthians are God's sanctuary, in which the Holy Spirit dwells.'[91] Paul's word for 'destroy' (*phtheirō*) reflects what Shanor wrote about penalty clauses. To damage God's shrine or his people amounts to sacrilege. Thus 1 Corinthians 3.2–17 has an impressive store of multiple metaphors or multiple pictures.

(9) Gale's next example comes from **1 Corinthians 4.9**, coupled with 15.30–32. In 1 Corinthians 4.9 he contrasts the apostolic image of **gladiators doomed to die in the arena** with the claim by some or many Corinthians 'to reign as kings' (see 4.8). Gaston Deluz sums up the situation very well, with some irony. He writes:

> These Corinthians are lucky. *Already* they enjoy favours that the apostles dare only hope for. They no longer 'hunger and thirst after righteousness'; they are *filled*; in the theory of the Spirit, they have eaten to satiety . . . In short, the Messianic kingdom seems to have come to Corinth and these people have been given their thrones, while the apostles dance attendance and are placed with servants.[92]

In other words, some of the Corinthians fall prey to an over-realized eschatology on the basis of a supposed 'spirituality' or an elite gift of the Holy Spirit. Barrett explains:

> The Corinthians are behaving as if the age to come had already been consummated, as if the Saints had already taken over the kingdom (Dan. 7:18); for them there is no 'not yet' to qualify the 'already' of realised eschatology.[93]

Wolff detects the influence of 'wisdom-gnosis' and 'Spirit-centred enthusiasm'.[94]

---

[90] See Otto Michel, '*naos*', in *TDNT*, vol. 4, pp. 880–90.

[91] L. S. Thornton, *The Common Life in the Body of Christ* (London: Dacre Press, 1950), p. 14.

[92] Gaston Deluz, *Companion to 1 Corinthians* (Eng., London: Darton, Longman & Todd, 1963), pp. 46–7 (his italics).

[93] C. K. Barrett, *A Commentary on the First Epistle to the Corinthians* (London: Black, 2nd edn, 1971), p. 109.

[94] C. Wolff, *Der erste Brief des Paulus an die Korinther* (Leipzig: Evangelische Verlagsanstalt, 1996), p. 86.

This is an exceptionally interesting example. For with skilful use of irony and caricature Paul paints a memorable picture of the contrasts between the self-assured 'strong' at Corinth, revelling in their supposed special status, and the labouring apostles, who appear as gladiatorial slaves or criminals fighting and struggling in the arena for their very survival. The 'picture' is unforgettable with its overdrawn contrast of the kind which elsewhere George Caird describes as being like a political cartoon. As Luther at the Reformation and Käsemann in the late twentieth century both insist, struggle is an integral part of the normal Christian life, in contrast to the exalted illusions of the 'enthusiasts'. It is important for Paul's argument that he uses the Greek term *apedeixen* (aorist of *apodeiknumi*), which NRSV translates 'exhibited', but for which I have suggested 'put on display'. Paul introduces the metaphor of a great pageant in which criminals, prisoners or professional gladiators process to the gladiatorial ring with the apostles bringing up the rear as those who must fight to the death. Paul states that the apostles have become a 'spectacle' (Gk, *theatron*, v. 9), at least in the fantasy world of the 'spiritual'. The Corinthians are the spectator audience who sit in comfortable seats and ironically applaud; Paul is the participant who continues to struggle! Hence Paul continues his irony in verse 10, 'We are fools for the sake of Christ, but you are wise.' He then emphasizes how he labours with his hands, that is, engages in manual toil (vv. 11–13). The apostles are 'the world's scum, and the scrapings from people's shoes' (my translation of *perikatharmata* and *peripsēma*). This makes the metaphor more striking, memorable and powerful.

Gale agrees with this emphasis, but also uses 1 Corinthians 15.30–32 as a foil where the picture or analogy of a struggling gladiator has a quite different application from that which it has in 4.8–9. The application of the same picture is utterly different in each case, and demonstrates the importance of correct interpretation, as well as the fact that no picture can be understood as a merely free-floating object or example. When in 15.32 Paul speaks of fighting with wild beasts at Ephesus, the analogy is also metaphorical, as the phrase in Greek *kata anthrōpon* ('humanly speaking', RSV) indicates. Further, no Roman citizen would normally be reduced to the criminal or slave status of a gladiator in the arena. In 4.9 Paul uses the analogy of the gladiator for a totally different reason, as Gale stresses.[95] In 15.32 he genuinely has a fight on his hands at Ephesus, which he describes in purely metaphorical terms.

---

[95] Gale, *The Use of Analogy*, p. 95.

(10) In **1 Corinthians 5.6** Paul repeats the analogy of **yeast and leaven**, previously used in Galatians 5.9. The key metaphor is the Greek, *zumē*, *leaven* or *fermented dough*. Its metaphorical use was not invented by Paul. Danker records it as a popular or proverbial metaphor for 'that which negatively penetrates attitude or behaviour', for example in Mark 8.15, Luke 12.1, Matthew 16.6, 11, and Ignatius.[96] In the exegesis of 1 Corinthians 5.6–8 two explanations of the analogy are offered. One suggests that the specific immoral conduct and stance of the man in question threatens to weaken the moral fibre of the community at Corinth. The other suggests that the 'old leaven' is a metaphor for all immoral acts or thoughts within the community. Verses 5 and 6, with the demand for the man's excommunication or expulsion from the local church, favour the first; the wider application of the metaphor in verse 8 suggests that all 'malice and evil' cause the corruption.

This is one of the ten times when Paul protests, 'Do you not know that?', once again implying both intensity and that this is a familiar piece of teaching. C. Leslie Mitton wrote, 'Leaven is not quite the same as yeast . . . [When] it was fermenting . . . it could cause fermentation in the new dough.'[97] Failure to distinguish between leaven and yeast could cause confusion.[98] Thus Wolfgang Schrage and F. Lang support this distinction.[99] Leaven always represents unstoppable effects, mainly of evil, but often of good. Thus the unmentionable sin could taint the whole congregation, as if it were an infection. The comment 'You are arrogant' (plural, v. 2) implies that the whole congregation was largely at fault; hence the new leaven needs to crowd out old in the church also. Perhaps either they mistakenly rejoiced in freedom from the law, or had special reasons for keeping the support of the immoral man, for example, financial gain.[100] Straub discussed the metaphor both in Galatians 5.9 and 1 Corinthians 5.6, citing Weiss and Lietzmann on leaven, and the ordinance of the Passover in Exodus 12.15.[101]

Leaven and dough constitute a useful visual representation or picture which is powerful and vivid, and stays in the mind. The notion of newness

---

96 BDAG, p. 429.

97 C. Leslie Mitton, *The Gospel According to St Mark* (London: Epworth Press, 1957), p. 61.

98 C. Leslie Mitton, 'New Wine in Old Wineskins; 4: Leaven', *ExpTim* 84 (1973), pp. 339–43.

99 W. Schrage, *Der erste Brief an die Korinther* (4 vols), vol. 1 (Zürich: Benziger Verlag, 1991), pp. 379–85; F. Lang, *Die Briefe an die Korinther* (Göttingen: Vandenhoeck & Ruprecht, 1994), pp. 73–4.

100 Anthony C. Thiselton, 'The Meaning of *Sarx* in 1 Cor. 5:5: A Fresh Approach', *SJT* 26 (1973), pp. 204–28.

101 Straub, *Die Bildersprache des Apostels Paulus*, pp. 67 and 80–1.

leads on to the celebration of the New Passover or Passover Lamb in verses 7–8.

(11) As was the case in 1 Corinthians 3, so also 1 Corinthians 9 becomes especially fruitful for examples of metaphors which can readily be visualized. Gale selected **1 Corinthians 9.4–14** as his fifth main example of analogies and metaphors in this epistle. The **living expenses of soldiers and farmers** provide analogies with *living expenses for Paul, Barnabas and other apostles.* Paul, Gale suggests, asks three questions: first the man who serves as a soldier (Gk, *strateuetai*) in military service receives his rations; should not this apply more widely? (v. 7). Second the man who plants in the vineyard (*phuteuei ampelōna*) eats from its fruit; should not this apply to others? Third, the man who tends a flock (Gk, *poimainei, poinēn*) partakes of the milk from the flock; should not this apply to other occupations?[102] These analogies, he adds, are not merely illustrative but constitute *arguments.* This strengthens the case made by Ricoeur and Soskice that metaphors can convey cognitive truth and realities. Paul then confirms his argument by appealing to the law of Moses (v. 8), when he quotes from Deuteronomy 25.4: 'You shall not muzzle an ox while it is treading out the grain' (v. 9).

Gale points out that in the strictest terms the three analogies apply only to granting a stipend or living expenses to Paul and Barnabas. Nevertheless the wider principle is often applied to ministers today in general. Perhaps the distinction is that it explicitly applied to Paul and Barnabas in these three analogies, but only implicitly applies to ministers in general. However, the principle laid down in verses 13–14 seems to presuppose a wider application. In verses 13 and 14, Paul introduces a fourth analogy:

> Do you not know that those who are employed in the temple service get their food from the temple, and those who serve at the altar share in what is sacrificed on the altar? In the same way, the Lord commanded that those who proclaim the gospel should get their living by the gospel.

Of course the word 'altar' and other features applied to the Jewish Temple, not to a Christian equivalent to it.

Does the allusion to 'an ox while it is treading out the grain' (v. 9) constitute a fifth analogy? Paul argues that Deuteronomy 25.4 serves as a revelation of God's will 'for our sake' (v. 10), since the larger context of

---

[102] Gale, *The Use of Analogy*, p. 101.

Deuteronomy 24 and 25 shows God's care and concern for all creatures, including humankind. Richard Hays sums up his use of this difficult passage as follows: Deuteronomy 25.4

> functions as an elegant metaphor for just the point that Paul wants to make: the ox being driven around and around on the threshing floor should not be cruelly restrained from eating the food that is its only labour . . . So, too, with the apostles.[103]

Elsewhere he argues:

> *di' hēmas* [for our sake] is not simply synonymous with the more neutral *di' anthrōpous* [on account of humankind] . . . We should probably understand him to be claiming that the words of the law . . . find their time and primary reference in the financial arrangements pertaining to his own ministry.[104]

Schrage argues that this passage, together with 10.4 and Galatians 4.2, is one of the very few which come near to using allegory.[105] Aageson regards this passage as having a double or extended context.[106] The allusion to Barnabas carries weight in view of his selling his possessions to give support to the church (Acts 4.36–37). R. F. Hock has expounded a hypothesis which highlights Paul's menial status as a leather-worker, tentmaker or manufacturer of stage properties.[107]

Paul's final quotation in verse 14, 'The Lord commanded that those who proclaim the gospel should get their living by the gospel', seems to confirm that this general principle applies to Christian ministers today. There are also abundant quotations from Deuteronomy and Proverbs which establish this principle. In verses 11–12 Paul also speaks of selling and reaping spiritual things. Nevertheless, as C. K. Barrett, Jean Héring and others have pointed out, the main point of the passage is Paul's emphasis upon renouncing 'rights' in more general terms. He establishes that he has a right to financial maintenance, *but chooses to renounce that right* and to teach *forbearance* to the church at Corinth.[108] Additionally, what Gale has placed under a single heading turns out to elaborate some half

[103] Richard Hays, *First Corinthians* (Interpretation; Louisville: Knox, 1997), p. 151.

[104] Richard Hays, *Echoes of Scripture in the Letters of Paul* (New Haven: Yale University Press, 1989), pp. 165–6.

[105] Schrage, *Der erste Brief*, pp. 299–301.

[106] J. W. Aageson, *Written Also for Our Sake* (Louisville: Westminster/Knox, 1993), p. 49.

[107] R. F. Hock, *The Social Context of Paul's Ministry* (Philadelphia: Fortress, 1980), pp. 50–68.

[108] Barrett, *First Epistle*, p. 202; Jean Héring, *First Epistle of Paul the Apostle to the Corinthians* (Eng., London: Epworth Press, 1962), p. 76.

a dozen metaphors or analogies. Straub considered these metaphors in various contexts.[109]

(12) Gale selected as his fifth example in 1 Corinthians the well-known metaphor of **the athlete and the need for self-control** (Gk, *egkrateia*) in **1 Corinthians 9.24–27**. He rightly observed that the picture cannot be applied in all its aspects: for example, only one receives the prize. It is not a free-floating picture, but includes detailed stage-setting.

Victor P. Pfitzner discussed this imagery in his *Paul and the Agon Motif*. He included well-researched material on the Hellenistic *agōn* tradition (one of struggle and strain). In the Greek world rivalry and self-assertion play a major role.[110] He examined Greek physical training, the Greek gymnasium and the tradition in Greek philosophy. He included Aristotle, Epictetus and Seneca. In his Part 2, he considered this tradition in Paul, and concluded that Paul used what had become a popular image in Greek thought.[111] His work on Greek thought is thorough. His comments are also useful on 1 Corinthians 9.24. He wrote that the *details*

> *set the stage for the theme of egkrateia* (self-control) which follows. All the endeavours of the athlete are in vain if he has not trained his body and abstained from all that may in any way harm his physical condition.[112]

Pfitzner also carefully examined the Pastoral Epistles, where metaphors of military warfare and striving play a greater part than in the major epistles (e.g. 1 Tim. 1.18; 4.10; and 2 Tim. 2.3). In 1 Corinthians 9.25, Paul urged, '*Run in such a way that you may win it* [the prize].' Clearly, rivalry and self-assertion cannot be a relevant part of Paul's metaphors. The picture serves to focus only on self-discipline and effort. That is why Pfitzner calls most of the details of the metaphor '*stage-setting*'.

Why does Paul spend so much time on mere stage-setting? We need to recall how much the city of Corinth was constantly mindful of the Isthmian Games. These Games were one of the four great pan-Hellenic festivals, and the Isthmian Games were second only to the Olympic Games. These Games were held close to Corinth. Murphy-O'Connor wrote:

> Paul could not have been unaware of the Isthmian Games, and was probably in Corinth when they took place; they were celebrated in the spring

[109] Straub, *Die Bildersprache des Apostels Paulus*, pp. 69, 72–3 and 81–2.
[110] Pfitzner, *Paul and the Agon Motif*, pp. 16–22.
[111] Pfitzner, *Paul and the Agon Motif*, pp. 165–86.
[112] Pfitzner, *Paul and the Agon Motif*, p. 87 (his italics).

> of A.D. 49 and 51. Athletic metaphors were commonplace in the popular philosophy of the period . . . But it can hardly be coincidence that Paul's first sustained development of this occurs in a letter to the Corinthians (1 Cor. 9:24–27).[113]

Kent argued that the city of Corinth underwrote financial sponsorship for the Games, including the renovation of buildings and the provision of banquets; although on the other hand Broneer pointed out that substantial revenue accrued to the Corinthian tradespeople and entrepreneurs from the 'huge crowds who stayed in the city and area for the duration of the games every alternate spring'. [114] Paul's readers were so intimately familiar with the Isthmian Games that his analogy would readily convey visual imagery or pictures of the events depicted.

As for details of the stage-setting, Paul's language about 'one' prize is not the only dissonant detail: what he says about the 'prize' suggests a point of contrast, not of similarity. He explicitly writes, 'They do it to receive a perishable wreath [Gk, *phtharton stephanon*], but we an imperishable one' (v. 25). In the Games the wreath, garland or crown was made from pine leaves, although some argue that it was made from celery. 'Crown' points up the contrast between two kinds of crown. The victor's crown is the crown here; it is not the royal crown.

In verses 26–27 Paul shows that he, too, plays his part. He keeps his eye on the target ('I do not run aimlessly'). Now he switches to the metaphor of boxing: he is 'not as though beating the air'. In verse 27 the Greek *hupōpiazō*, which NRSV translates as 'punish my body', may pedantically mean 'to hit under the eye'; but in boxing, according to Danker, it means 'to give a black eye, strike in the face', or 'to bring someone to submission'; 'to punish' is only the third and final listed option.[115] Robertson and Plummer and Findlay suggested, 'Beat black and blue'.[116] 'Body', as we have elsewhere argued, signifies the self in the public domain. Straub includes *trechō* (I run) in his first section of *Bildwörter*.[117] The analogies

---

[113] Jerome Murphy O'Connor, *St Paul's Corinth: Texts and Archaeology* (Wilmington: Glazier, 1983), pp. 16–17.

[114] J. H. Kent, *Corinth*, VIII/3: *The Inscriptions 1926–50* (Princeton: American School of Classical Studies at Athens, 1966), p. 70; Oscar Broneer, 'The Apostle Paul and the Isthmian Games', *Biblical Archaeologist*, 25 (1962), pp. 2–31.

[115] BDAG, p. 1043.

[116] A. T. Robertson and A. Plummer, *A Critical and Exegetical Commentary on the First Epistle of St. Paul to the Corinthians* (Edinburgh: T&T Clark, 1914), p. 196; G. G. Findlay, 'St. Paul's First Epistle to the Corinthians', in W. R. Nicoll (ed.), *Expositor's Greek Testament* (Grand Rapids: Eerdmans, 1961; from 1900), p. 856.

[117] Straub, *Die Bildersprache des Apostels Paulus*, p. 28.

of running and boxing, however, equally suggest vivid and powerful pictures.

(13) Gale's next example is **1 Corinthians 12.12–30, the body and limbs and organs** (specifically 12.12 and 14.26), which he rightly said 'dominates the entire section of the discussion of which it is a part'.[118] Like the previous athletic analogy, this picture was well known and popular in Hellenistic thought, and could be visualized.

Parallels to the metaphor of body and members can be found in Plato, Livy, Plutarch, Cicero, Dionysius of Halicarnassus, Epictetus and other writers. Livy places the analogy on the lips of the senator Menenius to persuade the plebeians, who have gone on strike, to return to work on the ground that the active manual 'members or limbs' of the body should resume feeding the belly or governing classes for the health of the whole body.[119] Dale Martin has recently shown that Paul applies this rhetoric in such a way as to turn it upside down. He pleads with the supposed elite or spiritually or socially 'strong' in Corinth to accept those whom they regard as 'weak', or probably those of lower social status, on the ground that this is profitable and necessary for the whole body of the church.[120] Although the NRSV translates verse 12 as 'The body is one and has many members, and all the members of the body, though many, are one body', in view of the innovative work of J. A. T. Robinson the translation 'members' is understated and therefore unacceptable. It is true that the Greek term *ta melē* strictly means 'the members'. But Robinson was concerned that today the word 'members' is too readily and popularly used of a social club and its members, for example being a member of the Automobile Association, or a golf club. This is *not* what Paul means by *ta melē*. In order to emphasize the unity of the body and its eyes, hands, arms and feet, we suggest the term 'limbs and organs'.[121] To value only one part of the body, or one set of limbs, at the expense of another is, in Paul's view, to tear apart the limbs of Christ, for the body *is* Christ (v. 12). Indeed Robinson speculated that the origin of Paul's phrase 'the body of Christ' lay in his encounter with the risen Christ on the road to Damascus, which is recounted in Acts 9.4, when Jesus said, 'Saul, Saul, why do you persecute me?'

Margaret Mitchell has made a special study of this passage in her book,

[118] Gale, *The Use of Analogy*, p. 116.
[119] Livy, *Ab Urbe Condita*, 2.32.7–11.
[120] Dale B. Martin, *The Corinthian Body* (New Haven: Yale University Press, 1995), pp. 94–103.
[121] John A. T. Robinson, *The Body: A Study in Pauline Theology* (London: SCM, 1952), p. 58.

Paul and the Rhetoric of Reconciliation. She stresses the use here of deliberative rhetoric (an appeal to advantage), to argue that unity in diversity profited the whole body (Gk, *pros to sumpheron*, v. 7).[122] She emphasizes 1 Corinthians 12.11: 'One and the same Spirit allots to each one individually just as the Spirit chooses.' Mitchell is mainly right, except that in 12.12 Paul's main emphasis falls upon Christ. This begins to bring out Paul's specific understanding and use of the metaphor from one that is often understood. The more popular usual meaning which is understood from the body and members image is that all stand in corporate solidarity with one another, and that as Paul says, 'If one member suffers, all suffer together with it: if one member is honoured, all rejoice together with it' (12.26). But when Paul first introduces the metaphor in verse 12, the significance of the body metaphor is that it is specifically the body of *Christ.*

This reveals the distinction between two understandings of the *body* picture. First, we may understand the metaphor strictly in terms of Paul's intention, in which 'the body' is the body not only because of its limbs and organs, but above all because of its relation with *Christ.* Second, many suggest a broader, quasi-sociological and less specific interpretation of what this picture really means, which is a more popular than Pauline view. Gale understands this first aspect very well. He wrote, 'In reality more than *likeness* is involved here, for there is a sense in which the Christians *are* the body of Christ. For Paul it is no simile, but a spiritual reality.'[123] This is not to deny that some have made extravagant claims about the literal meaning of 'the body of Christ', as if to imply that to become part of the visible body is thereby to become part of the spiritual Christ. Nevertheless the more basic point is well made. Gale also points out that the concept of unity in diversity is stated from both sides: from the point of view of the body, it stresses the unity or *oneness*; from the point of view of the members it stresses the *diversity.* Mitchell rightly stresses the *mutuality* of both viewpoints. The important point, however, is the relationship of the body to Christ. Without this Christological dimension the picture becomes similar to the exhibit in the Temple of Asclepius at Corinth, where body parts are laid side by side to show the consciousness at Corinth of Asclepius as the god of medicine and the human body.

We must also distinguish between the main metaphor and what we have called its 'stage-setting'. Paul vividly and powerfully expounds the need of one member for another, and the way in which no limb or organ

[122] Mitchell, *Paul and the Rhetoric of Reconciliation*, pp. 20–64, and 266–822, esp. 268–70.

[123] Gale, *The Use of Analogy*, p. 117 (his italics).

can be dismissed as somehow inferior or weaker (Gk, *asthenestera*, v. 22), for example 'I have no need of you' (v. 21). On the other hand, others cannot boast that they are somehow more important or less dispensable. Paul provides a powerful illustration that if one member is experiencing pain, the *whole body* is experiencing pain (not simply that one organ or limb). But this is not Paul's primary invention. It appears that Plato had used this example many years earlier. He wrote:

> The best ordered polity resembles an individual. For example, if one of our fingers is hurt, the entire community of the physical organism feels pain as a whole, although it is only one part that suffers. So we may say, a man has pain in his finger.[124]

As in the previous metaphor of athletic struggle and the principle of forbearance, 'stage-setting' should not be stressed. Its significance is to add power to the picture.

(14) Gale next considered the picture of **the mirror** in **1 Corinthians 13.12**. The NRSV translates, 'For now we see in a mirror, dimly, but then we shall see face to face. Now I know only in part; then I will know fully, even as I have been fully known.' The Greek is *dia esoptrou*, when *dia* with genitive could mean 'through a mirror', but equally it could mean 'by means of a mirror', as describing the medium or means of perception. The other Greek phrase is *en ainigmati*, which may allude to obscurity, distortions or puzzles, caused by the limitation of mirrors in the ancient world. The KJV/AV version translates 'darkly' in contrast to the future face-to-face vision of God and complete knowledge, which is reserved for the future.

Corinth was well known for the production of good-quality bronze mirrors, by the standards of the day. Robertson and Plummer correctly observed that the custom of frequently producing concave or convex mirrors led to 'somewhat distorted reflection'.[125] Nevertheless, they add, to describe the resulting image as puzzling, obscure or enigmatic seems to overstate 'their relative inadequacy by modern standards'. Polished bronze can offer quite reasonable images, even if, as the KJV/AV version *darkly* suggests, this entails a deterioration of brightness. This does not express Paul's main point, as Héring and Fee argue.[126] Perhaps the translation 'indistinctly' would be the nearest possible. Tertullian believed that

---

[124] Plato, *Republic*, 5.462.

[125] Robertson and Plummer, *First Epistle*, p. 298.

[126] Héring, *First Epistle*, p. 142; Gordon Fee, *The First Epistle to the Corinthians* (Grand Rapids: Eerdmans, 1987), p. 646.

esoptron denoted a semi-transparent, translucent pane of horn through which the shapes can be perceived.[127] But in Hellenistic Greek the term usually means a mirror, and there was a lively trade in the purchase of mirrors for the purpose of seeing one's face. Possibly in the background lies Plato's contrast between the indirect perception of an image, and the direct apprehension of ideas. He speaks of a 'mirror which receives impressions and provides visible images'.[128]

Paul declares, 'Now I know only in part; then I will know fully even as I have been fully known' (v. 12). The Greek *ek merous* means 'part by part', implying fragmentary knowledge which is accumulated by knowing parts rather than the whole. The future contrast is the perfection of uninterrupted personal intimacy with God, which is implied by the passive mood. The Greek *prosōpon pros prosōpon* expresses a continuing relationship of intimacy which is face to face. The wonder of this intimacy is increased when we grasp the individual uniqueness of a face, as David Ford has very well expounded it.[129] Gale also suggests that Paul may be alluding to Numbers 12.6–8, where Paul is represented as saying that to a prophet, God makes himself known only indirectly, namely in a vision or a dream, while he speaks 'mouth-to-mouth' to Moses.[130] On the main analogy, however, he rightly insists that Paul's emphasis is entirely on the limitations of the mirror in contrast to our knowledge of God in the future. It argues that the analogy can be used no other way. Straub considered mirrors among graphic figures of speech, alongside other images which allude to the eye.[131]

(15) Gale now selects as his fifteenth picture **notes of the military bugle**, either giving a *clear signal*, or making an *indistinct sound* (1 Cor. 14.6–12). 'Notes' (Gk, *phthoggois*) have been used in Wisdom of Solomon 19.18, LXX). The phrase 'what shall I profit you?' (Gk, *ti humas ōphelēsō*) prompts Margaret Mitchell to repeat her comment about deliberative rhetoric. Any sound that is meaningless helps no one. Paul applies this picture at once to speaking in tongues, unless this is interpreted by prophecy in a meaningful way. The issue for Paul is whether the word of God conveys revelation or disclosure clearly. The NRSV translates *salpyx* as *bugle*; the REB and NJB translate it as *trumpet*. The differentiations of pitch alone are not

[127] Tertullian, *On the Soul*, 53.

[128] Plato, *Timaeus*, 71 B.

[129] David Ford, *Self and Salvation: Being Transformed* (Cambridge: CUP, 1999), pp. 1–29.

[130] Gale, *The Use of Analogy*, p. 128.

[131] Straub, *Die Bildersprache des Apostels Paulus*, pp. 44–5.

strictly necessary for it to be an effective signal; the length of note, rhythm and other devices maintain its effectiveness as a communicative signal to prepare for battle. The Greek *adēlon . . . phōnēn* signifies an obscure or indistinct sound whereby the need for immediate action is ambivalent. Paul compares preaching or perhaps prophecy as belonging to the first category, while speaking in tongues, or *glōssolalia,* belongs to the second. Another key word is the Greek *eusēmos,* which means readily intelligible; linguisticians might translate the word as *transparent.*

In 14.10–11 Paul uses the further example of an intelligible language used between a speaker and an addressee. If the communication is not transparent and intelligible, one will appear to the other like an alien or stranger (Gk, *barbarous,* v. 11). Straub made a similar point in his discussion of the flute, trumpet and linguistic communication.[132] Paul does not belittle speaking in tongues, but intelligibility is his prime concern. If an outsider comes to the Christian assembly, and all that he or she can hear is *glōssolalia,* the outsider may well think that the congregation is mad. Paul concludes, 'I thank God that I speak in tongues more than all of you; nevertheless, in church I would rather speak five words with my mind, in order to instruct others also, than ten thousand words in a tongue' (vv. 18–19).

(16) Gale's last picture from 1 Corinthians is chapter 15 (vv. 35–50), mainly on what emerges from **sowing a seed and a related chain of metaphors.** He calls it 'a combination of pictures', and spends some 13 pages discussing the passage.[133] Although he normally insists that there is one meaning only which the metaphor conveys, here he rightly argues that this main metaphor gives rise to a chain of metaphors. At least three or more are entailed. First, the seed which is sown produces something that 'come[s] to life' (v. 36), pointing to the assurance and inevitability of resurrection. Second, the seed that is sown is quite different from the 'body' (or fruit or flower) which later comes into being (v. 37). The resurrection 'body' will be radically different from our earthly body. Third, verses 42–44 explain in four contrasts to what extent the two 'bodies' differ from each other. The earthly body is sown 'perishable' (NRSV; Gk, *en phthorai*); the resurrection body 'imperishable' (Gk, *aphtharsia*). Our earthly body will be sown in dishonour (*en atimiai*), but raised in glory (Gk, *en doxēi*). It will be sown in weakness (*en astheneiai*), but raised in power (*en dunamei*).

---

[132] Straub, *Der Bildersprache des Apostels Paulus,* pp. 83–4.

[133] Gale, *The Use of Analogy,* pp. 134–7.

It will be sown as a 'physical' body (NRSV, Gk, *psuchikon sōma*), but raised as a 'spiritual' (NRSV; Gk, *sōma pneumatikon*). NRSV's translations of the first three contrasts are acceptable, but, as we shall argue, the fourth is unacceptable: the fourth (physical–spiritual) is not Paul's meaning at all. The three metaphorical pictures, derived from one 'root' metaphor, make three points.

The 'root metaphor' is that of planting and new growth that Gale identified. The larger context *excludes* a mechanistic understanding of merely natural cause and effect because throughout 1 Corinthians 15.35–44 the theme of God's creative power always lies in the background. This is the major point behind 'Fool!' (v. 36) and 'Some people have no knowledge of God' (v. 34). Paul addresses the *conceptual* problem of how we can *conceive of* the resurrection of a body. How can we believe what seems unintelligible and inconceivable? Paul addresses both a logical and contingent question. He implies a rejection of any Jewish notion of the reassembly of the particles of the old body, as perhaps in 2 Baruch 49.2. 'Sowing' becomes quasi-metaphorical for letting oneself go in death, with a creative consequence. 'Fool', or better, 'You fool' (Gk, *aphrōn*) means 'You senseless person', because the picture or model of sowing should have provided the clue to what was conceivable. A kindred sub-metaphor was the manifold kinds of 'flesh' (Gk, *sarx*) already created by God. *Sarx*, I have argued elsewhere, is a polymorphous concept. It signifies an empirical or physical substance which can take many different forms: humans, animals, birds, fish, insects, sun, moon, stars or atmospheric entities. God has already demonstrated his creative, inexhaustible, sovereign power in the variety of created entities. 'God gives it a body as he has chosen, and to each kind of seed its own body . . . Star differs from star in glory' (vv. 38 and 41). Thus the 'root' metaphor has given rise to two more analogies, pictures or sub-metaphors, making, in effect, five so far.

We come now to the climactic metaphors of verses 42–44, which emphasize and expound the contrast between our earthly bodies and our resurrection 'bodies'. The first contrast between 'perishable' and 'imperishable' adequately translates the Greek. However, 'perishable' (*phthorai*) signifies not only temporal duration (it is mortal), but also the concept of decreasing capacities. In the LXX the word translates the Hebrew *chebel*, which usually means emptiness, fruitlessness, vanity or decay. Paul notes the decreasing capacities and increasing weaknesses, which issue in exhaustion and stagnation, that is, a state of decay. By contrast, 'imperishable' (NRSV) denotes decay's reversal, in other words a progressive, purposive flourishing in fullness of life. It is essential to retain the notion of progressive purposiveness, in contrast to static perfection, as we shall argue shortly. The new 'body' will not be 'trapped' in a timeless, static vacuum.

The second contrast between dishonour and glory is also a correct translation of the Greek. The NRSV, NIV and KJV/AV translate *dishonour*. But REB and Wolff translated this word *humiliation* (Ger. *Niedrigkeit*), which included its pitifulness and loneliness.[134] However, Danker retains the usual term *dishonour*.[135] The third contrast, weakness–power, is strictly correct. But in this epistle power regularly denotes the capacity to carry through purposes or actions with *operative effectiveness*. In this context it signifies the reversal of decay.

The fourth contrast (v. 44) provides most unease with the NRSV translation. The NRSV translation makes the final contrast *physical* and *spiritual*. But neither Greek term is used in this way in 1 Corinthians. The Greek *psuchikon* never means *physical* in Paul's discourse with the church at Corinth. The classic exposition of *psuchikon* is in 1 Corinthians 2.6–16 and 3.1–4. When it is used in contrast to *pneuma*, Danker suggests, it means 'natural, unspiritual, worldly'.[136] Sometimes it means 'on a purely human level'. The contrasting *sōma pneumatikon* (v. 44) clinches this meaning. For here *pneumatikos* means 'that which pertains to the Holy Spirit of God' (my translation).[137] It denotes a mode of existence in which the Holy Spirit of God animates, characterizes and renews it, in accordance with his transformative and ever-new nature. Recently, N. T. Wright has expounded this approach. He defines the spiritual body as 'a body animated by, enlivened by, the Spirit of the true God, exactly as Paul has said more extensively in several passages . . . The new body is the *result* of the Spirit's work.'[138] Joseph Fitzmyer also implies this approach. He writes, 'The real problem . . . is the meaning of *sōma pneumatikon*, which seems to attribute to *sōma* a meaning that is diametrically opposed to "body".'[139] Clearly he also rejects the view implied by the NRSV translation. All this enhances the contrast between the old and new modes of existence. This

134 Wolff, *Der erste Brief des Paulus an die Korinther*, p. 407.

135 BDAG, p. 149.

136 Danker, *Greek-English Lexicon*, p. 1100.

137 Thiselton, *First Epistle*, p. 1275; and Anthony C. Thiselton, *Life after Death: A New Approach to the Last Things* (Grand Rapids: Eerdmans, 2012) or *The Last Things: A New Approach* (London: SPCK, 2012), pp. 123–5.

138 N. T. Wright, *The Resurrection of the Son of God: Christian Origins and the Question of God*, vol. 3 (London: SPCK, 2003), p. 354 (his italics).

139 Joseph Fitzmyer, *First Corinthians* (Anchor Bible; New Haven: Yale University Press, 2008), p. 596.

does not *exclude* the physical meaning in *completely* different contexts, but it does not convey Paul's meaning here.

It has emerged that in this passage Paul has multiplied his metaphors. They all arise, however, from the main metaphor of planting seeds and awaiting the new creation, which is utterly transformed. When the chapter is viewed as a whole, clearly contrast and continuity are both involved in the resurrection. We have discussed other aspects elsewhere. Our aim here has been to examine Paul's pictures or metaphors. This is the last of Gale's examples from 1 Corinthians, but our survey is far from comprehensive. Our numerals refer to Gale's selection only.

Our examination of Paul's earlier epistles strengthens our argument that analogies, metaphors or mental pictures are vital not only for clarification, power and vividness, but to facilitate accurate understanding. Paul in his context of city life shared the concern of Jesus in his context of rural life and the domestic household. But in both cases we also saw that analogies, metaphors and mental pictures could be seriously misinterpreted, especially in popular modern culture. It is good to strive to multiply analogy and pictures; but we must beware of being seduced through ignorance or popular misunderstandings into misapplying them. The Pauline epistles underline both points.

8

The later letters of Paul: from 2 Corinthians to the Pastoral Epistles

Paul's metaphors in 2 Corinthians and Romans

Paul continued his use of metaphors and analogies in 2 Corinthians, Romans, Philippians, and later epistles including Colossians and Ephesians. Without prejudice concerning Paul's authorship we may also include the Pastoral Epistles. In the Corinthian correspondence, Paul proceeds from 16 examples in 1 Corinthians to the twenty-sixth at the end of 2 Corinthians.

It may seem unusual to begin a new chapter with a seventeenth example, but we are counting metaphors sequentially, and reach the seventeenth as we begin 2 Corinthians.

(17) 2 Corinthians 2.14–16 almost certainly uses the **picture of the triumphal procession**. A difficulty is raised by the Greek *thriambeuonti hēmas en Christōi*, for which Bultmann suggested four meanings, Furnish six meanings, and Harris even considered ten possible meanings.[1] Virtually every modern commentator rejects the KJV/AV rendering 'causeth us to triumph'. A first problem is that *thriambeuō* has as its first meaning in Danker's Lexicon 'lead in triumphal procession' (exemplified in Colossians 2.15 and in 2 Corinthians 2.14 (NRSV and REB); and its second meaning, 'to lead in triumph' (exemplified in 2 Cor. 2.14); but its sixth meaning as 'display, publicize, make known'.[2] Only Calvin, Beza and older commentators accept Danker's third meaning, 'cause to triumph', which Danker calls very questionable. His fourth meaning, 'triumph over', is supported by some for Colossians 2.15, but is not Danker's preferred meaning.

---

1 Rudolf Bultmann, *The Second Letter to the Corinthians* (Eng., Minneapolis: Augsburg, 1985), p. 66; Victor P. Furnish, *II Corinthians* (Anchor Bible; New York: Doubleday, 1984), pp. 174–6; and Murray J. Harris, *The Second Epistle to the Corinthians* (NIGTC; Grand Rapids: Eerdmans, 2005), p. 244.

2 BDAG, p. 459.

The resultant problem is the accusative *hēmas* (us). The traditional assumption is that the apostles are seen as *following* the triumphal procession, which is usually accorded to victorious Roman generals, but *not* as captives or prisoners. However, the accusative case seems to suggest that they are among the trophies, usually captives, which make up the festive triumphal procession. Yet several recent commentators argue that Paul has often called himself the slave of Christ, and that in this outburst of praise and thanksgiving, his praise is directed only towards God and Christ, and that he is a ready captive of Christ through such experiences as his conversion and call on the road to Damascus. Among those who adopt this approach are Collange, Barrett, Martin, Williamson, Harris and Furnish.[3] Egan rejected any connexion with a Roman triumph, but he remains in the minority of scholars, and Marshall has replied to him.[4] NJB avoids deciding about the accusative *hēmas* by translating 'gives us a part in the triumphal procession'.

This would not satisfy the emphasis, however, of Martin, Furnish, Harris and others. Paul's burst of thanksgiving and praise focuses on God in Christ, to whom the apostles are willing captives. Harris calls the apostle 'a willing and privileged captive, a trophy of the general's victory . . . who has been conquered'.[5] In Martin's words, it also coheres with Paul's description of apostles as 'clay jars' (4.7, NRSV), surrounding a treasure.[6]

Harris also provides a vivid image or pictorial representation of the victorious Roman triumph. Although some argue simply for 'festal procession', he pictures the Roman triumph as:

> a victory procession celebrated by Roman generals on their return to Rome after a successful foreign campaign, although during the Empire the privilege of celebrating a triumph became the prerogative of the Emperor . . . At the head of the procession came the magistrates and the Senate, followed by trumpeters and some spoils of war such as the vessels of gold or beaks of ships. Then came the flute players, ahead of white oxen destined to

---

3 J-F. Collange, *Enigmes de la deuxième épitre de Paul aux Corinthiens* (SNTSMS 18; Cambridge: CUP, 1972), pp. 24–5; C. K. Barrett, *The Second Epistle to the Corinthians* (London: Black, 1973), pp. 97–8; Ralph P. Martin, *2 Corinthians* (WBC; Dallas: Word, 1986), pp. 46–8; L. Williamson, 'Led in Triumph: Paul's Use of *Thriambeuō*', *Int.* 22 (1968), pp. 325–6, cf. 317–32; Harris, *The Second Epistle to the Corinthians*, pp. 244–7; and Furnish, *II Corinthians*, pp. 173–6.

4 R. B. Egan, 'Lexical Evidence on Two Pauline Passages', *NovT* 19 (1977), p. 41; cf. pp. 34–620; P. Marshall, 'A Metaphor of Social Shame: *thriambeuein* in 2 Cor. 2:14', *NovT* 25 (1983), p. 304; cf. pp. 302–17.

5 Harris, *The Second Epistle to the Corinthians*, p. 245.

6 Martin, *2 Corinthians*, p. 47.

> be sacrificed in the temples along with some representative captives from the conquered territory, including such dignitaries as the king, driven in chains in front of the ornate chariot of the general, the *triumphator*.[7]

Although Paul is borrowing a metaphor, it is impossible not to view it as an imaginative and powerful picture, which could be recalled by anyone who has heard about the phenomenon.

Festal processions and military triumphs both involved incense or sacrifices. As Barrett remarks, 'Incense was customary in triumphal and quasi-triumphal processions, both royal and religious.'[8] Hence in verses 11–15 Paul uses the derivative metaphor of 'fragrance' and 'aroma' (Gk, *osmē*), which usually means a pleasant *fragrance*, but may also mean a *deadly fume* or unpleasant odour. In verse 14 it is a sweet fragrance which spreads knowledge of God, but in verse 16 it becomes a deadly fume (hardly 'fragrance', NRSV). Harris points out that this corresponds with Paul's reference to believers and unbelievers in 1 Corinthians 1.18–19.[9] Hence a visual picture is complemented by an appeal to another of the senses. Gale called this a 'mingling of pictures'.[10] Straub refers only to the metaphor of *osmē*, which Paul offers as a priestly offering of thanks.[11]

(18) Gale's next example concerns **'Letters of recommendation'** (NRSV) in **2 Corinthians 3.1** (Gk, *sustatikōn epistolōn*). Paul introduces the thorny subject of self-commendation in 3.1. Clearly the so-called super-apostles claimed letters of commendation from a third party, and Paul at once responds by retorting that his Christian converts in Corinth are indeed his 'letter of commendation'. The Greek *sunistanō* is a late form of *sunistēmi*, which originally meant 'to combine', and hence 'to bring together as friends' or 'to introduce'; while the ending '*-ikos*' turns the word into an adjective. The adjective *introductory* became *commendatory*. Apart from renouncing self-commendation as such, the 'commendation letter' created by Christian believers points to the commendation being from *God*, not from oneself. Self-commendation is pejorative; Paul's boast is in the Lord (1 Cor. 1.31). Paul uses the negative *mē* (surely not) when he asserts, 'Surely we do not need commendatory letters!' Such an idea would be

[7] Harris, *The Second Epistle to the Corinthians*, pp. 243–4.

[8] Barrett, *The Second Epistle to the Corinthians*, p. 98.

[9] Harris, *The Second Epistle to the Corinthians*, p. 246.

[10] Herbert M. Gale, *The Use of Analogy in the Letters of Paul* (Philadelphia: Westminster Press, 1964), p. 150.

[11] Werner Straub, *Die Bildersprache des Apostels Paulus* (Tübingen: Mohr, 1937), p. 41.

ridiculous. This is personal to Paul's situation; he is a spiritual 'father' to the church at Corinth (1 Cor. 4.14–15).

On the other hand, travellers or emissaries could well benefit from letters commending or introducing them. Paul provided commendations of Phoebe (Rom. 16.1–2), Timothy (1 Cor. 6.10–11), Titus (2 Cor. 8.22–23) and Onesimus (Philem. 10–12, 17–19). Barrett, Furnish and others stress how letters of commendation abounded in the ancient world. Furnish writes:

> Such letters of introduction, whether official (certifying someone as a duly commissioned representative or messenger of another) or unofficial (commending a relative, friend, or associate to others), played a larger role in the ancient world, when communications were poorer and hospitality in distant places was more difficult, than they do today.[12]

Gale considered that 3.1–3 provide 'a somewhat confusing mixture of metaphors'.[13] This is largely because he regards 'a letter of Christ . . . written not with ink but with the Spirit of the living God, not on tablets of stone but on tablets of human hearts' (v. 3) as a separate metaphor. He repeated, 'Paul has mingled together a variety of analogies.'[14] But we have already argued that Paul regarded the earlier letters of commendation as coming primarily from God in Christ, in parallel with 1 Corinthians 1.31. Paul expands his allusion to the letter in terms of its being written not on stone tablets, probably reflecting Jeremiah 31.31, but this is hardly a separate mixed metaphor. He is saying that the Spirit of God, who caused his letter of recommendation to be written through his converts, continues to write about Paul's effective ministry in their hearts.

Some see a complicating problem in the manuscript reading of 'our hearts' (NRSV; NJB; NEB) and 'your hearts' (RSV) in verse 2.[15] *Your* (rather than *our*) is found in Sinaiticus and 33, and is preferable because 'our' may be an assimilation to 7.3. Here, Barrett said, Paul uses 'letter' to describe the Corinthians' testimony to his apostleship. It constitutes an extension of the application of the metaphor, not a 'confused' mixed metaphor. As Plummer indicates, the transition of all three verses constitutes a vindication of the office of apostle, as authenticated by God through the effective ministry of Paul.[16] Once we see the purpose and value of multiple meta-

[12] Furnish, *II Corinthians*, p. 193; Barrett, *Second Epistle to the Corinthians*, p. 106.

[13] Gale, *The Use of Analogy*, p. 152.

[14] Gale, *The Use of Analogy*, p. 155.

[15] Barrett, *The Second Epistle to the Corinthians*, p. 96.

[16] Alfred Plummer, *A Commentary on the Second Epistle of Paul to the Corinthians* (Edinburgh: T&T Clark, 1915), pp. 79–81.

phors, it is difficult to know where to stop. Does the letter written 'not with ink' (v. 3) mean a letter that could not be blotted out, underlining its permanency? This might owe more to a modern preacher's ingenuity than to Paul's intention. His emphasis is on the work of the Spirit of God. The contrast between the ministry of Moses and Christ brings this home. Straub does not list this among his examples of pictorial language.

(19) In **2 Corinthians 5.1–10** Paul uses *three metaphors*, according to Gale: '**earthly tent**', contrasted with 'house not made with hands' (v. 1); '**clothed with our heavenly dwelling**' (v. 2) contrasted with 'found naked' *(v.3);* and '**at home in the body**' (v. 6), contrasted with 'at home with the Lord' (v. 8). These are strictly not 'mixed metaphors', for this term properly applies to more than one incompatible metaphor when they control the same finite verb of a single sentence. Gale regarded both 'the earthly tent' and 'clothed', 'clothes' or 'putting on' as two 'pictures'.[17] The Greek *ependusasthai* (*putting clothes on over*) is used in verse 2 and verse 4. He called the third, 'at home in the body' (v. 6) or 'at home with the Lord' (v. 8), an analogy concerning one's homeland. This is signposted by *endēmeō*, to be at home, and *ekdēmeō*, to be away from home.[18] Each, however, presents a visual picture to the imagination.

Harris remarks, 'Clearly the "housing" and "clothing" metaphors are crucial.'[19] Martin similarly insists that the key contrasts in this section are 'between the temporary and permanent, and what is seen and the unseen'.[20] But in common with many he considers possible explanations for the arguable shift in content and theme in 5.2–4. He considers three possible explanations. First, one possible reason is that Paul has shifted his eschatology from the future to the present. But he dismisses this argument, as Kennedy and Thornton also do. Second, he considers the argument offered by Earle Ellis that 2 Corinthians 5.1–10 emphasizes the corporate body rather than individual bodies, and has nothing whatever to do with the so-called intermediate state. Martin is not entirely convinced by this explanation. Third, he argues that Paul may well be responding to a situation in Corinth, namely the theology of his opponents. He explains:

> How did the two understandings of being a Christian differ? The issue [according to his opponents] is not death and resurrection, but the distinction

[17] Gale, *The Use of Analogy*, p. 158.

[18] Gale, *The Use of Analogy*, p. 159.

[19] Harris, *The Second Epistle to the Corinthians*, p. 366.

[20] Martin, *2 Corinthians*, p. 97.

> between the soul and the body . . . From his opponents' viewpoint the soul could attain to God only by a mystical ascent.[21]

Paul's alternative is to present the vision of becoming a heavenly house of God, and putting on the new garments of the new creation. Barrett added:

> We may think of a man living in a house or tent; he wishes to put up another, larger house or tent round the one he already inhabits. Paul longs therefore to receive the new dwelling, which awaits his use in heaven without having to give up the old; that is, he hopes not to have the old tent taken down in death, but . . . to receive the new dwelling in addition – to put it on like an overcoat.[22]

2 Corinthians 5.6–10 constitutes the second part of the section. It begins with Greek *tharrountes*, 'We are always confident'. Admittedly, Paul argues, this earthly body is fragile and temporary, as the word 'tent' implies. But, he says, the Christians' true home is with the Lord. The image is that of leaving the body to be at home with the Lord. This would accord with Philippians 1.21. The picture of *homecoming* or even homesickness can easily be imagined. Straub included the tent and building, and the home, among his pictorial language, analogies or comparisons.[23] Paul has thus provided three more memorable visual pictures.

(20) 2 Corinthians 9.6, 'The one who sows sparingly will also reap sparingly' (Gk, *ho speirōn . . . therisei*), is probably a frozen or historical metaphor. That is to say, that as Gale and others suggest, it was already a metaphor in Proverbs 22.9 (LXX), and Paul probably has this in mind when he urges greater generosity with financial giving. He adds, 'For God loves a cheerful giver' (Gk, *hilaron gar dotēn agapai ho theos*), also from LXX of Proverbs 22.8. Since the principle is not always inevitable, Gale suggests, 'The picture, as introduced, can be applied only loosely.'[24] As Furnish observes, the metaphor was familiar in ancient literature, and Paul had already used the metaphor of sowing and reaping in Galatians 6.8.[25]

---

[21] Martin, *2 Corinthians*, p. 101; cf. E. E. Ellis, 'II Corinthians v.1–10 in Pauline Eschatology', *NTS* 6 (1959–60), pp. 211–24; and H. A. Kennedy, *St. Paul's Conception of the Last Things* (London: Hodder & Stoughton, 1904), pp. 264–81; L. S. Thornton, *The Common Life in the Body of Christ* (London: Dacre Press, 1942), pp. 284–6.

[22] Barrett, *The Second Epistle to the Corinthians*, pp. 152–3.

[23] Straub, *Die Bildersprache des Apostels Paulus*, pp. 84–5.

[24] Gale, *The Use of Analogy*, p. 163.

[25] Furnish, *II Corinthians*, p. 440.

(21) 2 Corinthians 10.3–6 draws *three metaphors* from '**waging war**' (Gk, *strateuometha,* v. 3), '**weapons of our warfare**' (Gk, *hopla tēs strateias,* v. 4), and '**power to destroy strongholds**' (v. 4, NRSV; Gk, *pros kathairesin ochurōmatōn).* We can readily appreciate, given that Paul's tone has changed in 2 Corinthians 1—9, that many argue that these two sections represent different letters. Suddenly Paul confronts what remains of his opponents at Corinth, with little of the earlier attempt at thanksgiving and reconciliation. But this change should not be exaggerated. Paul insists, 'The weapons of our warfare are not merely human' (v. 4, NRSV); or 'The weapons we fight with are not worldly weapons' (Martin).[26]

In Greek, the weapons of this war are not 'fleshly' (Gk, *sarkika*). In other words, this is not like a straightforward military conflict. Paul's 'power' is that of God, and he has already defined this as power in weakness (1 Cor. 1.21–25; 2.1–5). The analogies and metaphors, therefore, become strained and modified. Nevertheless, they do express conflict and warfare in a vivid, pictorial, way. Straub examined the metaphors of warfare briefly.[27] Personally, we do not subscribe to the view that 2 Corinthians 10—13 constitutes a separate letter from chapters 1—9.

(22) 2 Corinthians 11.2–3 presents a *picture* of **betrothal** (NRSV, promise; Gk, *ērmosamen*) **and marriage** (*heni andri parthenon agnēn parastēsai tō Christō*; NRSV, 'I promised you in marriage to one husband, to present you as a chaste virgin to Christ'). In one sense this might also be regarded as a historical metaphor (often called a 'dead' metaphor), since the Old and New Testaments are full of this analogy. Barrett, Martin and Furnish list, for example: 'I pledged myself to you and entered into a covenant with you' (Ezek. 16.8; cf. 16.8–14; Isa. 50.1–2; Hos. 1—3; Eph. 5.22–32; Rev. 19.7; 21.2, 9).[28] J. Paul Sampley also elaborates on Ephesians 5.21–33.[29] Gale is surely correct in claiming, 'Paul is not attempting consciously to apply it [i.e. the analogy] in detail.'[30] He is perhaps right, however, to apply 'jealousy' (also v. 2) to God's jealousy over Israel's unfaithfulness as a bride, and also in the following verse, to see the seduction of Eve in Genesis as a distraction from purity. Some doubt whether Paul regards himself as the

[26] Martin, *2 Corinthians*, p. 405.

[27] Straub, *Die Bildersprache des Apostels Paulus*, p. 92.

[28] Barrett, *Second Epistle to the Corinthians*, pp. 272–4; Martin, *2 Corinthians*, p. 332; and Furnish, *II Corinthians*, p. 499.

[29] J. Paul Sampley, *'And the Two Shall Become One Flesh': A Study of Traditions in Ephesians 5:21–23* (Cambridge: CUP, 1971), pp. 34–51 and throughout.

[30] Gale, *The Use of Analogy*, p. 165.

third person arranging the betrothal, but this is certainly possible. At all events, 'betrothal' remains a powerful and vivid picture of a close, covenantal relationship with God.

(23) 2 Corinthians 11.8 depends largely on the precise meaning of Greek *esulēsa*, translated '**robbed** other churches' in the NRSV and in most other versions. Gale insisted that the word 'was frequently employed with reference to the "despoiling" of a defeated enemy'.[31] He also claimed that 'taking pay' (NRSV, 'accepting support'; Gk, *labōn opsōnion*) was often used of a soldier's pay or allowance. Danker simply describes the meaning of *sulaō* as 'rob, sack' and alludes to 2 Corinthians 11.8 without any military connection, although he refers to the technical meaning of 'right of seizure'.[32] Harris points out that *sulaō* is extremely rare, that the military nuance is found mainly in earlier classical Greek, and that in the papyri it is used of the theft of tools.[33] Moreover, he stresses, both *sulaō* and *opsōnion* are symbolic, ironical and clearly figurative. If this analogy does convey a picture, it is weaker than most. Gale admits that the 'picture' of the despoiling soldier is highly irrelevant and inapplicable in numerous ways.

(24) 2 Corinthians 12.7 pictures '**the exceptional character of [Paul's] revelations**' (Gale, 'visions and revelations'; Gk, *tē huperbolē tōn apokalupseōn*). This is followed by 'a **thorn** was given me in the flesh' (Gk, *edothē moi skolops tē sarki*). *Skolops* is often translated as 'thorn', 'splinter' or 'stake', as Danker also translates it.[34] The exception is the NEB, which translates the term as 'a sharp physical pain', with the alternative of 'a painful wound to my pride (literally a stake or thorn for the flesh)'. The NEB removes the pictorial presentation, but in the Greek and the NRSV it presents a *powerful, concrete, pictorial metaphor.* Hence Gale places the two 'pictures' together. He also notes that Numbers 33.55 warns the Israelites of 'barbs in [their] eyes and thorns in [their] sides', if they do not drive out the inhabitants of the land. Ezekiel 28.24 also speaks of 'a pricking brier or a piercing thorn' for those who treat 'neighbours' with contempt. Hence, although it is vivid and powerful, this image has not been coined by Paul for the first time.

---

31 Gale, *The Use of Analogy*, p. 167.

32 BDAG, p. 955.

33 Harris, *The Second Epistle to the Corinthians*, p. 757; J. H. Moulton and G. Milligan, *The Vocabulary of the Greek Testament* (London: Hodder & Stoughton, 1952), p. 596.

34 BDAG, pp. 930–1.

There have been innumerable attempts to explain the meaning of 'the thorn in the flesh'. Martin concludes, 'The exact meaning of thorn remains elusive. No one has yet given an interpretation that is generally accepted.'[35] Mullins has argued that the term may allude to personal enemies of Paul.[36] In effect this broadly revives earlier interpretations. Others, however, have interpreted it as a physical pain (Tertullian and NEB).[37] Philip Hughes provides a historical survey of views.[38] From Tertullian to Augustine, the Western Fathers followed the 'physical' interpretation. Luther, however, argued that it referred to exceptional temptation and struggle. More recently some have argued that it is defective eyesight. At all events, it served to remind Paul of his weakness and need for humility in the face of exceptional revelations or perhaps exceptional mystical or charismatic experiences.

(25) In **2 Corinthians 12.14** Paul declares, **'I will not be a burden'** (Gk, *katanarkēsō*). The Greek word is rare. It is absent from the New Testament except for four uses by Paul, all in 2 Corinthians 11 and 12 (2 Cor. 11.19; 12.13, 14, 16). Danker comments, 'The Apostle's use of satire in the context suggests that in these passages the meaning approaches our colloquial "knock out".'[39] He adds, however, that Chrysostom and Theodoret take for granted the meaning *to burden*, or *to be a burden to someone*. Lampe's *Patristic Lexicon* understands it to mean 'lie heavy upon', for example of troubles in Gregory of Nazianzus.[40] Although Grimm-Thayer draw on the LXX meaning 'to grow numb', the New Testament meaning is almost certainly *to be burdensome to*, or *to weigh heavily upon*.[41] Moulton and Milligan give no specific meaning, but regard it as 'a medical term in regular use' in Hippocrates, but used in a distinctive way by Paul, which depends on the context.[42]

Thus whether this constitutes a vivid picture depends on how familiar the term is to the first readers. However, since virtually all translations render the term as *burden*, it has clearly become a vivid picture for subsequent generations of readers. Straub has only a reference to parents and children in this verse.[43] In spite of Danker's allusion to irony, the

35 Martin, *2 Corinthians*, p. 413.

36 T. Y. Mullins, 'Paul's Thorn in the Flesh', *JBL*. 76 (1957), pp. 299–303.

37 Tertullian, *De Pudicitia*, 13.17 (Eng., ANF, vol. 4, p. 87).

38 Philip E. Hughes, *Paul's Second Epistle to the Corinthians* (London: Marshall, Morgan & Scott, 1962), pp. 443–7.

39 BDAG, p. 522.

40 G. W. H. Lampe (ed.), *A Patristic Greek Lexicon* (Oxford: Clarendon Press, 1961), p. 712.

41 Joseph H. Thayer, *Greek-English Lexicon* (Edinburgh: T&T Clark, 4th edn, 1901), pp. 334–5.

42 Moulton and Milligan, *Vocabulary of the Greek Testament*, p. 330.

43 Straub, *Der Bildersprache des Apostels Paulus*, pp. 65–6.

meaning is clear. Unlike the innuendos of a minority of opponents in Corinth, Paul's motivation has nothing to do with financial gain. He simply hopes that the proposed third visit will not constitute any burden, but will give them the opportunity to share in solidarity with other churches in giving what they can to the church in Jerusalem.

We may now turn to Romans. 2 Corinthians often raises difficult questions concerning grammar and syntax, and hence we have spent longer than usual in clarifying meanings and analogies in this epistle.

(26) Romans 4.4 takes up the figure of **Abraham** and the picture of **workers and their pay.** Although he called this a 'picture', Gale argued, curiously, that the picture as such cannot be applied, because justification by grace demands its reversal.[44] But others argue that the picture remains relevant: God reckons righteousness by his grace as a response to faith, and Abraham's justification through faith remains relevant (Gen. 15.6). The context of Romans 4.1–5 clarifies this.

Certainly Abraham is not a worker labouring to earn 'pay' (Gk, *misthos*). Paul insists that it was Abraham's trust in God that meant that 'it was reckoned to him as righteousness' (Rom. 4.3). Righteousness came as a *gift* (Gk, *kata charin*). 'To one who, without works, trusts [Gk, *pisteuonti*] him who justifies the ungodly, such faith is reckoned as righteousness' (Rom. 4.5). James Denney regarded this single sentence as a summary of the whole gospel. This, as Barrett stressed, is the polar opposite to what was affirmed in the traditions of Judaism.[45]

Arguably the picture of labourers and pay remains a picture of what Paul does *not* mean, by contrast. But the image may still serve as a reminder of that, just as some parables of Jesus hit home because of surprising or shocking elements. More to the point, the *picture of Abraham* remains a lasting picture. The differences between Jewish and Christian interpretative traditions sharpen the image. Goppelt reminds us of the place of Abraham in Christian typology.[46]

(27) Romans 5.7 contrasts the *picture* of '**a righteous person**' (Gk, *dikaios*), for whom anyone would rarely die, with a *picture* of '**a good person**' (Gk, *agathos*), for whom 'someone might actually dare to die'.

---

[44] Gale, *The Use of Analogy*, p. 173.

[45] C. K. Barrett, *From First Adam to Last: A Study in Pauline Theology* (London: Black, 1962), p. 31.

[46] Leonhard Goppelt, *Typos: The Typological Interpretation of the Old Testament in the New* (Grand Rapids: Eerdmans, 1982), pp. 136–40.

In this analogy 'good' is clearly a stronger term than 'righteous': *good* traditionally denoted a person of more warmth and compassion than the *righteous* person. On the other hand Robert Jewett argues that good may often denote a benefactor.[47] The overall point of the verse is to demonstrate that God shows *his* love in the death of Christ, whether in theory we were righteous or good. Baillie, Jüngel and Moltmann have shown how important this understanding is for Christian faith. It denies the absurd thought that God the Father fails to be involved in the death of Jesus, and counteracts any false notion of division in the Godhead.[48] The Epistle to the Romans especially emphasizes the place of *God*, and the helplessness of humankind.

(28) Gale treats **Romans 6.1–14** as one picture or metaphor, although several verses serve to illustrate a single theme. The main analogies turn on **death and life**. He writes, 'In 6:1–14 he [Paul] addresses . . . particularly the idea that man [humankind] having entered into new life "in Christ", must now consider himself as "dead" to sin.'[49] The phrase '*dead to sin*' constitutes a reply to the hypothetical question, 'Does grace encourage sin?' Hence Paul continues his diatribe style with hypothetical rhetorical questions, and with practical examples. For some of the questions Paul uses a *deliberative subjunctive*. For example, 'What are we to say?' requires deliberation. Bultmann rightly observes, '"Sinlessness" is not a magical guarantee against the *possibility* of sin . . . But release from the compulsion of sin.'[50] The notion that 'death' brings many kinds of obligations to an end reflects legal and financial conventions in many places. The problem for some readers is that here 'death' is still metaphorical rather than natural, as the quotation from Bultmann illustrates. Sin is still operative, but no longer a dominant force. The converse metaphor is that baptism represents this new creation and a new life, which is also integrated with the picture of being 'raised with Christ'. The Christian life is already a 'post-resurrection' life in the spiritual and moral sense, although it will also be realized in physical terms at the end time. The old self 'dies'; the new self begins a new life. Barrett and Fitzmyer describe the tense in verse 5b as a

---

[47] Robert Jewett, *Romans: A Commentary* (Minneapolis: Fortress, 2007), p. 360.

[48] Donald Baillie, *God Was in Christ* (London: Faber & Faber, 1948), p. 124; Eberhard Jüngel, *God as the Mystery of the World* (Eng., Edinburgh: T&T Clark, 1983), p. 229; Jürgen Moltmann, *The Trinity and the Kingdom of God* (Eng., London: SCM, 1981), p. 16.

[49] Gale, *The Use of Analogy*, p. 177.

[50] Rudolf Bultmann, *Theology of the New Testament*, vol. 1 (London: SCM, 1952), p. 332 (his italics).

logical future ('will be united'), in the sense of the conditional sentence: 'If *X* happens, *Y* will follow.'[51] Holland and Zwiep underline the *corporate* nature of baptism.[52] Schnackenburg expounds usefully Paul's theology of baptism.[53]

(29) In **Romans 6.15–23** Paul elaborates the picture of **slavery**. In particular he points out that if Christian believers are dominated by sin they are behaving like 'obedient slaves' to sin (v. 16). Slavery is a condition which demands obedience and undivided service. The analogy of slavery reinforces the idea of *submission and obedience.* In terms of Roman law, a slave was merely a 'thing' (Lat., *res*), not really a person. Slavery could involve oppressive misery, including torture and corporal punishment. On the other hand, in the case of a male slave, the situation might be reasonably bearable if he belonged to a really benevolent owner, often a person to whom he was a literate secretary or manager; the slave owner would take care of his security and safety, and the welfare of his family if he were to die. In the past, Adolf Deissmann approached the problem of slavery in the New Testament from the point of view of liberation from slavery as illustrated from pagan deities. However, more recently Dale Martin has shown that the key in Paul is not so much 'freedom from slavery', as *transference from an evil master to a good master,* namely to Jesus Christ (v. 23).[54] Formerly, Christians had been slaves of sin and evil; now they have become slaves of Christ.

(30) In **Romans 7.1–6** Paul uses the picture of **marriage** as an analogy. Gale writes, 'Paul now introduces the picture of marriage to show that the Christian lives no longer in that condition where the law – and hence sin – prevails.'[55] The meaning of the law in Paul is extremely complex, for it is used in at least three separate ways. First, Paul regards the law in a positive light as one of Israel's privileges (Rom. 9.4); and as a tutor (Gk *paidagōgos,* Gal. 3.24) to bring us to Christ. Second, it is sometimes used

[51] Tom Holland, *Contours of Pauline Theology* (Fearn: Mentor, 2004), p. 152; Arie W. Zwiep, *Christ, the Spirit, and the Community of God* (WUNT 2; Tübingen: Mohr, 2010), pp. 100–19.

[52] C. K. Barrett, *The Epistle to the Romans* (London: Black, 1957) p. 124; Joseph A. Fitzmyer, *Romans: A New Translation with Introduction and Commentary* (New York: Doubleday, 1992), p. 435.

[53] Rudolf Schnackenburg, *Baptism in the Thought of St Paul* (Oxford: Blackwell, 1964), especially pp. 21–6.

[54] Dale B. Martin, *Slavery as Salvation* (New Haven: Yale University Press, 1990), pp. 15–22, 50–85, 122–4 and 145–9.

[55] Gale, *The Use of Analogy,* p. 190.

as God's self-revelation, or Holy Scripture (1 Cor. 14.21), which is 'holy and just and good' (Rom. 7.12). Third, however, in Dennis Whiteley's words, 'Wrongdoing . . . must be crystallised into conscious sin' on the basis of the activity of the law.[56] Hence the law and sin are inextricably bound together. 'The law is binding' translates Greek *kurieuei, has dominion* (KJV/AV). Hence Paul appeals to the analogy of death and marriage to argue, 'She is discharged from the law concerning her husband' (v. 2). Admittedly the interpretation of this verse is controversial: Barrett interprets the two terms in opposition, as if the husband represents the law, but Cranfield rejects this as unlikely.[57] Paul uses exactly this analogy in 1 Corinthians 7.39–40. The general meaning is clear, however, whatever the details. Paul compares two regimes, in which being in Christ redeems us from the curse of the law.

(31) Romans 9.20–24 more simply uses the analogy of **a potter and clay**, although Gale argued that the analogy cannot be pressed in every detail. Paul has expounded God's commitment to irrevocable covenant promises. In the light of this, the failure of Israel to believe in Jesus Christ constitutes a problem. Paul asks,

> Is there injustice on God's part? By no means! For he [God] says to Moses, 'I will have mercy on whom I have mercy, and I will have compassion on whom I have compassion.' So it depends not on human will or exertion, but on God, who shows mercy. (9.14–16)

In verses 20–21, Paul draws on a vivid analogy. He asks:

> Who indeed are you, a human being, to argue with God? Will what is moulded say to the one who moulds it, 'Why have you made me like this?' Has the potter no right over the clay to make out of the same lump one object for special use, and another for ordinary use?

Astonishingly C. H. Dodd called it 'the weakest point in the whole Epistle', for 'A mechanical determinism annihilates morality'.[58]

---

[56] D. E. H. Whiteley, *The Theology of St. Paul* (Oxford: Blackwell, 1970), pp. 79–80; J. D. G. Dunn, *Paul and the Mosaic Law* (WUNT 89; Tübingen: Mohr, 1998); J. D. G. Dunn, *The Theology of Paul the Apostle* (Edinburgh: T&T Clark, 1998), pp. 128–61; N. T. Wright, *Paul and the Faithfulness of God* (London: SPCK, 2013), pp. 851–79 and 892–914; E. P. Sanders, *Paul, the Law, and the Jewish People* (Philadelphia: Fortress, 1983).

[57] Barrett, *The Epistle to the Romans*, p. 136; C. E. B. Cranfield, *A Critical and Exegetical Commentary on the Epistle to the Romans*, vol. 1 (ICC; Edinburgh: T&T Clark, 1975), p. 333.

[58] C. H. Dodd, *The Epistle of Paul to the Romans* (London: Hodder & Stoughton, 1932), pp. 158–9.

F. F. Bruce, however, comments, 'God is not answerable to man.'[59] Further, Franz Leenhardt observes:

> If man presumes to dispute with God, he must at least try to share God's angle of vision, if he can . . . God's providential government must not be judged by the limited views of man. To help his readers adjust to this field of vision, Paul proposes they should consider the parable of the potter.[60]

The very same analogy is quoted in Isaiah 29.16 verbatim, and also reflects Isaiah 44.8; 45.8–10; Jeremiah 18.6; and Wisdom 12.12 and 15.7. Clearly how much, if at all, God's sovereignty is conditioned by human free will remains a matter of debate, and to some extent Paul discusses this in the remainder of chapters 9—11.

(32) **Romans 11.16–24** embodies at least two analogies within it. The first analogy is between the **dough** (Gk, *to phurama*) **or the root** (Gk, *hē rhiza*) and the **first fruits** (Gk, *hē aparchē*) **or the branches** (*hoi kladdoi*). Munck and Whiteley see Israel as the root or, to change the metaphor, the rudder that guided the Gentiles in.[61] We must recall the tense relation in the Roman church of the time between Jewish and Gentile Christians. This analogy invites humility on the part of Gentile Christians. God's promises to Abraham are the basis of Gentile salvation. The analogy is also probably an allusion to Numbers 15.19–21.

The second analogy concerns the **grafting** of new branches on to a tree. Christian Gentiles have been grafted on to the Jewish root-stock. Paul's notion of branches 'broken off' and yet becoming re-grafted into the cultivated olive has raised considerable exegetical debate. The majority of commentators consider this to be impossible in horticultural terms, although William Ramsay offers evidence for a wild olive becoming grafted on to a cultivated olive in the ancient world.[62] Richard Bell argues that Paul's phrase 'against nature' (in 11.24) shows that Paul was aware that the process he describes was contrary to the usual practice.[63] Ziesler and Jewett have updated Ramsay's arguments.[64] The grafting in and breaking

---

[59] F. F. Bruce, *The Epistle to the Romans* (London: Tyndale Press, 1963), p. 195.

[60] Franz Leenhardt, *The Epistle to the Romans* (London: Lutterworth Press, 1961), p. 255.

[61] Johannes Munck, *Paul and the Salvation of Mankind* (London: SCM, 1959), p. 45; Whiteley, *The Theology of St. Paul*, p. 87.

[62] William Ramsay, *Paul and Other Studies* (New York: Armstrong, 1906), pp. 219–21.

[63] Richard Bell, *Provoked to Jealousy: The Origin and Purpose of the Jealousy Motif in Romans 9–11* (WUNT 2, 63; Tübingen: Mohr, 1994), pp. 103–4.

[64] Jewett, *Romans*, pp. 684–6; John Ziesler, 'Paul and Arboriculture: Romans 11:17–24', *JSNT* 24 (1985), pp. 24–32.

off of branches must be seen as 'the kindness and the severity of God' (v. 22). Gale concludes that while Paul's analogies serve his purpose, they do not apply in every possible way.[65]

Analogies in Philippians, Philemon, Colossians and Ephesians

Gale includes Philippians and Philemon with the other Pauline epistles, but does not consider Colossians, Ephesians and the Pastoral Epistles, presumably because the Pauline authorship of Colossians, Ephesians and the Pastorals is doubtful, or at least debated.

(33) In Philippians 3.2 Paul warns his readers, '**Beware of the dogs** [Gk, *tous kunas*], beware of the evil workers'. The picture is used to illustrate very negative characteristics. Strack and Billerbeck call dogs the most despised, most shameless and most wretched creature, and Otto Michel concurs.[66] H. Koester calls this description one of the strongest in invective terms possible, claiming, 'the deliberate aim of the polemic here is not to describe the opponents, but to insult them'.[67] O'Brien calls it 'bitterly ironic'.[68] The allusion is probably to the herds of dogs which prowl about Eastern cities, and still do today in parts of South America and perhaps southern Europe. Whatever may be the exact definition of the culprits, they stand in contrast to 'the (true) circumcision, who worship in the Spirit of God' of verse 3. Ralph Martin commented, 'It is more to the point if Paul is ironically seizing upon a term which his Jewish enemies were using concerning his converts in the Gentile churches – uncircumcised Gentile believers.'[69] Paul evidently regarded the troublemakers as intruders and scavengers. Gale cites only this example in Philippians.

(34) Gale cites **Philemon verse 10**, however. Paul's use of **the father–son analogy** he calls 'more than a picture'.[70] C. F. D. Moule comments, 'The

---

65 Gale, *The Use of Analogy*, pp. 213–15.

66 Hermann L. Strack and Paul Billerbeck, *Kommentar zum Neuen Testament aus Talmud und Midrasch*, vol. 1 (Munich: C. H. Beck, 1926), p. 722; and Otto Michel, '*kuōn*', *TDNT*, vol. 3, pp. 1101–4.

67 H. Koester, 'The Purpose of the Polemic of a Pauline Fragment (Phil. 3)', *NTS* 8 (1961–2), p. 320; pp. 317–2.

68 Peter T. O'Brien, *The Epistle to the Philippians* (NIGTC; Grand Rapids: Eerdmans, 1991), p. 354.

69 Ralph P. Martin, *Philippians* (NCB; London: Oliphants, 1976), p. 125; F. W. Beare, *The Epistle to the Philippians* (London: Black, 1959), p. 103.

70 Gale, *The Use of Analogy*, p. 220.

metaphor of fatherhood – the evangelist "begetting" a convert – occurs also in 1 Cor. 4:15. For the metaphor of motherhood, see Gal. 4:19.'[71] Paul also used the analogy of 'nurse' or 'mother' in 1 Thessalonians 2.7. He has 'begotten' (Gk, *egennēsa*) Onesimus as his spiritual father. James Dunn observes, 'The imagery of father and son was a natural one to describe the relation of pupil and teacher . . . or one in a state of religious dependence on priest or select leader.'[72] We need not rehearse Elizabeth Castelli's arguments to the effect that the use of 'father' signifies authoritarianism and 'control' on Paul's part, especially since she bases much of her argument on the attacks of the postmodernist philosopher Michel Foucault on all forms of authoritarian institutions.[73]

Gale concludes, 'A picture is introduced for the sake of a single element in it that serves to illustrate or reinforce the particular idea involved in the immediate context.'[74] In a few cases, he concedes, more than one element in the analogy is used. Further, a great many pictures include elements that are quite inapplicable. Some pictures, he adds, are applied differently in different contexts. Finally, he added, Paul's analogies are intended to be applied in a limited way. Thus pictures retain great importance, but have to be used with accuracy and discrimination.

(35) We now move beyond Gale's considerations in exploring Colossians, Ephesians and the Pastoral Epistles. It is difficult to know how many of Paul's analogies are to be treated as genuine analogies, since many use established parallels in the tradition. For example, Paul refers in Colossians to 'the **inheritance** of the saints in the light' (**Col. 1.12**), when 'inheritance' has become an established word in Paul, which is not entirely analogical. Dunn observes that the term *inheritance* is 'unmistakably Jewish in character'.[75] J. D. Hester has written explicitly on the concept of inheritance.[76] Beginning with the inheritance of the Holy Land to Israel, the concept then embraces the eschatological future for Christians.

---

[71] C. F. D. Moule, *The Epistles to the Colossians and to Philemon* (Cambridge: CUP, 1962), p. 144.

[72] James D. G. Dunn, *The Epistles to the Colossians and to Philemon* (NIGNT; Grand Rapids: Eerdmans, 1996), p. 328.

[73] E. A. Castelli, *Imitating Paul: A Discussion of Power* (Louisville: Westminster/John Knox, 1991), pp. 97–115.

[74] Gale, *The Use of Analogy*, p. 223.

[75] Dunn, *Colossians and Philemon*, p. 75.

[76] J. D. Hester, *Paul's Concept of Inheritance* (SJT Occasional Papers 14; Edinburgh: Oliver & Boyd, 1968).

(36) The same dilemma confronts Paul's use of '**image** [Gk, *eikōn*] of the invisible God' (**Col. 1.15**), since 'image of God' has become a well-worn biblical phrase from Genesis 1.26 onwards. Indeed it has been widely agreed that verses 15–20 are probably derived from a pre-formed hymn, as Martin, O'Brien and Dunn all stress. The overall thought is that the hidden God can be known through his image, namely Jesus Christ, and secondarily through the Christian apostolic community. C. F. D. Moule regarded the theme as especially indebted to the Wisdom literature.[77] Among passages which use analogy, this perhaps constitutes a borderline case.

(37) The metaphor of '**struggling**' (Gk, *agōna echō*; **Col. 2.1**) is more clearly Pauline and analogical. Struggle refers to the ups and downs of Paul's ministry. Dunn comments, 'The metaphor of the athletic contest (*agōn*) is continued from the preceding verse – an image which Paul and his circle used to express the concentrated and sustained effort that his ministry demanded (Phil. 1:30; 1 Thess. 2:2; 1 Tim. 6:12).'[78] Victor Pfitzner has devoted a special study to this image.[79]

(38) Paul uses a mixed metaphor, if not perhaps incompatible and contradictory metaphors, in his description of the Church as '**rooted** [Gk, *errizōmenoi*] and **built up** [Gk, *epoikodomoumenoi*] in him [Christ], and established in the faith' (**Col. 2.7**). The term *rooted* depicts an organic metaphor of growth, whereas *built up* implies a more static model of a building which has been established. Dunn calls these 'forceful metaphors'.[80] But in the end, a root for a new plant, and a foundation for a new building are complementary, not contradictory. Fruit-bearing and building on (Gk, *epi*) what was already there are both metaphors of firmness and increase.

(39) In **Colossians 2.14** Paul uses a double metaphor: one analogy is that of being '**nailed to the cross**'. The context is that of being buried and being raised in baptism, and God's forgiving our trespasses. The other analogy is that of '**erasing**' (or smearing out or obliterating) 'the record that stood against us' (NRSV). Moule compared 'smoothing away' what had been

77 Moule, *Colossians and Philemon*, p. 59.

78 Dunn, *Colossians and Philemon*, p. 129.

79 Victor C. Pfitzner, *Paul and the Agon Motif: Traditional Athletic Imagery in the Pauline Literature* (Leiden: Brill, 1967).

80 Dunn, *Colossians and Philemon*, p. 141.

written on wax, and striking out 'the title nailed over a criminal's head . . . like an "IOU" . . . no longer valid'.[81] Dunn comments, 'The expunging of the record confirms that none of these transgressions is any longer held against us.'[82] He adds that 'Nailing it to the cross' is 'another way of saying "*by crucifying it*"'. There may be 'a play on the practice of attaching a crucified man's indictment to his cross to indicate to onlookers what his crime was'.[83] F. F. Bruce summarized the point of the metaphors: 'God has broken you clean away from your past.'[84] This is a carefully worked-out strong pictorial analogy.

(40) Allowing for the fact that 'put to death' (in 3.5) is more than an analogy, we come to Paul's analogy of a '**door**' for the word of God (**Col. 4.3**). Dunn comments that evidently Paul liked the metaphor of door for opportunity, since he also uses it in 1 Corinthians 16.9 and 2 Corinthians 2.12. It is characteristic of Paul to request prayer for his missionary work. Deissmann suggests that Paul's analogy of a '*door* for the word of God' was a borderline metaphor because it was an expression in current general speech.[85] If we were to assume that he wrote the whole Pauline corpus with the exception of Ephesians and the Pastoral Epistles, Paul would have used around 40 analogies or metaphors which are primarily pictorial.

(41) In **Ephesians 1.10** the well-known term '**to gather up all things**' (Gk, *anakephalaiōsasthi*) has become famous, especially as the '**recapitulation**' interpretation of Irenaeus. Irenaeus, Tertullian and Jerome translated the Greek by the Latin term *recapitulare*, often, *to sum up*. Paul perhaps meant the term to be understood literally, but the application of this term remains partly metaphorical. Paul uses the term to mean 'the typical union of all things in the Messiah, a final harmony answering to the idea of creation'.[86] Following Paul in Ephesians, Irenaeus wrote, 'One God the Father and one Christ Jesus . . . gathered together all things in himself.'[87]

---

[81] Moule, *Colossians and Philemon*, p. 98.

[82] Dunn, *Colossians and Philemon*, p. 166.

[83] Dunn, *Colossians and Philemon*, p. 166.

[84] F. F. Bruce and E. K. Simpson, *The Epistles of Paul to the Ephesians and to the Colossians* (London: Marshall, Morgan & Scott, 1957), p. 238.

[85] Adolf Deissmann, *Light from the Ancient East* (London: Hodder & Stoughton, 1910), p. 301, n. 2.

[86] Brooke F. Westcott, *St Paul's Epistle to the Ephesians: Greek Text* (London: Macmillan, 1906), p. 14.

[87] Irenaeus, *Against Heresies*, 3, 16, 7 (Eng., ANF, vol. 1, p. 443).

He also wrote, 'The Lord . . . summing up in Himself all things which are in heaven, and which are on earth . . . These things he [Christ] recapitulated in Himself, by uniting man to the Spirit to dwell in man.'[88] Third, he also wrote:

> The Son of God . . . became incarnate and was made man. He commenced afresh the long line of human beings . . . and furnished us . . . [with] what was lost in Adam, namely to be according to the image of God – that we might recover in Christ Jesus.[89]

Armitage Robinson does not hesitate to call the term a metaphor. He wrote:

> As the total is the result of the addition of separate actors, as a summary of events in one view the details of a complicated argument (*sic*) – these are the messages suggested by the apostle's word – so in the Divine councils Christ is the Son of all things.[90]

He added, 'The variety of the universe, with all its discordance and confusions' is also the principle of unity. 'In Christ', says St Paul in Colossians 1.17, 'all things consist'; in him, that is, they have their principle of cohesion and unity; even as 'through him and unto him they have been created'. If confusion seems to arise, it is 'not of the nature of things, and it is not the eternal'.[91]

(42) In **Ephesians 1.13** Paul speaks of being '**marked with the seal** of the promised Holy Spirit'. Robinson wrote, 'As if to remove all question and uncertainty, God sets his seal on you. The order of the words in the original is striking.'[92] Westcott commented, 'You were sealed (Gk, *asphragithēte*)' looks to the Greek noun *sphragis* (seal), which is

> used of the invisible attestation of the reality of a spiritual fact . . . The seal openly marked servants of God as belonging to him (2 Cor. 1:22), and assured them of his protection. So they were solemnly recognised as his sons . . . and . . . pledged to his service.[93]

Seal is often used in the epistles as a guaranteed mark of ownership in the present, which will be fully revealed as authentic at the end times. The

---

[88] Irenaeus, *Against Heresies*, 5, 20, 2 (Eng., ANF, vol. 1, p. 548).

[89] Irenaeus, *Against Heresies*, 3. 18, 1 (Eng., ANF, vol. 1, p. 446).

[90] J. Armitage Robinson, *St Paul's Epistle to the Ephesians* (London: Macmillan, 1987), p. 32.

[91] Robinson, *Ephesians*, pp. 32–3.

[92] Robinson, *Ephesians*, p. 35.

[93] Westcott, *Ephesians*, p. 17.

symbol or analogy is a familiar one in the commercial world. Robinson describes it as a metaphor from mercantile life.[94]

(43) One of the main problems of considering pictures in Ephesians is that many analogies are repeated from earlier Pauline letters. This provides a double-edged argument about Paul's authorship of Ephesians. Some consider this to be the work of a Pauline disciple, who is keen to copy whatever he can of Paul's authentic works and style. Others regard it as Paul himself using his favourite analogies and phrases. Whatever the explanation, we find such repeated pictures as '**pledge [and] inheritance**' (**Eph. 1.14**); 'his body' (1.23; 2.16); 'dead' and 'alive' (2.5); 'cornerstone' (Eph. 2.20); 'a holy temple' (2.21); 'heirs' (3.6); 'maturity' (4.13); 'cloth[ing] . . . the new self' (4.24); 'building up' (4.29); and so on. Because we have discussed these above, we need not rehearse them again as separate considerations. However, three (or perhaps four) metaphors are distinctive to Ephesians, and well known. These are 'aliens' and 'alienation', 'the dividing wall', the detailed picture of the Christian's armour, and perhaps the traditional passage about husbands and wives.

(44) The pictures surrounding '**aliens**' (**Eph. 2.12, 19**) includes some associated metaphors such as '**strangers**' (2.12, 19), and '**far off**' (2.13). These are counteracted by 'reconciled' and 'brought near', which happen to combine the typical Pauline concept of reconciliation with that of Hebrews' liturgical analogy of being brought near. The negative terms picture what it is to be 'without Christ' (Gk, *chōris Christou*, 2.12), that is, to lose this personal relationship with him. Being aliens (Gk, *apēllotriōmenoi*, from *apallotrioō*) indicates being estranged from the corporate life of Israel in 2.12, and estrangement from spouses in Ephesians 4.18 and 1 Corinthians 6.3.[95] In Colossians 1.21 it is associated with being an *enemy* (Gk, *echros*). It constitutes the antonym of 'drawing near' (Eph. 2.13).

(45) The metaphor, analogy or picture of **the 'dividing wall'** (Gk, *mesotoichon tou phragmou* (KJV/AV, 'middle wall of the partition', **Eph. 2.14**) refers directly to the physical wall in the Jerusalem Temple, which formed the barrier between the Court of the Jews and the outer Court of the Gentiles. The Jerusalem Temple of Paul's day had six courts. (a) The innermost of all was the Holy of Holies, which only the high priest could enter once

[94] Robinson, *Ephesians*, p. 36.

[95] BDAG, p. 96.

each year on the Day of Atonement. (b) The Holy Place was entered daily by a priest to offer incense, and sacrifice the morning and evening lamb. (c) The Court of the Priests contained the Altar of Burnt Offerings. (d) The Court of the Sons of Israel allowed entrance to Jewish men. (e) The Court of the Women invited entrance to Jewish women. Finally (f) the Court of the Gentiles permitted Gentiles to enter, but not to go beyond the 'dividing wall' on pain of death. The six 'Courts' stressed both the invitation of grace, and the degrees of holiness which also provided a barrier which prevented close access for some. In 1871, wrote Robinson, an inscription was discovered which said in Greek: 'No man of another nation to enter within the fence and enclosure . . . (or) death ensues'.[96] The inscription was found originally on the site of the Jerusalem Temple but is now preserved in the Istanbul Archaeology Museum.

Robinson vividly writes:

> That barrier, with its series of inscribed stones threatening death to the intruder, was still standing in the Temple courts at the moment when St Paul boldly proclaimed that Christ had broken it down. It still stood: but it was already antiquated, obsolete, out of date, as far as its spiritual meaning went. It still stood: but the thing signified was broken down. The thing signified was a separation between Gentile and Jew.[97]

This analogy brilliantly serves the central message of this epistle.

(46) The detailed picture of the **Christian's armour** is depicted in **Ephesians 6.11–17**, and has been the subject of many Sunday School lessons, children's talks and visual aids. In verse 11 Paul begins, 'Put on the whole armour of God [Gk, *endusasthe tēn panoplian tou Theou*], so that you may be able to stand against the wiles of the devil.' John A. T. Robinson rightly wrote, 'The contrast is not, as is commonly taken, between the visible and the invisible, but between the ineffectiveness of merely human forces against the "powers" (Gk, *exousias*) of the spirit-world.'[98] The particular 'weapons' which the Christian needs include 'the belt of truth', 'the breastplate of righteousness', 'the shield of faith' (Gk, *ton thureon tēs pisteōs*), 'the helmet of salvation' and 'the sword of the Spirit, which is the word of God'. 'Stand' (Gk, *stēnai*, v. 11) means to hold one's position.[99] Westcott added, 'The metaphor (Gk., *palē*, struggle, wrestling) is changed

96 Robinson, *Ephesians*, p. 60.
97 Robinson, *Ephesians*, p. 60.
98 John A. T. Robinson, *The Body: A Study in Pauline Theology* (London: SCM, 1957), p. 20.
99 Westcott, *Ephesians*, p. 93.

in order to bring out the personal individual conflict.'[100] These separate analogies serve the argument well.

(47) It is difficult to know whether the traditional passage about **husbands and wives (Eph. 5.25–33)** should be included among specific analogies, or whether the teaching is so traditional, especially in Judaism, that it hardly constitutes an analogy in the strictest sense of the term. Perhaps its appearance of being an authoritative series of commands encourages those who challenge the personal or direct Pauline authorship. An entire volume on this passage has been provided, however, by J. Paul Sampley.[101] Sampley concludes that the readers would have 'a certain fund of traditions . . . from Judaism and the early church, upon which he [the author] may draw to communicate his message to them'.[102] All the same, he argues, the traditions chosen by the author generally match his purposes and concerns. He writes, 'Marriage between Christians, reflecting the larger purposes of God, is to be understood as grounded firmly in the old Testament ordination of marriage, Gen. 2:24.'[103] The author, he argues further, shows a deep indebtedness to Leviticus 19.18, that is, you shall love your neighbour as yourself. His further argument is that 'Ephesians is directed to a congregation or to congregations exposed to, or partaking in schismatic talk'.[104]

Westcott's argument, however, may seem more convincing. He points out, 'The wife is to the husband as the church to Christ . . . Marriage is used in a vital unity which points to the ideal confirmation of humanity.'[105] Nevertheless, as Westcott asserts with equal emphasis, Christ's self-sacrifice on behalf of the Church seriously and deeply qualifies how the marriage relationship is to be interpreted and understood. Again, to what extent these verses should be recorded as an analogy alongside other analogies remains a matter of debate. Those who include Ephesians among directly and personally Pauline writings may conclude that Paul appears to use some *47 analogies, pictures or metaphors* in this extended Pauline canon.

[100] Westcott, *Ephesians*, p. 93; BDAG, p. 752.
[101] J. Paul Sampley, *'And the Two Shall Become One Flesh': A Study of Traditions in Ephesians 5:21–33* (SNTSMS 16; Cambridge: CUP, 1971).
[102] Sampley, *'The Two Shall Become One Flesh'*, p. 158.
[103] Sampley, *'The Two Shall Become One Flesh'*, p. 159.
[104] Sampley, *'The Two Shall Become One Flesh'*, p. 160.
[105] Westcott, *Ephesians*, p. 83.

Pictures and images in the Pastoral Epistles

The Pastoral Epistles have been treated in a different way by Walter Butcher, in his article 'The Metaphors of St Paul'.[106] We propose to follow his scheme. Butcher argues that Paul's writings, including the pastorals, 'are rich in metaphor . . . keeping in close touch with the fashions, tastes, habits and ways of his own time'.[107] He groups these metaphors in the pastorals under the headings, first, imperial warfare; second, classical architecture including building up; third, ancient agriculture; fourth, metaphors drawn from Greek games; fifth, metaphors from Roman law including adoption and becoming heirs; sixth, metaphors from medical science; seventh, metaphors from seafaring life; eighth, metaphors from mercantile life; and ninth, metaphors from the fowler's craft.

(1) Under **imperial warfare**, Paul or the writer mentions:
(i) 1 Timothy 1.18, 'Fight the good fight' (Gk, *strateuē . . . tēn kalēn strateian*).[108] The word *strateuō* means to do military service, to serve in the army or to engage in conflict. It is clearly a pictorial metaphor. Paul may well be using military terminology to urge Timothy to avoid the fate that befell Hymenaeus and Alexander who in verses 19–20 suffered shipwreck in the faith. Kelly comments:

> The battle, by its very nature noble [is] against other versions of the gospel message. Paul is fond of military metaphors, and in particular likes to depict the apostolic leader as a Christian warrior (1 Cor. 9:7; 2 Cor. 10:3; Phil. 2:25; 2 Tim. 2:3–4).[109]

(ii) In **1 Timothy 5.14** Paul urges widows 'to give the **adversary** no occasion to revile us'. 'Adversary (Gk., *ho antikeimenos*, from *antikeisthai*, to oppose) could refer either to the devil or the churches' detractors . . . the former is perhaps preferable.'[110]

(iii) and (iv) 2 Timothy 2.3 repeats the language 'a good **soldier** of Christ Jesus'. **2 Timothy 3.6** reads: '**captivate** [Gk, *aichmalōtizein*, to capture] silly women [Gk, *gunaikaria*, a scornful diminutive], overwhelmed by their sins and swayed by all kinds of desires'. Kelly describes this as 'biting sarcasm', but also 'a life-like picture of the tactics of religious propaganda'.

---

[106] Walter A. Butcher, 'The Metaphors of St. Paul', *Baptist Quarterly* 9 (1939), pp. 484–7.
[107] Butcher, 'The Metaphors of St Paul', p. 484.
[108] BDAG, p. 947.
[109] J. N. D. Kelly, *The Pastoral Epistles* (London: Black, 1963), p. 57.
[110] Kelly, *The Pastoral Epistles*, p. 219.

'Being captured' is metaphorical, with direct and obvious application. It has almost become a dead metaphor.

(2) Under **classical architecture and building**, Butcher includes:

(v) 1 Timothy 3.13, 'Those who serve well as deacons gain a **good standing** [Gk, *bathmon heautois kalon*] for themselves'. William Mounce comments that this alludes to one's standing or reputation before the outside world.[111] Danker regards *bathmos* as meaning a physical step, or a 'structured rest for the foot marking a stage in ascending or descending'.[112] Thus it is a metaphor from a building, but with clear application.

(vi) 1 Timothy 3.15 provides a cluster of metaphors connected with '**the household of God** [Gk, *en oikō Theou*], which is the church of the living God, the pillar and bulwark [Gk, *stulos kai hedraiōma*] of the truth'. The Greek *oikos* may be a house, a building or household. Kelly suggests, '*Buttress* is probably a more accurate rendering of the Greek *hedraiōma*.'[113] This would reflect the task of each congregation to support, bolster up and thus safeguard the teaching of the Church. In the same vein, Mounce points out that many other interpreters argue that the household metaphor had a dominating influence in the theology of the Pastoral Epistles, so that churches bolster up a hierarchical social structure which is threatened by disruptive forces.[114] Mounce himself, however, disagrees with this view, arguing that the household does *not* stand for the Church, and that the metaphor is *not* a dominating force. This issue, although not the architectural metaphor, is disputed. Too many interpreters seem to reflect their own theology of the church.

(vii) 1 Timothy 6.19 uses the metaphor of '**foundation**': 'storing up for themselves the treasure of a good foundation for the future'. Mounce comments:

> The difficulty of this verse is the mixing of metaphors. [The word] *apothēsaurizein* occurs only here in the New Testament. It means 'to store up, lay away' . . . But *themelios* means 'foundation', used in the New Testament both literally of a building, and figuratively of the foundation

[111] William D. Mounce, *Pastoral Epistles* (WBC; Nashville: Nelson, 2000), p. 207.

[112] BDAG, p. 162.

[113] Kelly, *The Pastoral Epistles*, p. 88.

[114] Mounce, *Pastoral Epistles*, p. 221; D. C. Verner, *The Household of God and the Social World of the Pastoral Epistles* (SBLDS; Chico, CA: Scholars Press, 1983), p. 186.

> built by a person's preaching of Christ (Rom. 15:20) . . . The mixing of metaphors is somewhat confusing.[115]

The mixed metaphor, however, need not be confusing, and Kelly notes that Paul frequently uses mixed metaphors.[116] Robert Wall simply asserts, 'To store up for themselves a good foundation [is] for eschatological ends.'[117]

(viii) 2 Timothy 2.19 asserts, 'God's firm **foundation** stands'. In spite of discouragement by the effects of the heretics' campaign, Paul gratefully recognizes the function of the main building. Kelly writes:

> Various interpretations have been proposed for the solid foundation: Christ and his apostles . . . the truth of the gospel, the church as a whole, or the unshakable core of genuine Christians at Ephesus. It almost certainly stands for the last, or at any rate for the Ephesian church considered as part of the great Christian Church.[118]

(3) Metaphors from **ancient agriculture**:

(ix) In **1 Timothy 4.10** Paul writes, **'We toil and struggle'** (NRSV; Gk, *kopiōmen kai agōnizometha*), or 'We labour and strive' (KJV/AV). Kelly calls this an athletic metaphor, rather than an agricultural one.[119] This is the regular meaning of the Greek, especially of *agōnizometha*. Butcher has misclassified this, but it clearly remains a metaphor, which ideally should belong in the next category. The same perhaps goes for Butcher's next example of 1 Timothy 5.17, which simply uses the word **labour** (Gk, *kopiōntes*) for labouring in preaching, that is, strenuously struggling to do a difficult task. In this case the word is scarcely metaphorical; it is used so frequently in this way. We have not added it to our list of metaphors.

(x) 1 Timothy 5.18 reads: **'The labourer** [Gk, *ho ergatēs*] **deserves to be paid'** (NRSV), or 'the labourer is worthy of his hire' (KLJV/AV). This is a quotation verbatim from Luke 10.7, and slightly differently from Matthew 10.10, which Paul repeats in 1 Corinthians 9.14. If it specifically reflects the teaching of Jesus, a rural and agricultural setting may be presupposed; but if it is quoted as a common proverb, whether it is commercial or agricultural is debatable. It remains, however, a metaphor of common popular currency.

---

[115] Mounce, *Pastoral Epistles*, p. 368.
[116] Kelly, *The Pastoral Epistles*, p. 149.
[117] Robert W. Wall, *1 & 2 Timothy and Titus* (Grand Rapids: Eerdmans, 2012), p. 200.
[118] Kelly, *The Pastoral Epistles*, p. 186.
[119] Kelly, *The Pastoral Epistles*, p. 102.

(xi) 1 Timothy 6.10 is a well-known saying: 'the love of money is **a root** [Gk, *riza*] of all kinds of evil'. It is misquoted in the popular song: 'Money is the root of all evil'. The root is not money, but the love of money. The metaphorical nature of the word is improved by translating 'a root', rather than '*the* root'. Once again, this is a popular proverb, which may be found in Diogenes Laertius 6.50, Philo and elsewhere. Mounce calls it 'figurative', partly because this use of 'root' is so widespread that some regard it as no longer a creative metaphor.[120] On the other hand it is suggestive for preachers and expositors.

(xii) In **Titus 1.13, 'Rebuke them sharply'** (NRSV) does not look at all like a metaphor. However the Greek, *elegche autous apotomōs*, according to Butcher, means 'cut them away as with a sharp pruning knife'. However, Danker renders the adverb *apotomōs* simply as *severely* or *rigorously*, the adjective *apotomos* as *relentless*, and the noun *apotomia* as *cut off*, without reference to horticulture. Only if we resort to historical etymology could we seriously claim that Paul is using a metaphor from agriculture. Hence we shall not include this use among our list of metaphors. On the other hand Titus 3.14, 'so that they may not be unproductive', suggests a different story. The Greek *akarpoi* does indeed mean 'fruitless'. Hence the terms therefore constitute an agricultural or horticultural metaphor.

(xiii) In 2 Timothy 2.6 Paul uses a genuine simile: **'It is the farmer who does the work** who ought to have the first share of the crops.' Kelly comments:

> The analogy is not, as some editors suggest, far-fetched, dragged in because the writer noticed its occurrence in 1 Cor. 9:10–11 . . . [Paul] has also had in mind, no less than in 1 Cor. 9:10–11, the ministerial support which the apostolic leader is entitled to expect from the community in which he has laboured.[121]

At least three or more of Butcher's five proposed metaphors of ancient agriculture are probably correct; others are more than open to question.

(4) Butcher's fourth characterization of metaphors is drawn from **Greek games.**

[120] Mounce, *Pastoral Epistles*, p. 347.

[121] Kelly, *The Pastoral Epistles*, p. 176.

(xiv) 1 Timothy 4.7 reads: '**Train yourself** [Gk, *gumnaze seauton*] in godliness'. The KJV/AV has 'exercise thyself unto godliness'. Danker confirms that *gumnazō* normally means to train, or even to exercise naked in much pagan literature, where it is also a metaphor for self-discipline.[122] Wall comments:

> The pericope opens with an exhortation to follow the habits of a well-trained athlete: 'train yourself for holy living' . . . The word for training is *gumnazō* from which 'gymnasium' derives, and envisages the practices and habits that form physical self-control.[123]

This example is well placed among metaphors drawn from Greek games.

(xv) The NRSV translates **1 Timothy 6.12**, '**Fight the good fight of faith**' (Gk, *agōnizou . . . to kalon agōna*). We have already noted Victor Pfitzner's survey of this theme. He explored the use of the *agōn* motif in the Hellenistic world and in Judaism, and has devoted a number of pages to the same theme in the Pastoral Epistles.[124] In this verse the classification of the metaphor seems to be appropriate, since it covers such athletic activities as boxing and other competitions.

(xvi) In **2 Timothy 2.5** Paul expounds the well-known metaphor: '**In the case of an athlete**, no one is crowned without competing according to the rules.' Paul has moved from considering the hardships involved in Christian service, to the reward which will crown it. The phrase 'according to the rules' renders 'lawfully' (Gk, *nominōs*). There has been much debate on the status of the 'rules': some advocate particular games; others argue for such contests as the Olympic Games. This is not specified.

(xvii) An even more famous passage comes in **2 Timothy 4.7**: '**I have fought the good fight,**

> I have finished the race, I have kept the faith. From now on there is reserved for me the crown of righteousness, which the Lord, the righteous judge, will give me on that day.

Here, Kelly comments:

> The picture is not of warfare, but of an athletic contest, probably a

[122] BDAG, p. 208.

[123] Wall, *1 & 2 Timothy and Titus*, p. 121.

[124] Pfitzner, *Paul and the Agon Motif*, pp. 23–38, 73–125 and 105–87 respectively.

wrestling-match. There is no note of arrogance, as if he [Paul] personally had distinguished himself. It is the game or sport, viz. his apostolic vocation and ministry, which is noble. The emphasis is on the verb, which is in the perfect tense: 'I have fought in the contest to the very end'.[125]

(5) Metaphors drawn from Roman law. Butcher proposes only one of these.

(xviii) Titus 3.7 asserts: 'Having been justified by his grace, we might become **heirs** according to the hope of eternal life.' Although other contexts of justification occur (such as vindication), the picture of the court verdict lies at the root of the concept. We have already discussed the term *heir*, which is used so regularly by Paul, which may imply that it is only partly a metaphor. We suggest that this constitutes another example of a borderline case of metaphor.

(6) Metaphors drawn from medical science.

(xix) 1 Timothy 6.3 is a regular example. At first sight the simple phrase 'sound words' (NRSV) appears not to be metaphorical. Nevertheless the Greek term *hugiainousin*, from *hugiainō*, means 'to be in good health, be healthy, or to be sound or correct'.[126] Danker himself favours the latter in the Pastorals, but the notion of *health-giving doctrine* does not seem irrelevant. Kelly's translation is 'wholesome', which combines both nuances.[127] Mounce prefers 'healthy'.[128] On balance, Butcher is justified in calling this a medical metaphor. Sound words bring vigour, nurture and health. Butcher's appeal to Titus 1.9, which has 'sound doctrine' in the NRSV and KJV/AV, may also be included as a *repeated* example of the same metaphor, since the Greek is *en tē didaskaliā hugiainousē* (dative noun and participle), meaning *by healthy teaching*, or *by health-giving teaching*. In Titus 1.13; 2.1; and 2 Timothy 4.3 the same analogy is repeated yet again. The Greek word is the same, or from the same verb. So Paul must have attached great importance to this metaphor to have repeated it four times.

(xx) A different medical metaphor appears in **2 Timothy 2.17**. Paul is speaking of the spread of heretical disruptive ideas and forces, including

[125] Kelly, *The Pastoral Epistles*, p. 208.
[126] BDAG, p. 1023.
[127] Kelly, *The Pastoral Epistles*, p. 133.
[128] Mounce, *Pastoral Epistles*, p. 337.

those of Hymenaeus and Philetus, who have 'swerved from the truth'. In verse 17 a powerful medical metaphor is used: 'Their talk will spread **like gangrene** (Gk, *hōs gaggraina*; KJV/AV, 'eat as doth a gangrene'). Danker in his *Lexicon* writes, 'Disease involving severe inflammation, which, if left unchecked can become a destructive, ulcerous condition, gangrene, cancer, of spreading ulcers . . . (medical term since Hippocrates).'[129] Mounce comments, 'The sickening effects of their teaching will spread throughout the church as if it were gangrene in a body.'[130] Kelly speaks of its 'insidious tendency to spread and infect other people, just as gangrene . . . eats up the neighbouring tissues'.[131]

(7) Metaphors from seafaring life. Butcher names two, of which one is certain.

(xxi) In **1 Timothy 1.19–20,** Paul says, 'By rejecting conscience, certain persons have suffered **shipwreck** [Gk, *enauagēsan*] in the faith; among them are Hymenaeus and Alexander.' The verb *nauageō* does indeed mean 'to suffer shipwreck', or 'to live through a ship's destruction', and is a cognate form with *naus,* a ship, and *nautēs*, a sailor; compare the English adjective 'nautical'.[132] The second example comes from 1 Timothy 6.9, and is more disputable. The KJV/AV translates, 'such as **drown** men in perdition'. But the Greek *buthizousin,* while often meaning to sink, may also mean to experience disastrous consequences, even if *buthos* usually means deep water.[133] This is another borderline case.

(8) Metaphors from mercantile life. This example mainly concerns Paul's use of the word *gain.* Is it genuinely metaphorical when Paul states that some people imagine that 'godliness is a means of gain' (1 Tim. 6.5)? Some might doubt whether the analogy is fully metaphorical when Paul exclaims, 'I am sure that he is able to guard until that day what I have entrusted to him' (2 Tim. 1.12). The term 'deposit' is the KJV/AV translation of the NRSV's 'what I have entrusted to him'. But the Greek word *parathēkē* means property entrusted to another as a deposit. It is either metaphorical or, at least, an accepted figurative part of the language.

---

[129] BDAG, p. 186.
[130] Mounce, *Pastoral Epistles*, p. 527.
[131] Kelly, *The Pastoral Epistles*, p. 184.
[132] BDAG, pp. 666–7.
[133] BDAG, p. 185.

(9) Metaphors drawn from the fowler's craft, that is, snares or traps. Clearly the first eight categories of metaphor are familiar in everyday life today. However, this last example cannot be said to be of the same familiarity, at least in urban life. Further, the metaphorical status of such examples may be questioned. Two of Butcher's examples concern 'the snare of the devil' (1 Tim. 3.7 and 2 Tim. 2.26). Technically the Greek term *pagis* does denote a device used to catch animals, the trap or snare, and is used as a piece of equipment for a bird catcher in Aesop and other pagan writers. Nevertheless it can also mean that which causes one to be suddenly or unexpectedly endangered, especially in battle. If the word is metaphorical it had become a rather pale metaphor by Paul's time. Similarly in 1 Timothy 6.9 the NRSV translates, 'Those who want to be rich . . . are trapped by many senseless and harmful desires.' Again, if this is metaphorical, it constitutes a borderline metaphor. We have not repeated again such familiar terms as 'adoption' and 'inheritance'.

We have discussed some *21 metaphors* from the Pastoral Epistles, of which only a very few may be disputed. If we were to regard the Pastoral Epistles, with Kelly and others, as genuinely Pauline, together with Ephesians and Colossians, this should be added to *47 metaphors* throughout the Pauline corpus. It may come as a positive surprise to review *68 uses of metaphors altogether.* This compares favourably with our expectations of pictures, symbols and metaphors in the Old Testament, the teaching of Jesus, and in the book of Revelation. Paul, as an effective preacher, pastor and communicator, draws constantly on his perceptions of, and practical involvements in, the physical and social world around him, and the spiritual parallels he draws. The book of Revelation, to which we now turn, constitutes a feast of visual imagery.

9

Pictures, symbols and images in the book of Revelation

Pictures and images in Revelation: their varied interpretation

The book of Revelation has more pictures and images than descriptive words. In this respect it constitutes a unique document in the New Testament. John, comments Robyn Whitaker, 'calls attention to the visual'.[1] John testifies to all that he is commanded to write down 'what he *saw*' (Gk, *hosa eiden*, Rev. 1.2). He is commissioned to write 'what you *see*' (Gk, *ho blepeis*, 1.11; *grapson ha eides*, 1.19).

The words 'I saw', Natasha and Anthony O'Hear comment, occur over 60 times (e.g. 1.12–13; 19.18; 22.8, etc.).[2] Often the term *ekphrasis* is used to describe a vivid, often dramatic, verbal description of a visual representation or work of art. Thus Whitaker observes that in the context of its times and culture, '*Ekphrasis*, particularly ekphrastic description of a deity, bridges the gap between word and image to create a means of access to the divine.'[3] *In the book of Revelation out of 404 verses some 440 pictures or images occur*, at least according to my reading of the text of the book. O'Hear and O'Hear observe:

> Rather than finding oneself in the midst of a straightforward linear narrative, one is plunged into a kaleidoscope of fantastic images and themes . . . The images have the vividness and potency of dreams – but also, at times, the elusiveness of dreams.[4]

In the ancient world, Whitaker argues, images and sight served to provide vividness (Gk, *enargeia*), clarity (Gk, *saphēneia*) and style appropriate for the subject matter (Gk, *lexis*). At once it seems that the book of Revelation

---

[1] Robyn J. Whitaker, *Ekphrasis, Vision, and Persuasion in the Book of Revelation* (WUNT 2, 410; Tübingen: Mohr, 2015), p. 7.

[2] Natasha and Anthony O'Hear, *Picturing the Apocalypse: The Book of Revelation in the Arts over Two Millennia* (Oxford: OUP, 2015), p. 18.

[3] Whitaker, *Ekphrasis*, p. 38.

[4] O'Hear and O'Hear, *Picturing the Apocalypse*, p. 15.

far outstrips the relevance of any other biblical book for demonstrating the power of pictures and images. Whitaker calls Revelation 'a visual feast'.[5] Richard Bauckham comments, 'The images of Revelation are symbols with evocative power inviting imaginative participation in the book's symbolic world.'[6]

At the beginning of this study we may note several claims about Revelation which are widely accepted. First, in his comprehensive commentary on the Greek text of the book, G. K. Beale begins, 'The revelation is not abstract but *pictorial*.'[7] He supports his claim partly by a comparison with Daniel 2.28–30, 45, where the Aramaic for 'made known' (*yeda'*) is rendered by the Greek Septuagint as the aorist tense of *sēmainō*, to signify. This allows for symbolic communication, including such visual imagery of the huge statue in Daniel as one of gold, silver, bronze and iron. This is Beale's starting point, although he adds much more.

Second, it is necessary to understand the nature of *metaphor*, as we have sought to do in Chapter 3, above. This is why to communicate through pictures is not a sharp alternative to revelation which can be retrospectively communicated through propositions. Thus, as we emphasized in Chapter 3, Janet Martin Soskice and Paul Ricoeur showed that metaphors can convey cognitive truth. On the other hand, George Caird rightly insists that to treat every vision or picture like an analytical catalogue would be 'to unweave the rainbow'.[8]

Third, many argue that the book of Revelation draws on a *transfigured mythology*. Brevard Childs, George Caird, and in effect Beale, insist that the New Testament writers use only 'broken' myth.[9] 'Broken myth' denotes what was formerly myth, but which has acquired a different, perhaps historical, cognitive or literal function. Mythical imagery, Childs argues, is used by biblical writers, for example to express the imposition of order on chaos in creation, but it has no longer its original *mythical function*. The key difference between myth and cognitive language is that in Ernst Cassirer's words, 'Mythical thinking comes to rest in the immediate experience'; mythical thinking is essentially *uncritical*.[10] Some suggest that myths are like dreams: they abound in pictorial imagery, but often at

5 Whitaker, *Ekphrasis*, p. 4.

6 Richard Bauckham, *The Theology of the Book of Revelation* (Cambridge: CUP, 1993), p. 18.

7 G. K. Beale, *The Book of Revelation: A Commentary on the Greek Text* (Grand Rapids: Eerdmans, 1999), p. 51 (my italics).

8 George B. Caird, *The Revelation of St. John the Divine* (London: Black, 1966), p. 25.

9 Brevard S. Childs, *Myth and Reality in the Old Testament* (London: SCM, 1962); G. B. Caird, *The Language and Imagery of the Bible* (London: Duckworth, 1980), p. 226.

10 Ernst Cassirer, *Language and Myth* (Eng., New York: Harper, 1946), p. 32.

first make little direct cognitive sense. We noted earlier that the O'Hears compared the images in Revelation to dreams. But when we reflect upon them critically and retrospectively, insights often begin to emerge.

Caird begins his commentary on Revelation by observing that modern readers are often put off by 'visions . . . about a throne and a scroll, seals, trumpets, and bowls, horsemen, locusts, a dragon and a monster . . .'[11] The place of visual representation should not surprise us, as we have already noted, when we recall that John received God's command to 'Write in a book what you *see*' (Rev. 1.11; Gk, *ho blepeis grapson*). Thus we can list: falling stars (Rev. 1.20; 6.13; 9.1); the tree of life (2.7; 22.2); a white stone (2.17); white robes (3.6, 18; 4.4; 6.11); the book of life (3.5; 17.8); the rainbow (4.3); the sea of glass (4.6); lion (4.7); flying eagle (4.7); scroll (5.1, 3, 7, 8, etc.); seven seals (5.1); seven horns (5.6); golden bowl (5.8); the white, red, black and pale-green horses (6.2–7); an earthquake (8.5); the 144,000 (7.4; 14.1); Wormwood (8.11); the bottomless pit (9.1, 11; 11.7; 20.1); locusts (9.3, 7); scorpions (9.3); Apollyon (9.11); trumpets (9.4; 10.7); the great red dragon (12.3; 16.13); the beast who arose from the sea (13.1); Babylon (14.8; 16.20); golden bowls (15.7; 17.1); the name which no one knows (19.12); the lake of fire (19.20); the great white throne (20.11); the New Jerusalem (21.2); and so on.

Nevertheless these visions are not mere description alone. At least two alternative motivations have been distinguished for this visual mode of communication. Whitaker, among others, argues that visual images also seek to *persuade*. This persuasion concerns the utter and unrivalled sovereignty of God, the Almighty, who is the Alpha and Omega of all world-history. The book is primarily written for an oppressed and persecuted people. The majority of scholars suggest that the writing is to be dated either in the time of Nero or perhaps more probably during the reign of Domitian. In this context, Whitaker argues, the visions may function as *proofs or evidence* of God's sovereignty. Yet before Edith Humphrey's work in 2007, relatively few studies were undertaken of the rhetorical function of visions in the book of Revelation. Humphrey cites 2 Corinthians 12.1–10 and Acts 7.54–60 as examples of visions which function as '*proofs*' in this way.[12] On the other hand, visions of the visual are notoriously subjective. That is why Paul insisted in 1 Corinthians 15 that 'proof' of the resurrection is provided not simply by visual impressions, but by *historical*

[11] Caird, *Revelation of St John*, p. 1.

[12] Edith M. Humphrey, *And I Turned to See the Voice: The Rhetoric of Vision in the New Testament* (Grand Rapids: Baker Academic, 2007), especially pp. 151–95. Cf. Whitaker, *Ekphrasis*, p. 25.

events. Whatever Conzelmann and Marxsen may claim about the 'spiritual' meaning of 'see', Pannenberg, Künneth, Wright and others insist that 'seeing' was historical, in line with the tradition of the empty tomb.[13]

Thus Richard Bauckham suggests a second (whether complementary or alternative) purpose or motivation of visual imagery. The pictures and images of Revelation also *counteract* the deluge of visual impressions which surrounded the first readers on behalf of the imperial cult of Rome. He writes:

> Readers in the great cities of the province of Asia were constantly confronted with powerful images of the Roman vision of the world . . . All provided powerful visual impressions of Roman imperial power and of the splendour of pagan religion.[14]

John, therefore, uses visual images as *counter-images* which provide alternative visions of how the world is and will be.

Further, Bauckham continues, Revelation is saturated with verbal allusions to the imagery of the Old Testament. He adds, 'It would be a serious mistake to understand the images of Revelation as *timeless* symbols. Their character conforms to the contextuality of Revelation.'[15] Very many of the pictures and images, it is agreed, find their origin in the book of Daniel, and in Ezekiel, as do the images about plagues from the plagues of Egypt which accompanied the exodus. Similarly the army of locusts was depicted in the prophecy of Joel. The interpretation of such images should clearly take full account of their original context and meaning in the Old Testament. The climax of visions of doom is the fall of Babylon in an earthquake of supernatural proportions (Rev. 16.17–21). This accompanies the theophany of the holy God. Bauckham comments:

> The sacking of Babylon by the beast and his allies alludes to the contemporary myth of the return of Nero to destroy Rome. It is an image of the self-destructive nature of evil, which on the level of theological meaning is not inconsistent with the idea of the destruction of evil by divine judgement.[16]

---

[13] Hans Conzelmann, 'On the Analysis of the Confessional Formula in 1 Cor. 15.3–5', *Int* 20 (1966), pp. 15–25; W. Marxsen, *The Resurrection of Jesus of Nazareth* (Eng., Philadelphia: Fortress, 1970), pp. 82–125; Wolfhart Pannenberg, *Systematic Theology*, vol. 3 ([Eng.] Grand Rapids: Eerdmans, 1998), pp. 555–80; Walther Künneth, *The Theology of the Resurrection* (Eng., London: SCM, 1965), pp. 40–53; N. T. Wright, *The Resurrection of the Son of God* (London: SPCK, 2003), pp. 207–374 and 401–79.

[14] Bauckham, *The Theology of the Book of Revelation*, p. 17.

[15] Bauckham, *The Theology of the Book of Revelation*, p. 19 (my italics).

[16] Bauckham, *The Theology of the Book of Revelation*, p. 21.

Craig Koester has produced what is probably the most definitive commentary on Revelation. It is nearly 900 pages.[17] His Introduction includes an extensive history of interpretation and influence.[18] What this mainly shows is the sheer diversity of ways in which Revelation has been understood. No consensus was reached until the twentieth century, if at all. Koester argues, 'Creating pictures in the minds of an audience is a powerful means of evoking emotion . . . Word pictures convey multiple meanings simultaneously.'[19]

The theocentric character of the pictures and images of Revelation

'The theology of Revelation', Bauckham observes, 'is highly theocentric.'[20] Thus in Revelation 1.8 we read: '"I am the Alpha and the Omega", says the Lord God, who is and who was and who is to come, the Almighty.' As Bauckham argues, this is strategically placed, and represents one of the two occasions in Revelation in which God himself speaks.[21] This is God's own self-manifestation and declaration. It is similar to the second passage, in which God's self-revelation is also expressed as 'the Alpha and Omega, the beginning and the end' (21.6). Further, Jesus Christ is also 'the first and the last' (1.17), and 'the Alpha and the Omega' (22.13).

'The seven spirits', representing the Holy Spirit, are parallel with the Spirit (2.7) and 'in the Spirit' (1.10), and indicate the fullness of the Holy Spirit, through the symbolic number 'seven'. This, in effect, constitutes a Trinitarian greeting and commission from God Almighty (Rev. 1.4b–5a).

Thus, whether we follow Whitaker in understanding the visions to be evidential, or follow Bauckham in seeing them as expressing the absolute sovereignty of God over all history from its beginning to its end, this opening vision demonstrates the sovereignty of God. It does so in the face of oppression of any kind and in the face of Roman imperial power. The oppressed readers may rest assured that God Almighty controls both the beginning and end of world history. God is the Alpha and the Omega, 'who is, and who was, and who is to come' (1.8).

This theme is repeated in 21.5–8 and 22.13. As is the case in many

---

[17] Craig R. Koester, *Revelation: A New Translation with Introduction and Commentary* (Anchor Bible; New Haven: Yale University Press, 2014).

[18] Koester, *Revelation*, pp. 27–65.

[19] Koester, *Revelation*, pp. 135 and 138.

[20] Bauckham, *The Theology of the Book of Revelation*, p. 23.

[21] Bauckham, *The Theology of the Book of Revelation*, p. 25.

declarations, it reflects the Old Testament: here, Isaiah 44.6. God is the origin and goal of all history, and Jewish writers reflect the same belief.[22] In total this is repeated five times: 1.4; 1.8; 4.8; 11.17; 16.5. It reflects the revelation to Moses in Exodus 3.14: 'I will be what I will be' (future imperfect, *'ehyeh 'ᵃsher 'ehyeh*, not simply 'I AM', as Greek LXX). Fiorenza comments, 'The central figure of the whole vision is clearly God enthroned in great splendour and surrounded by a court of angelic principalities and powers.'[23]

The image of the throne room in chapter 4 highlights God's sovereignty over all, as does also the word 'Almighty' (Gk, *pantokratōr*). The philosophers of religion Peter Geach and Gijsbert van den Brink insist that this is a much more appropriate word than the Latin-derived 'omnipotent' (Lat., *omnipotens*). Paul uses the Greek term in 2 Corinthians 6.18, and it occurs in Revelation in 1.8; 4.8; 11.17; 15.3; 19.6, 15; and 21.22. Van den Brink argues that *pantokratōr* means not only power over, but power for, that is, enabling power.[24] Richard Swinburne points out that 'omnipotence can allow unintended logical contradictions'.[25] The vision of God on the throne is granted when John is taken up into heaven (4.1). This is part of God's assurance to his oppressed people that he will accomplish his universal purpose of overcoming all evil and opposition to his rule. Heaven already acknowledges this universal rule. The vision is reminiscent of Isaiah 6 and Ezekiel 1.5–14. Revelation 4.3 begins to use more visual symbolism of precious stones to indicate God's majesty and splendour.

The vision of God's throne room is also set in the heavenly sanctuary in Revelation 11.19 and 15.5–8. The whole creation worships God and the Lamb (5.13). In the throne room 'the twenty-four elders' are present, interpreted by Bauckham as 'a political term . . . angelic beings who compose the divine council . . . who are themselves rulers', as their own thrones and crowns indicate.[26] Koester likewise comments, 'The portrayal of the elders gives the readers a glimpse of what awaits the faithful. Christ promised that those who conquer would wear white robes (3:5), be given wreaths (2:10), and have a place on his throne.'[27] The four creatures speak

[22] Josephus, *Antiquities*, 8.280; Philo, *De Plantatione*, 95.

[23] Elisabeth Schüssler Fiorenza, *Revelation: Vision of a Just World* (Minneapolis: Fortress, 1991), p. 59.

[24] Gijsbert van den Brink, *Almighty God: A Study of the Doctrine of Divine Omnipotence* (Studies in Philosophical Theology; Kampen: Kok Pharos, 1993).

[25] Richard Swinburne, *The Coherence of Theism* (Oxford: Clarendon Press, 1977), pp. 149–62.

[26] Bauckham, *The Theology of the Book of Revelation*, p. 34.

[27] Koester, *Revelation*, p. 368.

ceaselessly of God day and night (4.8). The picture and image of the slain Lamb, who shares absolute sovereignty with God, softens the image of the sovereignty of God, as not one of sheer force as such, because sovereignty is also through self-sacrifice.

God's almightyness receives further definition when compared and contrasted with John's critique of Roman imperial power. Bauckham writes:

> Revelation itself allows no neutral perception: either one shares Rome's own ideology . . . or one sees it from the perspective of heaven, which unmasks the pretensions of Rome . . . The two major symbols for Rome, which represent different aspects of the empire, are the sea-monster ('the beast': especially chapters 13 and 17) and the harlot of Babylon (especially chapters 17–18). The beast represents the military and political power of the Roman Emperors.[28]

Babylon is the city of Rome; its prosperity is gained by exploitation of the empire. The O'Hears similarly comment, 'There . . . can be no compromise between good and evil; for the unrighteous the lake of fire; for the righteous the New Jerusalem of Revelation 21–22.'[29] In 13.3–4 the beast receives a mortal wound in one of its seven heads. The Christian vision which John promoted is that of the incomparable God, who relativizes all Rome's pretensions and power. Thus the throne room of chapter 4 is foundational for the rest of the book.

Many of the visual symbols of Revelation witness to this theme. Thus trumpets (Rev. 1.10; 8.6, 10, 12; 9.14; 10.7) are a symbol of God's authoritative speaking (cf. Exod. 19.19). White hair constitutes a symbol of God's wisdom and eternity (Rev. 2.17). Thunder, lightning, cloud and smoke (4.5; 8.5; 11.19) are symbols of his majesty and glory. The tree of life (2.7; 22.2) represents the joy and growth of paradisal happiness, which comes with union with God. God holds 'the key of David, which opens and shuts' (3.7). Koester argues that this is drawn from Isaiah 22.22, where the house of David has authority to open and shut the way.[30] In Revelation God holds this authority.

One powerful symbol is the sealed scroll (5.1–5). No one but God can read it; it is sealed in mystery, with seven seals. The seals indicate the gravity of its contents. God holds the scroll, but the Lamb receives it, and opens all the seals. The disclosure of its mysteries comes through

---

28 Bauckham, *The Theology of Revelation*, p. 35.

29 O'Hear and O'Hear, *Picturing the Apocalypse*, p. 17.

30 Koester, *Revelation*, p. 323.

Christ alone. Revelation 11 probably discloses its content: on one hand the destruction of God's enemies in the 'bottomless pit', on the other hand the absolute sovereignty of God.[31] Like the whole of Revelation, the scroll discloses the secret of world history and beyond.

The section of the four horsemen and seven seals follows directly after the throne-room scene of Chapters 4 and 5. In Revelation 6 the Lamb is deemed worthy to open the scrolls. The first seal sets in motion the release of the four horsemen (Rev. 6.1, 2). As the O'Hears observe, the four horsemen are not satanic forces, because their existence is brought about by the Lamb.[32] This might seem to constitute a problem for theodicy. For in Revelation 6.8 the first 'white' horseman is described as representing conquest and a sword or war: in Koester's words, 'It is linked to conquest and victory.'[33] The second horseman is bright red, or fiery red (6.3–4), and represents war and famine. The third horseman is black, and represents famine and pestilence. The fourth horseman is sickly green (Gk, unusual word, *chlōros*), and represents death and wild beasts.[34] In relation to the problem of evil, this shows that world history constitutes a mixture of pain and blessing. It includes the suffering and death of Christ.

Bauckham points out that the symbols are not anthropomorphic; indeed they avoid anthropomorphic language, especially any similarity between the brute force of Roman imperial power and God's absolute sovereignty. The pictorial imagery 'suggests the incomparability of God's sovereignty'.[35] Fiorenza also underlines this point. She states:

> No attempt . . . is made to visualize God in human form. The glorious presence of the 'One on the throne' manifests itself in the brilliance of light reflected by precious stones of opaque diamondlike jasper, blood-red sardis, and colourless emerald refracting a rainbow of prismatic colours, the sign of God's covenant with creation.[36]

The O'Hears point out that the ninth-century *Trier Apocalypse* has its picture of the four horsemen below a heavy black line, to distinguish world history from the purity of the throne room, depicted above the line.[37]

---

31 Koester, *Revelation*, pp. 383–4.
32 O'Hear and O'Hear, *Picturing the Apocalypse*, p. 73.
33 Koester, *Revelation*, p. 393.
34 O'Hear and O'Hear, *Picturing the Apocalypse*, p. 73.
35 Bauckham, *The Theology of the Book of Revelation*, p. 43.
36 Fiorenza, *Revelation: Vision of a Just World*, p. 59.
37 O'Hear and O'Hear, *Picturing the Apocalypse*, pp. 72 and 76.

By the twelfth century the four horsemen were depicted separately, as illustrated by the thirteenth-century *Lambeth Apocalypse*.[38]

But by the fourteenth century, errors concerning the text of Revelation began to creep in. The colour of the third horseman was wrong in the *Angers Tapestry*, and the fourth horseman was depicted as a skeleton.[39] By the fifteenth century Memling's visualization of the four horsemen 'presents a completely different picture', including a possible association with the dragon in Revelation 12.[40] By the time of Albrecht Dürer and Lucas Cranach many imaginative details are added. The biblical pictures can now serve other purposes than those intended by John. By the eighteenth century, the pale horse has become confused with the horse which was a symbol of the house of Hanover. In *The Presages of the Millennium* (1795), satirist James Gillray depicts Prime Minister William Pitt as a skeletal apocalyptic figure, riding such a horse. The O'Hears write, 'The monkey seated behind Pitt is the Prince of Wales. Pitt had formerly supported his accession to the throne during George III's period of mental illness, an act which linked them in a sort of alliance.'[41]

William Blake's *Death on a Pale Horse* appears to have conflated the four horsemen into two, with a figure of reptilian skin and an angel with unfurled scroll.[42] Finally, the twentieth century produced some modern satire. The *Sunday Express* produced in August 1943, at the height of the war, a satire involving Heinrich Himmler, ironically without horses, to indicate the evil of the Nazi regime, while the *Sunday Times* in May 1977 utilized the four horsemen to comment on the unofficial meeting of the G7, involving James Callaghan, Jimmy Carter and Helmut Schmidt. Their banners indicate world crises.[43] *The four horsemen exercise a powerful spell, but have been radically decontextualized.*

O'Hear and O'Hear conclude:

> Clint Eastwood's *Pale Rider*, a film from 1985, serves as a good example of this sort of decontextualized usage. The film . . . is set in a mining village in California in the 1880s. A mysterious pale rider known as the Preacher appears . . . [His] main enemy is a man named Sheriff Stockburn . . . Eastwood has appropriated the name and the idea of the pale rider . . . in a somewhat perverse way.[44]

---

[38] O'Hear and O'Hear, *Picturing the Apocalypse*, pp. 76 and 77.

[39] O'Hear and O'Hear, *Picturing the Apocalypse*, pp. 76 and 77.

[40] O'Hear and O'Hear, *Picturing the Apocalypse*, p. 78 and Plate 3 in colour.

[41] O'Hear and O'Hear, *Picturing the Apocalypse*, p. 83; see also p. 85, Figure 3.8.

[42] O'Hear and O'Hear, *Picturing the Apocalypse*, pp. 83–7.

[43] O'Hear and O'Hear, *Picturing the Apocalypse*, pp. 87–9; cf. pp. 89–92.

[44] O'Hear and O'Hear, *Picturing the Apocalypse*, p. 91.

However, 'The most decontextualized of all', they argue, is the work of the 'new atheists', Richard Dawkins, Sam Harris, Daniel Dennett and the late Christopher Hitchens, in their 2007 DVD, *The Four Horsemen in Conversation*. They introduce 'memes' or 'selfish genes' which capture and direct the behaviour of humankind.[45] *These examples brilliantly substantiate our claim throughout this book that vivid pictures are powerful and necessary, but without careful interpretation can mislead and seduce us.*

The picture of the four horsemen is dominant in Revelation chapter 6. Revelation 7 then paints an anticipatory eschatological vision of the sealing of the redeemed. Chapter 8 picks up the allusion to the seven seals in 6.1–17, and expounds them further in 8.1—11.7, ending with the vision of the 'bottomless pit' or abyss. Some have regarded the destruction unleashed by the seven Seals, the trumpets, and the bowls or vials as cyclical repetitions of the four horsemen, or even messianic woes, as in *4 Ezra*. But the repetition is not exact; it is not replication. Yet neither is it linear or chronological.

One of the few modern commentators who understood the structure to be chronological was R. H. Charles, who at the same time described the author as a 'shallow-brained fanatic', and found it necessary to propose a different sequence in the text.[46] From Victorinus of Pettau (third century) onwards most have judged that Revelation proceeds by some sort of recapitulation. Caird argues that any attempt to force John into some chronological framework

> founders on a reef of difficulties . . . John is like an expert guide in an art gallery . . . First he makes [people] stand back to absorb a general impression, then he takes them to study the details . . . The unity of John's book, then, is neither chronological nor arithmetical, but artistic.[47]

Before the trumpets of judgement are introduced in Revelation 8—11, the anticipatory vision of chapter 7, to which we referred briefly, the Church militant, is sealed against all harm.[48] Chapter 7 interrupts the seal septet, and keeps the reader in suspense. The centre of the vision is the lion-like Lamb, who symbolizes the risen Christ. His earlier symbols of the seven horns and seven eyes 'signify . . . fullness of power and omniscient control

[45] O'Hear and O'Hear, *Picturing the Apocalypse*, p. 92.
[46] R. H. Charles, *A Critical and Exegetical Commentary on the Revelation of St. John* (ICC; 2 vols, Edinburgh: T&T Clark, 1929), vol. 1, p. liv.
[47] Caird, *The Revelation of St. John the Divine*, pp. 105–6.
[48] W. Hendriksen, *More Than Conquerors* (London: Tyndale Press, 1962), p. 116.

over the world'.[49] The sealing provides a mark by which the sealed are recognized as belonging to Christ, and are under his protection. In the second part of the chapter (7.9–17) the great multitude from all nations are clothed in white, with palms of victory in their hands. They have 'washed their robes in the blood of the Lamb', and God's presence shines on them.

There is some advance in chapters 8—11, including the vision of the seven trumpets and seven bowls or vials. But in the main these chapters recapitulate and escalate much of what has gone before. The fifth, sixth and seventh seals are expanded, while the seven woes are reminiscent of the plagues, including locusts and hail, which were visited upon Egypt (Exodus 8—11). The destruction in these chapters comes through angels, not through the demonic beasts of Revelation 11, 13 or 17. O'Hear and O'Hear trace some of the historical attempts to visualize these visions in art. The *Trinity Apocalypse* (*c*.1260) pictures the sixth seal, but associates the darkening of the sun with the alleged punishment of the Jews for rejecting Christ. The *Gulbenkian Apocalypse* (*c*.1270) separates good and bad Jews. Francis Danby's *The Opening of the sixth seal* (1828) portrays a tiny humanity crushed by overpowering natural forces. Thereby it anticipates many modern disaster films.[50]

In the vision of the seven trumpets, Aune observes that a series of plagues is unleashed, beginning with hail, fire and blood, and a great mountain is thrown into the sea.[51] This depicts genuinely apocalyptic events. The third trumpet depicts the appearance of a star named Wormwood (Gk, *apsinthos*, Rev. 8.12), which poisons rivers and springs. The fifth trumpet also causes a star to fall from heaven to earth, 'and releases from the bottomless pit a plague of locusts, who harm only those lacking God's seal' (9.1–12). Aune regards this as an army of demons. John's narrative of the plagues, he says, does not have repentance as its aim. The O'Hears agree, observing:

> We see John and the sixth angel looking at the 'myriad' horsemen (said to number 200 million in Rev. 9:16), here depicted as demonic riders aboard monstrous horses with heads of lions and tails of serpents, as described in Rev. 9.17–19.[52]

They provide an artistic visualization of the seven trumpets from Albrecht Dürer's 'Apocalypse' series (*c*.1498). Dürer's images are detailed

---

[49] Fiorenza, *Revelation: Vision of a Just World*, p. 60.

[50] O'Hear and O'Hear, *Picturing the Apocalypse*, pp. 93–102.

[51] David Aune, *Revelation 6–16* (WBC; Nashville: Nelson, 1998), p. 495.

[52] O'Hear and O'Hear, *Picturing the Apocalypse*, p. 104.

and literalistic in content. The seven bowls or vials (Gk, *phialē*) were broad, shallow bowls, from which liquid content could readily be poured out. Caird comments:

> It cannot be accidental that John has used in such quick succession echoes of two Old Testament prophecies [Jer. 51.25, 42, and Isa. 14.12–20] which have to do with the fall of ancient Babylon. We are justified therefore in supposing that Wormwood is the star of the new Babylon, which was poisoned by its idolatry and the springs of its own life . . . Babylon's ruin is at hand.[53]

Pictures and images in the remainder of Revelation

It is unnecessary to trace the content and theme of every chapter. But we may select visualizations and images which leave an indelible impression on popular imagination and the history of art. Chapter 10.1–11 concerns the little scroll; 11.1–3, 4–14, the measuring of the Temple; 12.1–6, the two witnesses; 12.7–12, the woman clothed with the sun, and the birth of the Messiah; 13.1–18, war in heaven and the monsters from the abyss and from the land; chapter 17, the whore of Babylon; chapter 20, arguably Armageddon, the millennium and the Last Judgement; and 21, the New Jerusalem.[54]

The O'Hears write, 'The Woman Clothed with the Sun (Revelation 12) is one of the most strikingly beautiful images in Revelation.'[55] This picture perhaps draws on Genesis 3, with possible echoes of Eve and the serpent; Exodus 14 and 19, in which Israel is pursued by Pharaoh; and possibly traditions from the Gospels about Mary and messianic woes. Some also speculate about non-biblical sources. The woman's being clothed with the sun denotes her heavenly status, and she is about to give birth, but is pursued by the red dragon. The dragon is part of the satanic trinity of beasts, and is later identified as Satan. The consensus of modern commentaries is that the woman is certainly not Mary, the mother of Jesus, but the messianic community, or perhaps an imaginative figure projected on to the starry skies, representing the cosmic struggle between good and evil. This consensus is evidenced by Caird, Mounce, Kiddle, Fiorenza, Beasley-Murray and Koester, among others.[56]

---

[53] Caird, *The Revelation of St John*, p. 115.

[54] Caird, *The Revelation of St John*, pp. 124–281.

[55] O'Hear and O'Hear, *Picturing the Apocalypse*, p. 111.

[56] Caird, *The Revelation of St John*, pp. 149–50; Robert H. Mounce, *The Book of Revelation* (London: Marshall, Morgan & Scott, 1977), pp. 235–6; Martin Kiddle, *The Revelation of*

David Aune considers a variety of interpretations: (1) the Virgin Mary, as advocated by Oecumenicus, (2) the Christian Church, as advocated by Hippolytus, (3) the heavenly Jerusalem, as advocated today by Harrington, (4) the persecuted people of God, as advocated today by Yarbro Collins, (5) an astrological figure, perhaps Virgo, as advocated by F. Boll, and (6) Isis, an Egyptian cosmic queen, as suggested by J. Bergman.[57] Aune and Koester, however, regard cosmic conflict as the dominant theme.[58]

In the mediaeval period, however, especially in the thirteenth century, most commentators took the view that the woman was the Virgin Mary. But there are exceptions. The O'Hears examine the *Bamberg Apocalypse* (*c.*1000), in which the woman is huge, with a sun wheel around her head, standing on the moon, holding a male child, who is to become the messianic King. Below them hisses the dragon or serpent menacingly. Because of her size, they argue, it is unlikely that she is the Virgin Mary, but rather 'the Church, presiding over Salvation History'.[59] The *Bamberg Apocalypse* has a second picture which represents the woman fleeing into the wilderness. She is a contending cosmic force. The serpent is coiled and spitting. The O'Hears next consider the Solos manuscript of *Beatus* Apocalypses (1109), which has a huge seven-headed snake, in turn associated with the beast that represents Rome. However, they point out, this time the snake was associated 'with Islam, which posed a serious threat to Spanish Christianity by the eighth century. This image follows a pattern established in many *Beatus* manuscripts'.[60] Its inset alludes to the second battle of Revelation 20. It well portrays the insidious power of evil, but does not follow the text of Revelation in its context.

By the thirteenth century the *Trinity Apocalypse* (*c.*1260) pictures the woman

> in a convent-like setting . . . [and] depicts [her] with a gentle demeanour and cloak of blue and gold [which] would certainly suggest an identification with the Virgin . . . Her calmness and inner repose are very typical of contemporary representations of the Virgin Mary.[61]

St John (London: Hodder & Stoughton, 1940), p. 220; G. R. Beasley-Murray, *The Book of Revelation* (London: Oliphants, 1974), p. 197; Koester, *Revelation*, pp. 525–6; Fiorenza, *Revelation: Vision of a Just World*, p. 80.

57 Aune, *Revelation*, p. 680.

58 Koester, *Revelation*, p. 525.

59 O'Hear and O'Hear, *Picturing the Apocalypse*, p. 116; cf. p. 117.

60 O'Hear and O'Hear, *Picturing the Apocalypse*, p. 118; cf. Plate 23.

61 O'Hear and O'Hear, *Picturing the Apocalypse*, pp. 120–1.

By now, devotion to the Virgin Mary is becoming interwoven with apocalyptic struggle. This is perpetuated in the fourteenth and fifteenth centuries. In the *St John Altarpiece* (1474–9) the woman is Mary, who wears a deep blue cloak and a golden crown. There is an upper and lower level, representing heavenly and earthly domains: 'She appears in her heavenly incarnation standing in a bright yellow, oval-shaped sun just to the right of the heavenly throne room.'[62] Nevertheless, in Dürer's image of *Revelation 12* (1498), 'strangely' the woman is not clearly Mary. She is perhaps neither Mary nor the Church, but 'a sort of every-woman figure'.[63]

Diego Velázquez (1599–1660), the Spanish painter, painted in the wake of a papal decree defending the doctrine of the Immaculate Conception (1617). Velázquez's *Immaculate Conception* symbolizes the purity of the Virgin Mary, and draws on the Song of Solomon. It would be difficult to see her as the Church. Two centuries later, William Blake (1757–1827) produced an image of the woman clothed in the sun attacked by the dragon (Blake's *The Great Red Dragon and the Woman Clothed with the Sun: the Devil Is Come Down*). This is striking, but 'fantastical and enclosed in what looks like his own private constructions and interpretations, hard to place within the linear tradition of Christian interpretation'.[64] It is 'hard to interpret'. Later on, Odilon Redon's *A Woman Clothed with the Sun* (Rev. 12.1; 1899) is 'sensually seductive, half-mythical', and is 'on the cusp of becoming a secularized text, a compendium of images'.[65] All this confirms that pictures and images are powerful, but can readily seduce us when they wander from their appropriate context.

O'Hear and O'Hear choose as their next example what they call 'The Satanic Trinity', while others call them a hybrid figure of satanic beasts. It is relatively easy to distinguish the two beasts of Revelation 13. Koester calls these the beast from the sea (12.18—13.10) and the beast from the land (13.11–18).[66] Revelation 13.1–2 reads:

> And I saw a beast rising out of the sea . . . and on its horns were ten diadems, and on its heads were blasphemous names. And the beast that I saw was like a leopard, its feet were like a bear's, and its mouth was like a lion's mouth. And the dragon gave it his power and his throne and great authority.

[62] O'Hear and O'Hear, *Picturing the Apocalypse*, p. 122.
[63] O'Hear and O'Hear, *Picturing the Apocalypse*, p. 122.
[64] O'Hear and O'Hear, *Picturing the Apocalypse*, p. 127.
[65] O'Hear and O'Hear, *Picturing the Apocalypse*, p. 127.
[66] Koester, *Revelation*, pp. 568–606.

In verse 3 'One of its heads seemed to have received a death-blow, but its mortal wound had been healed.' This is often interpreted as a reference to the Nero myth. Koester comments, 'Revelation invokes the Nero legend to show that Nero's legacy defines Roman rule as a whole . . . The tale of surviving death was linked particularly to Nero, who was remembered as the great persecutor (13:7).'[67] Caird similarly writes, 'Nero will indeed return, reincarnated in a new persecuting emperor, an eighth who is [additionally] one of the seven.'[68] Many regard the current emperor as Domitian.

The monster out of the sea, Caird continues, is described as rising from the abyss (Rev. 11.7). John, he says, takes the abyss to be synonymous with the underworld or the cosmic depths. The dragon conferred on the monster his own power and throne. The sea-beast exercises authority for 'forty-two months' (Rev. 13.5). The second beast, the earth-beast, works for the sea-beast (Rev. 13.16). It is difficult to explicate 'a deeply mysterious passage in Rev. 13.8 . . . We simply do not know what exactly John meant by these words, beyond an insistence that unlike the Roman . . . empire God's law and rule . . . are eternal'.[69] The earth-beast parodies some of the actions of Christ. Hence it has lamb-like horns, and masquerades as a prophet. In view of this, although the term *Antichrist* does not occur in Revelation, this theme gave rise to mediaeval language about the Antichrist. Albrecht Dürer (*c.*1498) depicted the two beasts of Revelation 13.

But what is the third beast? O'Hear and O'Hear speak of the sea-beast, the earth-beast and the dragon. The *Trinity Apocalypse* (*c.*1260) pictures the dragon next to the sea-beast, handing him a sceptre. The sea-beast resembles a leopard (Rev. 13.2), has a bear's feet and seven lion-like heads. The *Gulbenkian Apocalypse* (*c.*1280) depicts the beast rising from the sea as the Antichrist, teaching blasphemy and sinfulness. The *Angers Apocalypse Tapestry* (*c.*1373–80) depicts the worship of the beast, and the three beasts vomiting frogs. *The Flemish Apocalypse* (*c.*1400), they argue, depicts the sea-beast, the earth-beast and the dragon, with the earth-beast parody of the Lamb.[70]

In the Reformation era, directly anti-papist pictures and images began to be associated with the monsters or beasts of Revelation. Some call the pictures an anti-Catholic visual polemic. Hendrick Hondius, the Dutch artist, produced the *Papist Pyramid* (1599) depicting a pyramid of snakes

---

[67] Koester, *Revelation*, p. 581.
[68] Caird, *The Revelation of St. John*, p. 165.
[69] O'Hear and O'Hear, *Picturing the Apocalypse*, pp. 134 and 136.
[70] O'Hear and O'Hear, *Picturing the Apocalypse*, Plate 29.

wearing Roman Catholic headdresses, which culminate in a more threatening snake wearing the papal triple tiara.[71] Lucas Cranach the Elder includes illustrations for Luther's Bible, which are similarly anti-Catholic pictures of the earth-beast. Centuries later, William Blake has a horrific picture of the satanic trinity in his *The Number of the Beast Is 666* (*c.*1810).[72] His picture *The Great Red Dragon and the Beast from the Sea* (*c.*1805) appears to portray the dragon giving birth to the sea-beast. Both beasts have ram's horns.

In modern times the beasts of Revelation are depicted as functioning in numerous ways. O'Hear and O'Hear comment:

> The polyvalency of the imagery used to describe the Beasts in Revelation 12–13 and elsewhere means that many different groups can find comfort in the imagery by identifying their oppressors with the oppressed nations of Revelation 13. Firstly, the polyvalency of the imagery means that others can hijack it for more sinister events.[73]

They see many of the most *context-free suggestions* as coming from America. In the twentieth century they cite a range of 'apocalyptic' scenarios, beginning with the First World War. In the Der Krieg series (Dix, 1924), horror gave way to anti-Nazi developments in the 1940s and finally to post-war pictures of nuclear holocausts. These include the so-called *Manchester Apocalypse* (2011, by James Chadderton) and the 'Apocalypse V2' series (2014, also by James Chadderton), which depict a collapsed, post-nuclear wasteland of Manchester and London.[74]

In popular imagination O'Hear and O'Hear cite Tim LaHaye and Jerry Jenkins' Left Behind series, which is widely influential in America (apparently selling 65 million copies), based on a particular understanding of 'the rapture', and Hal Lindsey's *The Late Great Planet Earth*.[75] These, however, represent generalized pictures of the End, rather than specific portrayals of the three satanic monsters. They also note that in secularized pictures of the End, the redemptive aspect found in Revelation is virtually absent.

Other chapters in Revelation feature pictures, metaphors and symbols which we have not yet fully explored. From chapter 11 onwards these include the bottomless abyss (11.7), Michael (12.7), marks on foreheads

---

[71] O'Hear and O'Hear, *Picturing the Apocalypse*, p. 148.

[72] O'Hear and O'Hear, *Picturing the Apocalypse*, Plate 31.

[73] O'Hear and O'Hear, *Picturing the Apocalypse*, p. 152.

[74] O'Hear and O'Hear, *Picturing the Apocalypse*, p. 250.

[75] O'Hear and O'Hear, *Picturing the Apocalypse*, pp. 245–74.

(12.16), 666 (13.18), the 144,000 (14.1), the fall of Babylon (14.8; 17.5; 18.2, 21), the sea of glass (15.1), white robes (15.6), Harmageddon or Armageddon (16.16), the woman in scarlet (17.3–4), the book of life (17.8), the marriage of the Lamb (19.7), the name which no one knows (19.12), the lake of fire (19.20), Gog and Magog (20.8), the New Jerusalem (21.2), the spring of the water of life ((21.6), the 12 gates (21.12), the 12 jewels (21.20) and the river of the water of life (22.1). This list is far from exhaustive, but includes only some of the more widely known examples.

Nevertheless, we must heed George Caird's warnings, already noted, that we must not try 'to unweave the rainbow' by attempting to 'decode' these symbols one by one in a crude literalism. To attempt this would undermine John's purpose of presenting *visual* imagery, even with the hope that it would not be entirely decontextualized. It would in effect replace the visual entirely by a written text.

Yet some images seem better left as suggestive internal mental images than as external visual phenomena. For example, 'the River of Life' has been depicted by William Blake through a visual depiction that to me, at least, is less suggestive of John's intent than his verbal image (Rev. 22.1).[76] The same might be said of 'the New Jerusalem Descending' in the *Angers Apocalypse Tapestry.*[77] Rather than depicting the people of God, it portrays buildings with five stone towers or steeples, in spite of the huge dimensions of the city in Revelation, demonstrating that the 'city' is entirely symbolic. Gundry is emphatic that the New Jerusalem represents the redeemed people of God.[78] Koester and Mathewson discuss the New Jerusalem and the Bride of the Lamb (Gk, both *gynē* and *nymphē*, Rev. 21.2 and 9) extensively.[79]

Koester and Mathewson refer to such Old Testament passages as Isaiah 65.17–19, Jeremiah 31.38–40, and especially Ezekiel 48.30–35 and also 43.1–5; 47.1, 12. Jerusalem is the opponent of Babylon. Koester comments, 'The bride is taken to the bridegroom's house . . . [and] enters the life or presence of God.'[80] Bauckham regards this as paradise.[81] The *Angers Apocalypse Tapestry* conveys little, if anything, of this, except perhaps

[76] See O'Hear and O'Hear, *Picturing the Apocalypse*, Plate 44.

[77] See O'Hear and O'Hear, *Picturing the Apocalypse,* Plate 46.

[78] Robert H. Gundry, 'The New Jerusalem', in Gundry, *The Old Is Better* (Tübingen: Mohr, 2005), pp. 399–411.

[79] Koester, *Revelation*, pp. 810–25; David Mathewson, *A New Heaven and New Earth: The Meaning and Function of the Old Testament in Revelation 21:1 – 22:5* (JSNTSup 238; London: Sheffield Academic Press, 2003).

[80] Koester, *Revelation*, p. 812.

[81] Bauckham, *The Theology of the Book of Revelation*, p. 133.

indirectly through angels. In this *Tapestry*, the river of the water of life shows how a concrete picture falls far short of John's imaginative (verbal) vision.[82] This may sometimes happen when a favourite book is turned into a film. Gordon Cheung, *Rivers of Bliss* (2007), goes further, but not everyone will regard it as adequately matching John's vision.[83]

Armageddon (or NRSV and near Hebrew, Harmageddon, Rev. 16.16) was historically a hill of Megiddo, which was the site of a great battle between King Neco of Egypt and King Josiah, in which Josiah died (2 Chron. 35.22), although only Megiddo, not Armageddon, is explicitly mentioned. Symbolically, however, Armageddon constitutes a visual representation of violent catastrophe, which we have not yet explored. O'Hear and O'Hear observe:

> No term from Revelation is more widely found in common usage, and arguably more misinterpreted, than Armageddon. In popular thought and culture, Armageddon is practically synonymous with the term Apocalypse itself, and the two of them seem virtually interchangeable as a sort of shorthand for the end of the world, particularly if there is some idea of a nuclear disaster in the background. References in the popular media abound, from the humorous 'Dial 00000000 for Armageddon. US's top secret launch code was frighteningly simple' to the biblical [question], 'Is Syria the latest sign of Armageddon?'[84]

They conclude: 'So the word Armageddon has become an all-purpose cliché, used almost as a knee-jerk reaction, to describe any environmental, nuclear, or financial disaster, real or imagined.'[85]

The O'Hears further cite *The Independent* of July 2013, which applies Armageddon to global warming. They also cite Bruce Willis' *Armageddon* (1998), which concerns destroying an asteroid which travels towards the Earth. They even cite a yearly comic book convention in New Zealand known as Armageddon Expo, although they do point out that the notion of a *yearly* Armageddon is paradoxical. They admit that this extravagant decontextualized use of Revelation 16.16 is not entirely 'wrong', since Revelation does use the term to symbolize a decisive battle between good and evil, and the final catastrophe. But John also stresses that God through Christ will decisively destroy Satan, the beasts and their followers. Thus Armageddon should not be gloomy, but joyous.

---

[82] O'Hear and O'Hear, *Picturing the Apocalypse*, Plate 47.

[83] O'Hear and O'Hear, *Picturing the Apocalypse*, Plate 49.

[84] O'Hear and O'Hear, *Picturing the Apocalypse*, p. 178; and the *Daily Mail*, November 2013 and September 2013.

[85] O'Hear and O'Hear, *Picturing the Apocalypse*, p. 178.

Armageddon was pictured in the mediaeval era in different ways. The *St Sever Beatus Manuscript* of *c.*1076 provides an early visualization of a simple three-tier design which it calls Armageddon (Rev. 19.11–21 and 20.7–10), but combines the Lamb standing in judgement and the death of the beast and Satan.[86] By the time of the *Lambeth Apocalypse* (*c.*1260) the picture of Armageddon becomes more complex, with the defeat of the army of the beast (Rev. 19.20). It also portrays Armageddon 2 in which Satan or the dragon is cast into the abyss of fire with the two beasts.[87] The *Gulbenkian Apocalypse* (*c.*1270) portrays the defeated armies of Satan overcome by the elect; the former with mediaeval weapons, the latter with mitres and crosiers.[88] The *Flemish Apocalypse* (*c.*1400) depicts events from Revelation 19—21, including the marriage of the Lamb, the beasts and Armageddon.[89]

The modern era brings a completely new mindset. The Belgian artist Frans Masereel produced *Aeroplanes over Mankind* (1944), which has become more of a notion of apocalypse than an interpretation of Revelation. The popular secular press, however, is not alone in very loosely interpreting or misinterpreting the message of Revelation and Armageddon. There are strands in Dispensationalist expositions of Revelation which relate the final battle to political consequences supporting the establishment and continuance of the State of Israel. Some refer to a battle of the First World War in September 1918, which ensured the end of the Ottoman domination of the Middle East. Some even called Field Marshal Viscount Allenby of Megiddo and Felixstowe 'Conqueror of Syria, and Liberator of the Holy Land'. Hence it is by no means entirely fanciful to associate the founding of the State of Israel by the Balfour Declaration of 1917 to some extent with Armageddon, provided that it is clear that this would not have entered John's mind.

Bernard McGinn has provided a classic treatment of apocalyptic, the Antichrist and Armageddon.[90] He brilliantly shows how in some influential American circles these are intermingled with dispensationalism and the founding and establishment of the modern Jewish state. He refers to the preaching of John Nelson Darby and others with a 'premillennialist' account of the events of the End. Millenarianism is the belief in a thousand-year period in which saints will rule, while the devil is bound. This

[86] O'Hear and O'Hear, *Picturing the Apocalypse*, Plate 39.

[87] O'Hear and O'Hear, *Picturing the Apocalypse*, Plate 40.

[88] O'Hear and O'Hear, *Picturing the Apocalypse*, pp. 185–6, Figure 8.3.

[89] O'Hear and O'Hear, *Picturing the Apocalypse*, pp. 186–8 and Figure 8.4.

[90] Bernard McGinn, *Antichrist: Two Thousand Years of the Human Fascination with the Devil* (San Francisco: Harper, 1994), pp. 250–80.

depends on a debatable reading of Revelation 20.1–10, and some other passages such as the so-called rapture in 1 Thessalonians 4.16–17. 'Premillennialists' believe that the millennium will *follow* the Parousia (or future return of Christ); 'post-millennialists' believe that it will occur *before* the return of Christ. A premillennial view was defended by Darby and the *Scofield Reference Bible* (1909), together with J. F. Walvoord and the popular writer Hal Lindsey. Caird calls the theory 'demonstrably false'. These also encouraged Zionist hopes for the establishment of the Jewish state. Dispensationalism, McGinn insists, involves

> the conviction that after predicting ancient history quite fully for many centuries, biblical prophecy took a holiday for almost two thousand years (the dispensation of the Gentiles) between the fall of the Second Temple of Jerusalem in 70 C.E. and the restoration of the Jewish state in 1948.[91]

McGinn adds that 'Dispensationalist apocalypticism had been obsessed with the place of the Jews in the end-time'.[92]

Some premillennialist views after the Second World War alluded to the explosion of the atomic bomb, allegedly the European Common Market, Russian interest in the Middle East, and other events. Lindsey's *The Late Great Planet Earth* (1970) sold more than 25 million copies by the mid 1990s. Some predicted the invasion of Israel by Russia as the prelude to Armageddon. Lindsey interprets Armageddon as a symbol of the Third World War, with its cataclysmic threat.[93] He also understands the symbol of Gog and Magog as representing a Russian invasion of Israel. McGinn concludes, 'Apocalyptic symbols are capable of retaining an archaic power to reveal meaning even when the precise beliefs they originally expressed have become outmoded.'[94]

Yet dispensationalists can find precedents for a literal interpretation of the millennium as 1,000 years. The *Epistle of Barnabas* (the first or early second century) wrote on the days of creation, at which on the seventh day 'the Lord will finish all things in six thousand years' of human history.[95] The Montanists looked to Revelation 21, their notion of an earthly kingdom, and Tertullian believed in a literal millennium. Tertullian argued:

> After its thousand years are over, within which period is completed the resurrection of the Saints, who rise sooner or later according to their deserts,

[91] McGinn, *Antichrist*, p. 253.
[92] McGinn, *Antichrist*, p. 255.
[93] Hal Lindsey, *The Late Great Planet Earth* (Grand Rapids: Zondervan, 1970), pp. 152–7.
[94] McGinn, *Antichrist*, p. 277.
[95] *Epistle of Barnabas* 15.3–5 (Eng., ANF, vol. 1, p. 146).

> there will come the destruction of the world and the conflagration of all things at the judgement.[96]

Origen, Methodius and Eusebius, however, reject the notion of a literal thousand years, while Tyconius and Augustine of Hippo understand the millennium to represent the whole of the Church's history.[97] The contrast continues with Jerome, who insisted on a spiritual kingdom, and Joachim of Fiore, who argued for an earthly fulfilment. However, the critique of a literal millennium or of chiliasm persisted in modernity. Kovacs and Rowland comment:

> The difficulties of Rev. 20.4–6 were widely recognized . . . The critique of chiliasm [known as amillennialism] developed in post-Constantinian Christianity and re-emerges with Beza . . . This is being fulfilled in the work of the Reformation . . . The millennium signifies eternity.[98]

One further set of symbols concerns the false prophet (Rev. 16.13; 19.20; 20.10; Gk, *pseudoprophētēs*), those who 'practise abomination or falsehood' (Rev. 21.27; 22.15; Gk, *pseusma*) and related themes of deception or hypocrisy (Rev. 12:19; 13.14; 18.23; 19.20; 20.3, 8, 10). Often, as in John Wycliffe, this is part of the visible Church, in contrast to the invisible Church of true believers. Although the term *Antichrist* does not explicitly occur in Revelation, this theme dominated late mediaeval thought, as McGinn thoroughly documents.

Craig Koester has a full exposition of false prophecy in the shape of the Beast from the Land in Revelation 13.11–18. He offers five interpretations of the land-beast, four of which relate to aspects of the imperial cult. Under the fourth interpretation, he discusses 'Christians who accommodate pagan practice'. He writes,

> The land beast is a false prophet (16:13; 19:20; 20:10). Within the Christian community there was a false prophet nicknamed Jezebel, who taught that it was acceptable to eat what had been sacrificed to Graeco-Roman deities . . . Just as the beast masquerades as a lamb, Jezebel [cf. Rev. 2.20] purports to follow Jesus the Lamb, yet both deceive people into false worship.[99]

---

[96] Tertullian, *Against Marcion*, Bk 3, ch. 24 (Eng., ANF, vol. 3, p. 343).

[97] Cf. Judith Kovacs and Christopher Rowland, *Revelation* (Blackwell Bible Commentaries; Oxford: Blackwell, 2004), pp. 203–7.

[98] Kovacs and Rowland, *Revelation*, p. 211.

[99] Koester, *Revelation*, p. 589.

He comments on 13.13, 'he makes the earth . . . worship the beast', and he and the beast will 'make' people worship the ruler through deception and coercion.[100] He observes that to host banquets that promoted pagan temples could be a source of civic pride. Moreover, in 13.14, he says, 'false prophets used miracles to lure people into forced worship', hence the beast provides 'signs'. In 13.15 the beast gives breath to the image of the beast: 'Giving statues breath and power of speech was identified with sorcery.'[101]

McGinn points out how great a contribution was made to pictorial presentations of revelation between 1200 and 1335. Joachim of Fiore wrote in 1200, and more than a century later, the imperious John XXII (1316–34) was widely identified as Antichrist and false pope by Franciscans and others.[102] Antichrist became a symbol of tyranny and deception. Joachim also described four ways by which the Antichrist would deceive the world: by cunning persuasion, by the working of miracles, by the giving of gifts and by displaying tortures. In the thirteenth and fourteenth centuries the papacy was experiencing probably its lowest ebb. Hence it is not surprising that several reform groups identified the papacy with Antichrist and the false prophet. Long before the major Reformers, several groups were regarding the papacy as the source of what McGinn calls 'counterfeit holiness'.[103] Peter Olivi (*c.*1248–98) was a student of Bonaventura, an apocalyptic propagandist and charismatic leader, who based his theology on Joachim of Fiore. He wrote a commentary on Revelation in which the papacy was the 'Mystical Antichrist', false prophet or great deceiver.[104] Similarly Dante attacked 'the Simoniac popes Nicholas III, Boniface VII, and Clement V' with torture by flames, and imagined the false Simon Magus falling from heaven.[105] In 1378 there was a split papal election, and Western Christendom was divided. In the end the Italian cardinals chose Urban VI.

In England John Wycliffe (1330–84), Master of Balliol College, Oxford, attacked the papacy, drawing a sharp distinction between the visible and invisible Church. In McGinn's words, 'The visible church – sunk in vice, loaded down with endowments, beset by hypocritical friars – was clearly opposed to Scripture.'[106] In his view, the papacy of Innocent III, which

---

[100] Koester, *Revelation*, p. 590.
[101] Koester, *Revelation*, p. 593.
[102] McGinn, *Antichrist*, p. 143.
[103] McGinn, *Antichrist*, pp. 143–72.
[104] McGinn, *Antichrist*, pp. 159–66.
[105] Dante, *Inferno*, XIX.22–30; cf. XIX.103–17.
[106] McGinn, *Antichrist*, p. 181.

saw the beginnings of the friars and the doctrine of transubstantiation, signalled the loosing of Satan (Rev. 20.7). Gog symbolized the papacy, and Magog its followers. The Lollards followed Wycliffe's example. John (or Jan) Huss (*c.*1372–1415) of Prague University followed Wycliffe's teaching, and became a national hero of Bohemia, or among the Czechs, contrasting Scripture with a power-hungry Church. Huss was excommunicated in 1411, but he and his followers continued to use Antichrist rhetoric against the papacy.

Karel Stejskal produced a visual picture of the papal antichrist adored by monks (*c.*1500). Among a multiplicity of anti-papal antichrists, *Piers Plowman* produced the Chester *Play of Antichrist.* It depicted the assault of Antichrist on the Church. McGinn comments, 'Antichrist iconography flourished as never before between 1335 and 1500.'[107] He offers examples of such imagery. He concludes, 'Antichrist's iniquity came to be seen more and more as religious evil, specifically hypocrisy and corruption in the Church.'[108] Eventually, alongside false popes, the Antichrist was also regarded as a symbol of Jews, Muslims and heretics. At the Reformation, Martin Luther readily saw the papacy as symbolized by the Antichrist. But this had less hold in England, and John Jewel (1522–71) dismissed what he regarded as mediaeval and legendary. The use of the Antichrist theme, however, was defended by the 'Radical Reformers' such as Thomas Müntzer (*c.*1480–1525), who was a notorious opponent of Luther. Some, but not all, of the English Puritans followed him. After 1660 the Antichrist figure suffered decline, except perhaps in the Russian Orthodox Church, and among American millenarians, whom we have discussed above.

We have probably ransacked enough of the pictures and images of the book of Revelation to provide further striking confirmation of the two claims of this book. We have shown that God often communicates through visual expressions or pictures, some of which cannot be fully conveyed by writing alone. But we have also seen how some have hijacked pictures to convey messages quite different from those communicated to John. We shall consider contemporary communication in the light of the foregoing. The power and uniqueness of pictures suggest that we cannot dispense with them in Christian communication, whether teaching or preaching. Yet the ease with which pictures can convey a content alien to their intended meaning also suggests that we should be cautious about their interpretation. We shall illustrate this further in our final chapter.

[107] McGinn, *Antichrist*, p. 191.

[108] McGinn, *Antichrist*, p. 198.

Visions and mental constructions may suggest content that is far from Christian truth. Many of us have experienced someone's saying: 'God gave me a picture; so we should do so-and-so.' It is possible that this may sometimes be right; but we need to test it. We shall consider some mediaeval mystic visions, some of which seem right, while others remain open to question. We also explore Gnostic and Charismatic visions, which need to be tested for truth. Either way, the issue demands further debate for the health of the Church.

Part 3

COMMUNICATION IN HISTORY AND TODAY

10

Pictures and symbols in post-biblical sources and Christian communication today

Three of many post-biblical examples of symbolism and the use of pictures are perhaps the most striking. (1) Very soon after the close of the New Testament canon Gnostic writings were beginning to draw on biblical symbols, but also give them a new and distinctive meaning. Thus Gnosticism provides an excellent example of how symbols and pictures can seduce us, as well as at times enrich us. Further, many examples spring from the Reception History of post-biblical interpretations of parables of Jesus, analogies in Paul, and especially the imagery and symbols of the book of Revelation. (2) The second striking example comes from some of the mediaeval mystics. Mystics often see visions which they express through visual imagery. The majority of such writers are sufficiently embedded in a biblical tradition to use these pictures with reasonable accuracy. Nevertheless some become less disciplined, and offer bizarre or misleading suggestions about the meaning of these pictures. (3) Some examples occur also in a few Pentecostal and Charismatic movements, when some people claim to see visions, which are then interpreted as God's direct guidance, with practical outcomes in church or personal life.

Pictures and symbols in some Church Fathers and in Gnostic writings

One of the most informative writers on the language of Gnosticism is Samuel Laeuchli in his book *The Language of Faith*. He argues:

> There is a tension between the meaning in its original frame and the new frame into which it is inserted . . . An interpreter can never speak exactly the language of the Bible, because he also speaks the language of his environment . . . Gnosticism demonstrates that this exegetical conflict is not

merely a matter of translation . . .*The same words have other implications; phrases stand in another light.*[1]

Laeuchli also expresses this in another way. He says, 'It is not the concept itself which can furnish an answer, but only the relation in which it stands to other concepts.'[2] Bertil Gärtner, alluding to Irenaeus, says: 'They [the Gnostics] recognize the authority of Scripture, it is true, but make irresponsible alterations, rephrasing and rearranging our Lord's words, *changing their meaning altogether.*'[3] Jean Doresse writes, 'Sometimes *The Gospel according to Thomas* uses the words of the New Testament, but attaches a different teaching to it.'[4]

The *Gospel of Thomas* provides one of many such examples. Some of the sayings which this gospel attributes to Jesus are close paraphrases of sayings in the Synoptic Gospels. Some are quotations with additions or with a twist, or augment the meaning in the Synoptic Gospels. Still in relation to the teaching, the parables of Jesus provide many further examples in Gnostic writings.[5] On this subject, it is helpful that we have classified the Gnostics in the same section as the Church Fathers, because some, for example Clement of Alexandria, use Gnostic language, while others, for example Tertullian and Origen, simply provide descriptions or quotations from Gnostic writers.

One of the earliest Fathers, Irenaeus (*c.*130–*c.*200), attacks the Gnostic writer, Valentinus. On the interpretation of Scripture, he writes:

> They disregard the order and the connection of Scripture, and so far as in them lies, dismember and destroy the truth. By transferring passages, and dressing them up anew, and making one thing out of another, they succeed in deluding many through their wicked part in adapting the oracles of the Lord to their opinions. Their manner of acting is just as if one, when a beautiful image of a king has been constructed by some skilful artist out of precious jewels, should then take this likeness of a man all to pieces, and should re-arrange the gems, and so fit them together and re-arrange them into the form of a dog or of a fox, and even that but poorly executed; and should then maintain and declare that this was the beautiful image of a king.[6]

1 Samuel Laeuchli, *The Language of Faith: An Introduction to the Semantic Dilemma of the Early Church* (London: Epworth Press, 1965), p. 19 (my italics).

2 Laeuchli, Th*e Language of Faith*, p. 16.

3 Bertil Gärtner, *The Theology of the Gospel of Thomas* (London: Collins, 1961), p. 78 (my italics); cf. Irenaeus, *Against Heresies*, 1, 8, 1; and 3, 12, 12.

4 Jean Doresse, *The Secret Books of the Egyptian Gnostics* (London: Hollis and Carter, 1960), p. 342.

5 Doresse, *The Secret Books*, pp. 342–3.

6 Irenaeus, *Against Heresies*, Bk 1, 8, 1. (Eng., ANF, vol. 1, p.326).

For example, in interpreting the Parable of the Leaven, Valentinus says that 'the three measures of meal' (Matt. 13.33/Luke 13.20–21/*Thomas* 96) represent three types of people: spiritual, animal and material, while the leaven represents Christ himself.[7] These three categories constitute the heart of Gnostic theology, and have nothing to do with the parable as Jesus taught it.

Clement of Alexandria (*c.*150–215) was both a bad example of an early interpreter of Scripture, and also was heavily influenced by Gnosticism. The Parable of the Mustard Seed (Mark 4.30–32/Matt. 13.31–32/Luke 13.18–19/*Thomas* 20) provides an example of the former. Instead of stating the message of Jesus that the kingdom of God hugely increased from very small beginnings, Clement centres his attention on the *taste and medicinal qualities of mustard*! Thus, he says: 'Mustard represses bile, that is, anger, and checks inflammation, that is pride'. Thus, according to Clement, the mustard seed guarantees the health of the soul.[8]

On the Parable of the Lost Son (Luke 15.11–32) Clement says that 'the best robe' (v. 22) represents 'the robe of immortality', while the ring represents a divine seal and the 'impress of consecration, signature of glory, pledge of testimony'.[9] The shoes stand for what is imperishable, in contrast to the crippling bondage of sin. In a second interpretation the younger brother represents the squandering of a rational creature, whose reason has been darkened, while the ring represents the mystery of the Holy Trinity.[10]

The Gnostic sympathies of Clement can be seen from his exposition of Matthew 13.13, 'The reason I speak to them in parables is that "seeing they do not perceive, and hearing they do not listen, nor do they understand".' In accordance with Gnostic teaching, Clement writes, 'Knowledge belongs not to all.'[11] Similarly he appeals to 1 Corinthians 2.6–7, 'We speak wisdom among those who are perfect . . . We speak the wisdom of God hidden in a mystery.'[12] The notion of revealing truth only to a specific class is central to Gnostic theology, as is the idea of a secret, in contrast to public, tradition. Clement urges the former; Irenaeus, the latter.

Tertullian (*c.*150–*c.*225) composed a treatise 'Against the Valentinians'. Valentinus was a major Gnostic theologian, who came to Rome in *c.*156,

---

[7] Irenaeus, *Against Heresies*, 1, 8, 3 (Eng., ANF, vol. 1, p. 327).

[8] Clement of Alexandria, *Fragments from the Hypotyposes*, 4 (Eng., ANF, vol. 2, p. 578).

[9] Clement of Alexandria, *Fragments*, 11.1 (Eng., ANF, vol. 2, p. 582).

[10] Clement of Alexandria, *Fragments*, 11.2 (Eng., ANF, vol. 2, p. 582).

[11] Clement of Alexandria, *Stromata*, Bk 1.1 (Eng., ANF, vol. 2, p. 299).

[12] Clement of Alexandria, *Stromata*, Bk 5.12 (Eng., ANF, vol. 2, p. 463).

with hopes of being elected bishop, and died in *c.*165. His teaching is primarily preserved by Clement of Alexandria. He probably came from Egypt, and produced some Coptic texts, from the Nag Hammadi library. The Valentinian sect produced the apocryphal *Gospel of Truth*, and perhaps the *Gospel of Philip*. In his book Tertullian remarks, 'They have fabricated the vainest and foulest figment . . . out of the . . . suggestions of Holy Scripture, since from its many springs many errors may well emanate.'[13] Tertullian argues that the Valentinians called Christians 'simple'.[14] Further, they regarded God as having 'emanations', which provided a bridge to earth.[15] In chapters 12–14, Tertullian accuses Valentinus of using the term *plērōma* (fullness) in terms which superficially copy Paul, but with a different meaning. In other works Tertullian argues that Valentinians 'twist' Scripture, including such parables as the Parable of the Prodigal Son and the Lost Sheep.[16]

Tertullian himself often allegorizes the parables. For example, in the Parable of the Lost Coin (Luke 15.8–10) he understands that the coin was lost in the church, and in the parable of the Prodigal Son, the citizen of the far country who employed the prodigal was 'the prince of this age', or the devil, while the ring given by his father represented baptism, and the feast was the Eucharist.[17]

Origen (*c.*185–*c.*254) was well known for his principles of biblical interpretation, yet also notorious for his leanings often towards Hellenistic philosophy and Gnosticism. He states, for example, that he interprets Holy Scripture 'in a threefold manner', its meaning as body, its meaning as soul and its meaning as spirit. He wrote, 'The very body of Scripture' is

> the common or historical sense . . . something more may be edified by the very soul of Scripture . . . Then again there is the wisdom of God, hidden in a mystery [as spirit] . . . For as man is said to consist of body and soul and spirit, so also does sacred Scripture.[18]

In Book 1.3 he has a partly parallel passage. Origen regards Scripture as full of mysteries and hidden truths, much as Clement, his predecessor, did. Thus, he says, the Parable of the Treasure Hidden in a Field points to Christ as One 'in whom are hid all the treasures of wisdom and knowledge'

---

[13] Tertullian, *Against the Valentinians,* 1 (Eng., ANF, vol. 3, p. 503).
[14] Tertullian, *Against the Valentinians,* 2 (Eng., ANF, vol. 3, p.504).
[15] Tertullian, *Against the Valentinians,* 7–10 (Eng., ANF, vol. 3, pp. 506–9).
[16] Tertullian, *On Modesty,* 9 (Eng., ANF, vol. 4, p. 82).
[17] Tertullian, *On Modesty,* 7 and 8 (Eng., ANF, vol. 4, pp. 80–2).
[18] Origen, *On First Principles,* Bk 4.1.11 (Eng., ANF, vol. 4, p. 359).

(Col. 2.3). Sometimes Origen extends the meaning of a parable to elucidate his own concerns. In explaining the Saying about the Asking Son (Matt. 7.7–11), he comments, 'God therefore will give the good gift, perfect purity in celibacy and chastity, to those who ask him with the whole soul, and with faith.'[19]

Still more striking, the everyday tale of the Good Samaritan (Luke 10.29–37) receives an allegorical meaning from Origen. The man who travelled from Jerusalem to Jericho is not an unfortunate traveller, but Adam, travelling from paradise to the world. The robbers are powerful demons. The wounds are sins. The traveller is half dead, because human nature is dead, while the soul is immortal. The priest represents the law; the Levites represent the prophets. The Samaritan is Christ; the inn represents the Church. The two denarii are the two Testaments, and the return of the Samaritan is the Parousia or the Second Coming of Christ.[20]

After the Council of Nicaea, the Church Fathers are more restrained in their interpretation of Scripture, most especially the Antiochene School, and in particular John Chrysostom (*c*.347–407). He very largely rejects the allegorical method of interpretation, and was noted for the success of his practical preaching, which earned him the title 'Golden-mouth' for his popularity and success. He rightly argues that many of the parables of Jesus 'make his discourse more vivid, and fix the memory of it in them [the hearers] more perfectly, and bring the things before their sight'.[21] This is almost exactly what C. H. Dodd and J. Jeremias have written in the twentieth century about the purpose of the parables. For example, on the Parable of the Mustard Seed, Chrysostom sees that this provides encouragement for the disciples, because it shows the great power of the seed to multiply, just as the word of God multiplies. He writes, 'The mustard seed was spoken with a view to the power of the gospel, and its surely prevailing over the world . . . It extends itself like mustard seed and prevails like leaven . . . It is precious like a pearl.'[22]

One of the few exceptions to the full rejection of allegorical interpretation after the Council of Nicaea was Augustine (354–430). He was attracted to allegorical interpretation mainly through the influence of Ambrose. In the Parable of the Wise and Foolish Maidens (Matt. 25.1–13),

---

[19] Origen, *Commentary on Matthew*, 14.25 (Eng., New Advent, Church Fathers, *Origen's Commentary on Matthew*, 14:25).

[20] Origen, *Homilies on Luke*, Fragment 71; described in Warren S. Kissinger, *The Parables of Jesus: A History of Interpretation and Bibliography* (London: Scarecrow Press, 1979), p. 18.

[21] Chrysostom, *The Gospel of Matthew*, Homily 44.3 (Eng., NPNF, ser. 1, vol. 10, p. 281).

[22] Chrysostom, *The Gospel of Matthew*, Homily 47.2 (Eng., NPNF, ser. 1, vol. 10, p. 293).

he focuses on the meaning of the oil that powered the lamps. He associates the oil with the need for love.[23] But in general, Augustine's expositions of Scripture are so extensive that it is difficult to generalize, and he has little about early forms of Gnosticism.

At this point we may turn more directly to Gnostic writings themselves. (1) We begin with the *Gospel of Truth*, which is a Gnostic treatise included among the Coptic texts discovered relatively recently (around 1945–6) at Nag Hammadi, in Egypt. It is thought to be the work produced by the disciples of Valentinus, and was probably composed before around AD 180, although it may represent thought from the earlier period of AD 140. It claims to expound the mission of Jesus as the Word or Name of the Father, and alludes to his death on the cross, but also uses a personalized female figure called Error or (Greek) *Planē*. Further, it often embodies biblical allusions and vocabulary to which it often gives its own distinctive meaning. We shall follow the translation and edition of Kendrick Grobel.[24]

We may select examples of biblical quotations and terminology as follows. In 18.5, the *Gospel of Truth* writes:

> By the mercies of the Father the secret mystery, Jesus the Christ . . . gave them a Way and the Way is the Truth, which it showed them. Because of this *Planē* was enraged at it, she persecuted it: she was endangered by it . . . He was nailed to a tree.

Grobel claims that the 'secret mystery' or 'hidden secret' is probably an allusion to Colossians 1.26, while the allusion to the Way and the Truth may well be an allusion to John 14.6.[25] In terms of content and teaching, however, the biblical passages are jumbled together from different contexts, and the cause of the crucifixion is supposedly the rage of *Planē* or Error. Further, the secret mystery, and the Way and the Truth, are not Jesus Christ, but the *Gospel of Truth* itself. For the most part, 'it' refers to the *Gospel of Truth*. In 18.40 the *Gospel of Truth* refers to 'members', using Paul's word *melos* from 1 Corinthians 12 and Romans 12. Grobel comments, 'Here Paul's ecclesiology seems transformed into cosmology.'[26] In 16.25 the *Gospel of Truth* uses the word '*Plērōma*' (fullness), which occurs 11 times, but more probably in a Gnostic sense of the word than in its fully biblical sense. Examples can be multiplied.

---

23 Augustine, *Sermons on New Testament Lessons*, 43.5 (Eng., NPNF, ser. 1, vol. 6, p. 402).

24 Kendrick Grobel, *The Gospel of Truth: A Valentinian Meditation on the Gospel* (London: Black, 1960).

25 Grobel, *The Gospel of Truth*, p. 51.

26 Grobel, *The Gospel of Truth*, p. 55.

One passage in the *Gospel of Truth* may shed some light on fullness or 'completion'. In 24.34—25.3 the Valentinians say:

> As in the case of anyone's ignorance: when one comes to know, *then* one's ignorance is wont to melt away, if the light appears – just so on the case of 'the Lack' [presumably lack of knowledge]: it is wont to melt away in the Completion.

Grobel suggests that this mimics Paul's notion of eschatological completeness or perfection.[27] In other ways it is what Wittgenstein would call a conceptual or 'grammatical' remark. It is not in the domain of Paul's theology at all, nor in that of Jesus. The *Gospel of Truth* also refers to God as 'Him who created the Totality, in whom the Totality is and whom the Totality lacks' (18.34–35). Grobel comments on *Totality,* 'The meaning seems to fluctuate: in 34a most naturally [it means] the universe, but 34b [is] more likely personal: men.' At first sight it looks like Paul's use of 'all things', but is far from Pauline thought.

The *Gospel of Thomas* is often closer to the teaching of Jesus than the *Gospel of Truth.* This is also a Coptic document discovered at Nag Hammadi in 1945–6, and professes to contain the 'secret words' of Jesus, perhaps written by Matthias, and perhaps written in Syria. Bertil Gärtner writes that it supports the view, common among Gnostics, that their concern was less with Jesus on earth, but with the heavenly Christ after the resurrection.[28] N. T. Wright observes:

> The influence of Gnostic theology is clearly present in the Gospel of Thomas . . . According to the Gospel of Thomas, the basic religious experience is not only the recognition of *one's divine identity, but more specifically the recognition of one's origin (light) and destiny (the repose, anapausis)*.[29]

He cites not only *Logion* 21 (with its 'kaleidoscopic imagery'), but also 37 and 51. Some of the Sayings of Jesus closely follow our canonical Gospels. For example, 'Jesus said: blessed are the poor, for yours is the kingdom of heaven' (*Logion* 54). The Parable of the Weeds is also fairly accurately rendered in *Logion* 57, and the Parable of the Sower in *Logion* 9.[30] As we noted above in Chapter 6, Jeremias gives numerous parallels from the *Gospel of Thomas* to various parables.[31] On the other hand, some alleged Sayings

[27] Grobel, *The Gospel of Truth*, p. 99.

[28] Gärtner, *Gospel of Thomas*, pp. 78–9.

[29] N. T. Wright, *The Resurrection of the Son of God* (London: SPCK, 2003), p. 534.

[30] Gärtner, *Gospel of Thomas, Logion* 57.

[31] Joachim Jeremias, *The Parables of Jesus* (Eng., London: SCM, rev. edn, 1963), p. 247.

have *no* New Testament support. For example, *Logion* 47 reads: 'Jesus said: It is not possible for a man to ride two horses, or to draw two bows' [like 'serve two masters'?].[32] Some are mixed: 'Jesus said: No prophet is well received in his own home town. The doctor does not cure those who know him' (*Logion* 31). Some are simply marginally distorted: '[Jesus said] If you do not fast from the world, you shall not find the kingdom. If you do not keep the Sabbath as Sabbath, you shall not see the Father' (*Logion* 27).

The Prologue of the *Gospel of Thomas* begins: 'These are the secret words spoken by the living Jesus, and Didymus Thomas wrote them down.'[33] Some Sayings are then taken out of context, and combined with others which are not necessarily authentic. For example, *Logion* 53 states: 'If two people are with each other in peace in the same house, they will say to the mountain: "Move!" and it will move.'[34] In *Logion* 63: 'Jesus says: "Blessed is the man who has laboured; he has found Life".'

Among the books of the Nag Hammadi library the *Treatise on the Resurrection*, or *Letter to Rheginos*, was also found as a significant Gnostic source.[35] Its central message is 'the restoration of *Plērōma* . . . a seed of truth'. It adds, 'The Saviour . . . transformed himself into an imperishable Aeon, and raised himself up, having swallowed the visible by the invisible.' Further, 'Strong is the system of the *Plērōma*'. Virtually none of this corresponds with Scripture. Both its introduction of *Plērōma*, and its devaluation of the visible, is glaringly unbiblical, and 'raising himself' is contrary to the logic of Paul, even if it might find a possible allusion to John. Wright insists that its central message is '"spiritual" resurrection in the present'.[36]

To return to general comments on the Gnostic view of Jesus Christ, Elaine Pagels writes, 'Gnostic critics claim that the basic error of "the many" (i.e. orthodox Christians) involves their preoccupation with the historical reality of Jesus.'[37] She adds, 'They reject the "earthly Jesus" along with the "simple" reading of the gospels.'[38] Even the word 'to know' has a non-biblical meaning in the Gnostic writings. Pagels further argues that Gnostic exegesis of John is dominated by the 'pleromic' and the 'cosmic', and illustrates her

32 Gärtner, *Gospel of Thomas*, p. 51.
33 Gärtner, *Gospel of Thomas*, p. 95.
34 Doresse, *The Secret Books*, p. 363.
35 Malcolm Lee Peel, *The Epistle to Rheginos: A Valentinian Letter on the Resurrection: Introduction, Analysis and Exposition* (London: SCM, 1969).
36 Wright, *The Resurrection of the Son of God*, p. 538.
37 Elaine H. Pagels, *The Johannine Gospel in Gnostic Exegesis: Heracleon's Commentary on John* (SBLMS 17; Nashville: Abingdon Press, 1973), p. 11.
38 Pagels, *Johannine Gospel*, p. 15.

argument especially from John 1.3.[39] In other parts of John, she shows that Clement and Origen indicate more difficulties, and, 'In terms of Valentinian analysis, [exegesis] once hylic [i.e. relating to matter, material or ordinary], wholly "sensible", has now become psychic.'[40] Similarly on the Temple in John 2, she says, 'Heracleon . . . understands his exegesis as a method of systematically translating somatic "images" into spiritual truth.'[41]

The fragments of Basilides constitute a notorious example of Gnostic texts. But they can be reconstructed generally only through Irenaeus, Clement of Alexandria and Hippolytus. If Irenaeus' account is accurate, Basilides claimed that Jesus did not die on the cross: 'He did not suffer, but a certain Simon of Cyrene was compelled to carry his cross for him; and this [Simon] was transformed by him [Jesus] so that he was thought to be Jesus himself.'[42] This is by no means an exhaustive account of Gnostic texts, but we have considered enough to give a sample of how biblical words and texts can be given an alien meaning when placed within an alien frame of reference, or system of interpretation.

Twelve mediaeval and post-mediaeval mystics, and claims about visions in the Pentecostal and Charismatic movements

The period from about 1000 to 1500 is generally known as the High Middle Ages, in which the visual was a very important factor in stimulating devotion. This period was therefore for many mystics an era of images and pictures. But of these Walter Hilton warned fellow mystics about the limits of pictorial language. We shall consider about 12 specific mystics, of which seven or eight are female mystics for whom pictorial language sometimes verged on the extravagant to a greater or lesser degree.

We must recall, however, that the term 'mystic' is loose and difficult to define with precision. In a major study of mysticism, William R. Inge (1860–1954), a great advocate of mysticism, stated that above all mysticism entails 'shutting the eyes to external things'.[43] Inge was Dean of Saint Paul's and Lady Margaret Professor of Divinity at Cambridge. However broad the term, the following are generally accepted as the main mediaeval and post-mediaeval mystics of the day.

---

39 Pagels, *Johannine Gospel*, pp. 34–5.

40 Pagels, *Johannine Gospel*, p. 54.

41 Pagels, *Johannine Gospel*, p. 67.

42 Werner Foerster, *Gnosis: A Selection of Gnostic Texts* (Oxford: Clarendon Press, 1972), vol. 1, p. 60; Irenaeus, *Against Heresies*, 1, 24, 3–7.

43 William Ralph Inge, *Christian Mysticism* (London and New York: Scribner, 1899), p. 4.

(1) Bernard of Clairvaux (1090–1153) founded the monastery of Clairvaux, of which he became Abbot. From this sprang the Cistercian Order. He urged contemplation and the mystical life. In his work *On the Love of God*, he explores 'four degrees' of love (*caritas*). In the first degree a person loves God, but not for God's sake, but for his or her own sake. In the second degree he or she loves God without self-interest, tasting the sweetness of the Lord. In the third degree a person loves God entirely for the Lord himself. The fourth degree is perfection beyond words (*On the Love of God*, chs 8–10). He similarly wrote *On the Steps of Humility and Pride*, and composed sermons on the Song of Solomon. He opposed the theology of Peter Abelard and Anselm, and supported the Second Crusade. But in general he was one of the most balanced and restrained mystics, and so remains less relevant to our argument than several others.

(2) Hildegard of Bingen (1098–1179) was noted especially for her visions, as well as for her writings, preaching and musical compositions. She became Abbess of her convent in 1136. Bernard of Clairvaux advised and encouraged her. From 1141 she wrote *Scivias*, or *Know the Ways of the Lord*. Her visions involved 'pictures'. *Fire* and flashes represented the Holy Spirit (*Scivias*, 2.2) who drives out sin (*Scivias*, 1.6; 3.9). *Fire and light* also represented Christ.

In the *Scivias*, Hildegard sometimes quotes Scripture, and often goes not *against* Scripture, but frequently *beyond* Scripture. For example, she sees in her vision 'the vast army of heavenly spirits, shining in the blessed life'.[44] In general terms, this may accord with the book of Revelation, but the claim to 'see' so many remains a claim. A better example would be her vision of hell. She speaks of it as 'the pit of great breadth and depth', of which the mouth was 'emitting a fiery smoke with great stench . . . to swallow up souls . . . a burning fire with black smoke pouring out, and a boiling, deadly stench'.[45] In the Catholic tradition, she urged, 'Do penance for all your iniquities.'[46]

When she discusses the fall of humankind and the deception of Eve, Hildegard writes, 'Because he [(Satan] knew the susceptibility of the woman would be more easily conquered than the strength of the man', he initially tempted Eve. This claim seems to be fantasy regarding Eve, clearly

[44] Hildegard, *Scivias*, 1.
[45] Hildegard, *Scivias*, 5.
[46] Hildegard, *Scivias*, 8.

external to the Bible, even if it is popularly fashionable. In her painting which accompanies Book 3, Vision 9, Hildegard draws a building inside which there are

> seven white marble pillars, each seven cubits high, supporting a round dome of iron which stands for wisdom of God . . . The seven white marble pillars are the seven gifts of the Spirit – seven modes of the purifying inspiration of the Holy Spirit, which drives away all adverse storms.[47]

There are several more speculations, for example one on sexual relations with a relative, all of which Hildegard claims to have 'seen'.[48] In this respect Hildegard provides a better support for the dual argument of this book than Bernard.

(3) Marguerite Porete (1250–1310) was a French Beguine. She published *The Mirror of Simple Souls* in vernacular French. Marguerite's text claims that humans can in fact become God by ceasing to be themselves. By stripping away human anxieties, ambitions and the human will, a person can cease to be a person and actually become the divine – for a few moments only, before being put back into the earthly body. The *Mirror* describes the human becoming *lost in God*, as a river flowing into and getting lost in the sea. This claim to having not only known but been a part of the divine gives Marguerite the spiritual authority to write her text. She was arrested on charges of heresy in 1310, and refused to give testimony during her inquisition trial. The University of Paris, after surveying some passages of her book, deemed her a relapsed heretic. She had been accused of instances of heresy prior to her last arrest. Unlike other female mystics, Porete publicly taught the message of her revelations. Marguerite was found guilty by the Inquisition and burned at the stake in 1310.

In *The Mirror of Simple Souls* Porete also explains the different states of the soul:

> And therefore this Soul knows only him, and loves only him, praises only him, for there is only he. Because what is exists by his goodness, and God loves his goodness whenever he has bestowed it, and his goodness bestowed is God himself, and God cannot depart from his goodness so that it doesn't dwell in him.

---

[47] Stanley M. Burgess, *The Holy Spirit: Mediaeval Roman Catholic and Reformation Traditions* (Peabody, MA: Hendrickson, 1997), p. 94.

[48] Hildegard, *Scivias*, 17–22.

She continues, 'Thus he is what goodness is, and goodness is what God is. And therefore Goodness sees itself by means of his goodness, through divine light in the sixth state, by which the Soul is purified.' Chapters 8, 16 and 17 depict dialogue between Love, Reason, the Soul and Virtue, and Chapter 12 speaks of the annihilation of the soul. It is difficult to offer an assessment of Marguerite, especially since she has fierce critics and admirers. However, she cannot be understood as an orthodox biblical Christian.

(4) Gertrude of Helfta (1256–1301) began to receive a series of visions from her twenty-sixth year until her death. In 1281, without warning, she had a vision of Jesus, and renounced all secular studies, studying the Scriptures with seriousness and diligence. Gertrude produced a work called *The Revelations of Saint Gertrude*, which comprises five books, containing her life and a record of divine blessings, although only Book 2 alone may be Gertrude's own work. She also composed seven long chapters of *Spiritual Exercises.* In view of her careful study of Scripture, it is not surprising that she is one of the most exclusively biblical of the mediaeval mystics, offering perhaps less imaginative or speculative visions than many. In her *Exercises* she writes, 'Jesus, fountain of life . . . Fill me with thy Spirit and take possession of my whole being in purity both of body and soul . . . Anoint me with the chrism of thy Spirit unto eternal life.'[49]

(5) Brigitta of Sweden (also spelt Bridget, Brigit, Bridget, 1303–73) was also a very influential mystic, who founded the Bridgettine nuns and then monks. She is venerated by many as a saint of Sweden, and patron saint of Europe, although Luther was to call her 'the crazy Bridget'. In about 1344 she entertained the idea of founding a religious community. She undertook pilgrimages to Rome and Jerusalem. Her first vision, said to have been of Christ on the cross, occurred at the age of ten. She then had a number of 'Celestial Revelations'. Some of these made her controversial. She described seeing the nativity of Jesus, including the sight of the Virgin Mary as blond-haired, and Jesus as on the ground emitting light. This was according to the practice of imagining oneself into the biblical narrative, which can be seen later in imagination spirituality. Mary and Joseph allegedly pray to the child. Brigitta prayed to know how much Jesus Christ suffered on the cross, and learned that Jesus 'received 5,480 blows on My [his] body'. Allegedly Christ told her that she could honour those

[49] Gertrude, *Gertrude of Helfta: The Herald of Divine Love* (New York: Paulist Press, 1993), 2.23, and 3.30 (Exercises 1, Prologue 4.1, quoted by Burgess, *The Holy Spirit*, p. 101).

wounds by reciting 15 'Our Fathers' and 15 'Hail Marys'. Some, including Eamon Duffy, doubt whether Brigitta actually made such claims.[50] They are strongly influenced by Catholic dogma, for example the use of indulgences, which would be so strongly opposed by Luther and the Reformers. In 1999 Pope John Paul II named her a patron saint of Europe, but she remains a controversial figure.

Bridget appears to owe more to visual speculation than to biblical orthodoxy. This is not necessarily to discount reasons why many admire her devotion.

(6) Walter Hilton (*c.*1343–96), however, warns us explicitly that visions too readily encourage '*imaginary*' notions, and deception by a wicked angel.[51] Different modern editions entitle his book *The Scale of Perfection*, or *The Ladder of Perfection*; we use both editions. The devil, he writes, can too easily create 'counterfeit visions and imaginings'.[52] The first section of *The Scale of Perfection* was written to correct an ex-anchoress from 'Perverted visionary experiences' and 'inordinate love and fears of earthly things'.[53] Even in Book 2 Hilton writes, 'Beware of the devil who walks at noon, and who makes his false light appear to come from Jerusalem . . . He shows a false light in place of the true light to deceive the unwary.'[54] On the other hand, Hilton encourages due contemplation: 'Contemplative life consists in perfect love and charity', and himself uses the metaphor.[55] 'Knowing God', however, must include 'study in holy Scripture'.[56] He stands both in the mystical tradition and as a judicious critic of it. Hilton was one of the earliest students of the University of Cambridge. *The Scale* (or Ladder) *of Perfection* probably came from the late period of 1390–6, and he also wrote *Mixed Life* and *Meditation on Seven Deadly Sins.*

(7) Julian of Norwich (1342–1416) lived as an anchoress, that is, one of those who withdrew from the world to live a solitary life of meditation and prayer. She was a classic example of mysticism. Her major work is

[50] Eamon Duffy, *The Stripping of the Altars: Traditional Religion in England c.1400–1580* (New Haven: Yale University Press, 1992), p. 249.

[51] Walter Hilton, *The Scale of Perfection* (Kalamazoo, MI: Mediaeval Institute Publications, 2000), ch. 10.

[52] Hilton, *The Scale of Perfection*, ch. 11.

[53] Hilton, *The Scale of Perfection*, ch 1.

[54] Walter Hilton, *The Ladder of Perfection* (London: Penguin, 1957), Bk 2, ch. 26, p. 170.

[55] Hilton, *The Scale of Perfection*, ch. 3.

[56] Hilton, *The Scale of Perfection*, ch. 4.

Revelations of Divine Showings.[57] She writes, 'God was showing . . . the bodily sight of the plentiful bleeding from Christ's head . . . Great drops fell down under the crown of thorns.'[58] The visual communication is explicit: she speaks of 'the bodily sight'. The *Revelations* take a longer and shorter form, of which we follow the longer version by Wolters. She writes, 'Our Saviour is our true mother in whom we are eternally born.'[59] On one side the *Revelations* are pictorial; on the other side they focus mainly on Christ's sufferings, especially in Chapters 1–26, in accordance with their biblical and historical foundation. Perhaps more speculative and imaginative is the dialogue between Julian and God. For example, much of the writings of the Protestant mystic, Amy Carmichael, take this form of dialogue with God.

The 'showings' seem to have begun in May 1373. In one of her earliest visions Julian recalls that darkness began to surround her but 'the image of the cross was somehow lighted up'.[60] She recalls,

> At once I saw the red blood trickling down under the Garland, hot, fresh, and plentiful, just as it did at the time of his passion when the Crown of thorns was pressed onto the precious head of God-and-Man, who suffered for me.[61]

Later she recalls, 'I saw the head bleeding so freely . . . I saw the maid who is his beloved Mother.'[62] In her second revelation she sees 'a picture and a likeness of the shame that our foul deeds caused'.[63] In her third revelation, she writes, 'I saw the whole Godhead concentrated as it were in a single point . . . God is the focal point of everything . . . He never changes.'[64] She continues:

> For me his passion was shown primarily through his blessed face, and particularly by his lips. Thereto I saw these four colours . . . Fresh, red, and lovely . . . But his dear body became black and brown as it dried up in death.[65]

57 Julian of Norwich, *Revelations of Divine Showings* (London: Penguin, 1998), ed. and trans. Clifton Wolters.
58 Julian, *Revelations*, 7, pp. 50–1.
59 Julian, *Revelations*, p. 57.
60 Julian, *Revelations*, ch. 3, p. 65.
61 Julian, *Revelations*, ch. 4, p. 66.
62 Julian, *Revelations*, ch. 8, p. 73.
63 Julian, *Revelations*, ch. 10, p. 77.
64 Julian, *Revelations*, ch. 11, pp. 80–1.
65 Julian, *Revelations*, ch. 16, pp. 87–8.

She adds, 'What could be seen of the skin of the face was covered with tiny wrinkles, and was tan coloured.'[66] This may perhaps reflect an experience of witnessing in literal detail what happens when blood dries and a body dies. We may acknowledge her intensity of devotion, and that for the most part her biblical theology was correct. Again, this is part of imaginatively projecting oneself into the biblical narrative, popular in these times. There is no need to cite further examples of this kind.

(8) Margery Kempe (*c.*1373–*c.*1438) is very different from Julian of Norwich. Both had mystical visions, and both came from Norfolk (Norwich and King's Lynn), but Margery remained a laywoman, and her account of her visions and dialogue with Christ is unrestrained and sometimes regarded as 'odd'. She dictated her book which chronicled her visions, and which has become known as *The Book of Margery Kempe.* She believed that she was called to 'greater intimacy with Christ'. She had multiple visions.

Margery grew up as a middle-class woman in King's Lynn, but suffered a nervous breakdown after the birth of her first child. She supposedly 'saw' numerous hideous devils surrounding her. Today this might well be regarded as a case of mental illness, to be treated by a psychiatrist. But she recovered after 'seeing' a vision of Jesus Christ, and determined to spend her life in devotion to him. Her 'Book' contains biographical tales, and intense devotion to Christ. She had several intense visions, after which she had uncontrollable weeping and sobbing. She urged her husband to live a celibate life, but succeeded only after bearing 14 children. Her visions included Christ, the Virgin Mary and several saints. She antagonized numerous enemies. Her devotional practices provoked opposition, yet her biographical comments show her absolute dedication to submit to the will of God, 'leaving [matters] to the Holy Ghost'. She regularly calls herself 'the creature' (in her English, the 'forsed [aforesaid] creatur'). Often she quotes Scripture, as in 'If God be for us, who shall be against us?', and was accused of being a Lollard.[67]

(9) Catherine of Siena (*c.*1347–80) was a Dominican nun, who lived much of her life in solitude and silence. Her major work was *The Dialogue of Divine Presence*, said to have been dictated in 1377–8, when she was in

---

[66] Julian, *Revelations*, ch. 17, p. 89.

[67] Margery Kempe, *The Book of Margery Kempe*, Pt 2, sect. 2 (based on Robbins Digital Projects).

a state of ecstasy.[68] It contains four treatises: first, 'A Treatise of Divine Providence'; second, 'A Treatise of Discretion'; third, 'A Treatise of Prayer'; and fourth, 'A Treatise of Obedience'. Her first vision was granted when she was five or six years of age, which was the vision of Christ seated in glory, with Peter, Paul and John. At seven, she committed her life fully to Christ. At 16 she was to be married, but built an 'inner cell' around herself. When she was 21, she came to believe that she was mystically espoused to Christ. There is some controversy about whether any 'physical' dimension accompanied the mystical. She practised extreme abstinence from food and sleep.

In 1370 Catherine experienced what she called 'mystical death', when after four hours of apparent lifelessness she experienced 'ecstatic union' with God. After this she felt led to become involved in some political matters, engaging in extensive correspondence, visiting Florence and Pisa, and in 1376 experienced a vision in which she urged Pope Gregory XI to return to Rome. In 1377 she reported a multitude of visions, some of which came in a five-day period of ecstasy. Many of these involved visual images and metaphors. These involved such phenomena as ladders and especially bridges. She saw a bridge from earth to heaven and from heaven to earth. Bridges can be vivid expressions of relations between the earthly and the heavenly, although Luther later affirmed the priority of divine grace as represented by a bridge from God to humankind. Such a bridge, Catherine said, was 'moistened with his [Christ's] blood'.[69] She was a true mystic, imagining God as addressing her: 'O best beloved, dearest, and sweetest daughter, my spouse, rise out of yourself.'[70] Catherine died at 33 through self-denial and exhaustion. She was canonized in 1461.

(10) Catherine of Genoa (1447–1510) is probably best known for her visions concerning purgatory. She regarded purgatory as an interior, rather than exterior, fire, which people experience within themselves. 'The soul presents itself to God still bound to the desires and suffering that derive from sin, and this makes it impossible for it to enjoy the beatific vision of God.' Pope Benedict XVI described this as a 'unitive life', that is, closeness and intimacy with God. Catherine also dedicated her life to caring for the sick, which she did until her death. Those Protestants who reject the doctrine of purgatory may have problems with this wording.

---

[68] Catherine of Siena, *The Dialogue of Divine Presence* (London: Kegan Paul, Trench, Trübner, 1907; digitalized, 1995).

[69] Catherine of Siena, *Dialogue*, 11.

[70] Catherine of Siena, 'Treatise on Prayer', in *Dialogue*, 18.

(11) Teresa of Avila (1515–82) was a Spanish Carmelite nun. As a mystic, she typically speaks of the journey of the soul. She frequently uses symbols and pictures. Her book, *The Way of Perfection* (begun in 1562), was outshone by her even more famous work, *The Interior Castle*, which she began in 1577.[71] She progresses through seven 'mansions' of the Castle. In the First Mansions she writes, 'The door of entry into this Castle is prayer and meditation', and this stage entails careful self-examination, allowing for the possibility of being 'tricked by all kinds of deceptions'.[72] The Second Mansions focuses on the need for perseverance, 'For the world is full of falsehoods and these pleasures which the devil pictures to it are accompanied by trials and cares and annoyances.'[73] In the Fourth Mansions she speaks of the sweetness of deeper prayer, and of the relationship between bride and bridegroom in the Song of Solomon. The Bible often uses the image of the bride and bridegroom to indicate an intimate relation with Christ, but frequently it is corporate rather than individual, referring to the whole community of believers (e.g. the New Jerusalem, prepared as a bride, Rev. 21.2; cf. Eph. 5.27–32; Rev. 22.17).

Teresa comments:

> The will is fixed so firmly upon its God that this disturbed condition of understanding is in great distress; but it (the soul) must not take any notice of this, for if it does so it will lose a great part of what it is enjoying.[74]

Finally in the Seventh Mansions she describes 'a supreme state of ecstasy', in spite of assaults of the devils, and observes:

> Often the body appears to feel nothing but the strength derived from the vigour gained by the soul after it is drunk from the wine from [God's] cellar, where its Spouse has brought it and which he will not allow it to leave.[75]

Teresa elaborates the imagery of the Castle: rooms, garden fountains and labyrinths. Such images may stimulate the imagination, and may relate indirectly to 'many dwelling places' in John 14.2. But in general her spiritual work is less speculative and more clearly biblical than many. She also collaborated with John of the Cross.

---

[71] Teresa of Avila, *Interior Castle* (New York: Dover, 1946), p. 9.

[72] Teresa of Avila, *Interior Castle*, First Mansions, ch. 1, p. 18, and ch. 2, p. 24.

[73] Teresa of Avila, *Interior Castle*, Second Mansions, ch. 3, p. 30.

[74] Teresa of Avila, *Interior Castle*, Fourth Mansions, ch. 3, p. 60.

[75] Teresa of Avila, *Interior Castle*, Seventh Mansions, ch. 4, p. 165.

(12) John of the Cross (1542–91) was also a Spanish mystic, who wrote *The Dark Night of the Soul.* The soul is 'moved to greater heights . . . The soul is nurtured and caressed by the Spirit'.[76] The 'dark night' of the soul denotes experiences which are a necessary purgation on the path towards union with God. Like Hilton, John also corrects the more arbitrary interpretations of mystical visions.

It will have become clear that there were considerable variations between the 12 examples of mystics which we have examined. At one end of the spectrum, Walter Hilton and Gertrude of Helfta seem to represent more sober and biblical interpretations of visions, images and pictures. At the other end of the spectrum, Margery Kempe, Hildegard of Bingen, Brigitta of Sweden, Julian of Norwich, Catherine of Siena, and probably more, draw on a mixture of biblical and speculative images in their devotional practice. It will be easier for Roman Catholic readers to give credence to some images and pictures than Protestants, who, for example, would have grave reservations about purgatory or the special veneration of the Virgin Mary. On the other hand, many may be legitimate applications of biblical imagery, and we should not, like some Puritans, exclude all but biblical pictures and images, but only exclude what is *incompatible* with biblical teaching. For readers who are Anglicans, Article VI of the 39 Articles makes this clear: 'whatever is *not* therein . . . is not to be required . . . that it should be believed' (my italics). Visions, as such, have biblical precedent, as in the book of Revelation and some Old Testament prophets; but that does not exempt them from critical testing.

The modern Pentecostal movement and Charismatic movement will be much shorter in our consideration because their *official* literature makes less of 'visions' than we might imagine from *more informal, local* encounters. Local Charismatic church groups may set greater store by pictures and visions supposedly given by God than many Charismatic or Pentecostal writers. It may be that the latter are more conscious of possible imaginings than the former. For example, the *New International Dictionary of Pentecostal and Charismatic Movements* has nothing in the Index or headings of articles under 'pictures', 'images', 'visual representations' or indeed 'visions'.[77]

By contrast, we may find dozens of local-church sponsored blogs if we

[76] John of the Cross, *The Dark Night of the Soul,* ed. Alison Peters (Image Books, 3rd edn., 1959), 1.1.2.

[77] Stanley M. Burgess and Eduard M. van der Mass (eds), *New International Dictionary of Pentecostal and Charismatic Movements* (Grand Rapids: Zondervan, 2002).

search the Internet. To quote only one example, Charity Virkler Keyembe writes:

> I enjoy the company of heaven, doing life together with Jesus and His holy angels through visions by day, and living into the kingdom of God through my dreams, my visions of the night. We are created in God's image, and He is Spirit (Jn. 4:24). So we, too, were made for the supernatural. We were created to live into the spirit realm and live out of it . . . My favorite thing is living into heaven here and now. My second favorite thing is sharing those revelatory encounters with others.

On the other hand, the dynamic Baptist preacher, Charles Haddon Spurgeon, once made the very opposite comment. He wrote:

> I have heard many fanatical persons say the Holy Spirit revealed this and that to them. Now that is very generally revealed nonsense. The Holy Ghost does not reveal anything fresh now. He brings old things to our remembrance. 'He shall teach you all things, and bring all things to your remembrance whatsoever I have told you,' (John 14:26). The canon of revelation is closed; there is no more to be added. God does not give a fresh revelation . . . There are no new doctrines, but the old ones are often revived . . . There is enough in the Bible for thee to live upon forever.[78]

In point of fact Spurgeon was not entirely 'cessationalist' (i.e. believing that all gifts of the Holy Spirit ceased after the close of the biblical canon), because in his preaching he regularly identified those individuals who especially needed his word. Today what he sometimes addressed might have been called 'a word of knowledge'. However, he did argue that the human mind is too easily *seduced* into *imagined* beliefs.

The issue of 'visions' has become one of lively debate among a less-than-formal or scholarly leadership. Ken Matto, for example, poses a series of questions, which he regards as temptations to give a positive but mistaken answer. Most relevant to the present enquiry is the following, where he writes:

> If there is one thing which no one questions in [the Charismatic movement], it is the dreams and visions which are taught. This is especially true when the person proclaiming their vision is on national TV . . . The problem is that with visions and dreams the Word of God takes second place and all eyes are on the individual with their claim . . . Satan has the ability

[78] Charles Haddon Spurgeon, *The New Park Street Pulpit*, vol. I (1855), p. 38.

> to give massive visions for deception. Paul was not allowed to discuss his journey into the third heaven.[79]

Kevin Reeves urges the positive importance of visions, but appeals to Old Testament precedents. He writes, 'There is perhaps nothing so powerful as a vision. When the heavens open and our eyes look upon fantastic things once hidden, it can alter the course of our lives.'[80] Then he cites Isaiah 6.1 (KJV/AV): 'In the year that king Uzziah died I saw also the Lord sitting upon a throne, high and lifted up, and his train filled the temple. Above it stood the seraphim.' On the other hand, Reeves points to contemporary phenomena of visions in his church. He writes:

> The cries of 'I saw!' reverberated throughout my church my whole tenure there. Sometimes the visions were two-dimensional, sometimes 3-D, and sometimes the person was actually caught up into them, in the same way the apostle John was translated into the heavenly realms in the book of Revelation. They moved as participants in the vision itself, walking, feeling, etc. As our pastor consistently reminded the congregation of its prophetic calling, dreams and visions grew to paramount importance. They were used to chart our congregation's very course, and any resistance or verbal doubt was severely frowned upon or openly dismissed.

We have cited two or three examples from each side, in order to expose the debate and controversy in this issue of 'seeing visions'. The examples seem to reflect the same issues as we witness in the mediaeval mystics. For many, 'seeing' is vital; but the interpretation of what is seen may be controversial, ambiguous, or seductive and misleading. Our argument in this book is that on the one hand pictures and images are powerful, vivid and necessary; but on the other hand, some may be seductive and misleading. The most questionable kind occurs when a visionary claims that a 'picture' comes from God as a directive for practical conduct, when no one attempts to test the authenticity of the 'vision' or picture.

The need for, and danger of, visual communication in the Church today

James Black, the author of *The Mystery of Preaching*, comments, 'It is certainly easier to get at the average mind by a picture than by an idea. There

---

79 Ken Matto, online article: <www.scionofzion.com/18dangers.htm>.

80 Kevin Reeves, 'The Lighthouse Trail Blog', 11 May 2008.

is a fine Arab proverb which says, "He is the best speaker who can turn the ear into an eye".'[81] Black compares the proportion of parable and illustration in the preserved teaching of Jesus with the proportion of illustrative images used in the average sermon. He further comments, 'An illustration is a window to let in air and light.'[82] He recommends keeping a 'Common-Place Book' in which illustrations from everyday life and from books of various kinds may be noted and indexed appropriately. In practice, many current books on preaching appear to say less about the use of illustrations, analogies or metaphors than can be implied by Jesus and Paul.

Our ultimate Master in matters of preaching and communication remains Jesus Christ himself. He was a master of preaching and teaching. He leaves no gap between the concepts which he wished to teach and the everyday world which he addressed. Among the many who have commented on this, we may cite Ernst Fuchs. To repeat a quotation which we have used earlier in Chapter 6, pictures and images often form the 'common world' of the hearers. In the words of Ernst Fuchs:

> Without a doubt Jesus speaks in this sphere of provincial and family life as it takes place in peaceful or normal times. It is from this life that he takes the examples of his parables. One observes the people walking along the street and knocking on the window; one hears the loud voice of their festivities. The farmer goes to his field, sows and harvests. The wife plants the small plot of land adjoining her house. There are the rich and the poor, the honest and the frauds; there is happiness and need, sadness and thankfulness. But all that is not only . . . 'source material' . . . not only a kind of 'point of contact'; instead he has in mind precisely this 'world'.[83]

Jesus was seeking to reach what Fuchs calls 'mutual understanding' (*Einverständnis*) by fully entering the world of the hearers, rather than expecting that they would enter into *his* theological world directly. Here, Fuchs asserts, 'He [Jesus] calls for faith – that is, for decision.'[84] Robert Funk, following C. H. Dodd, further declares that the meaning and application of pictures or parables is often 'left imprecise in order to tease the hearer into making his own application'.[85] This is broadly correct, although, as we noted, it raises the problem of 'right' interpretation.

[81] James Black, *The Mystery of Preaching* (London: James Clarke, rev. edn, 1934), p. 110.

[82] *Black, The Mystery of Preaching*, p. 111.

[83] Ernst Fuchs, 'The New Testament and the Hermeneutical Problem', in James M. Robinson and John B. Cobb (eds), *New Frontiers in Theology, vol. 2, The New Hermeneutic* (New York: Harper & Row, 1964), p. 126; cf. pp. 111–45.

[84] Fuchs, 'The Hermeneutical Problem', p. 129.

[85] Robert Funk, *Language, Hermeneutic and Word of God* (New York: Harper, 1966), p. 133.

The practice of Jesus shows us that the task of teaching and preaching is not finished when the message or concepts of what we seek to communicate has been formulated. Reflection must include what effect certain styles of teaching or preaching have upon the hearers themselves. In literary theory this concerns what since the 1980s we have come to know as Reader-Response Theory. This was elucidated through Wolfgang Iser and many others, and ultimately from Edmund Husserl's theory of perception, his student Roman Ingarden and more recently from Robert Jauss. Any attempt to formulate a communicative act must include the reader as well as a speaker. This is exactly what Jesus achieved in his strategy of teaching and preaching through the parables of the kingdom.

Within the overall argument of this book, the use of pictures and images by Jesus is part of this strategy of concern for the reader. Indeed in my first major book, *The Two Horizons* (1980), I had as my aim the engagement and interaction of the horizon of the biblical text and the horizon of the modern reader. This first volume on hermeneutics engaged especially with the philosophical and hermeneutical dimension of the problem. The second major volume in this series, *New Horizons in Hermeneutics* (1992), attempted to show in detail how a particular genre of biblical texts could match a particular type of readers.[86] This was partly a reaction against the tendency in systematic theology to generalize about the relation between the Bible and modern readers. This second book stressed the need for absolute particularity in assessing how the two horizons could engage and interact more efficiently and correctly. It therefore considered more explicitly the particular details presented by biblical studies, as well as the sociology of knowledge, in relation to the situation of modern readers.

In the teaching of Jesus, we noted in Chapter 6, the imagery of parables is seldom abstract, and usually concrete or particular. For example, Jesus said, 'Whenever you give alms, do not sound a trumpet before you' (Matt. 6.2). By comparison, to say in the abstract, 'Beneficence should not be ostentatious', would be without punch. A second example that Dodd cites is the memorable saying, 'It is easier for a camel to go through the eye of a needle than for someone who is rich to enter the kingdom of God' (Matt. 19.24). The sheer power and readily remembered nature of such images in teaching or preaching is beyond question. Amos Wilder

---

[86] Anthony C. Thiselton, *The Two Horizons: New Testament Hermeneutics and Philosophical Description* (Grand Rapids: Eerdmans, 1980), and Anthony C. Thiselton, *New Horizons in Hermeneutics: The Theory and Practice of Transforming Biblical Reading* (London: HarperCollins, and Grand Rapids: Zondervan, 1992 and 2012).

distinguishes between the functions of a variety of parables. The word *parable*, he writes, 'included a wide variety of metaphors, similitudes, riddles, mysteries and illustrations. Many of these were brief tropes' (e.g. salt of the earth), 'but many of the Jewish parables reflect a narrative character, as do many of those in the Gospels' (e.g. the Good Samaritan, the Rich Fool, and the Pharisee and the Publican). He continues, 'Here we have "example-stories", not symbolic narrative.' But, he writes, 'In the parable of the Lost Sheep, on the other hand . . . [w]e have rather an extended image – the shepherd's retrieval of the lost sheep and his joy.'[87] In his list of parables J. Jeremias counts some 40, including the parables which he conflates from the three Synoptic Gospels.[88]

One surprising conclusion which follows from examining analogies and metaphors in Paul is that analogies were abundant in Paul, matching, if not in some contexts perhaps exceeding, analogies and metaphors in Jesus and in the book of Revelation, despite the latter's focus on *visual* imagery. If we restrict our attention to the Pauline corpus excluding the Pastoral Epistles, Herbert Gale, we saw, counts some 47 analogies or metaphors, while if we include Butcher's total within the Pastoral Epistles, the total reaches some 68 examples. The Pastoral Epistles alone, we noted, include analogies or metaphors from imperial warfare, from architecture and building, from agriculture and horticulture, from Greek games and athletics, from Roman law and from medical science. This alone provides a fruitful example for teachers and preachers today.

If we turn from the Pastorals to the major Pauline epistles, we may recall that 1 Corinthians alone contained some ten analogies or metaphors, including: planting, watering and growth (1 Cor. 3.6–7); milk and solid food (3.1–2); fields and buildings (3.16); gladiators and theatre (4.9); yeast and leaven (5.6); and competition between athletes (9.24–27). The eight analogies or metaphors in Romans are not far behind. They include work and pay (Rom. 4.4); the righteous and the good (5.7); slavery (6.15–23); death and life (6.1–14); marriage (7.1–6); the potter and the clay (9.20–24); athletes and their training (9.24–27); and roots, fruit and grafting (11.16–24). Of the four major epistles, Galatians has four; 1 Corinthians, ten; 2 Corinthians, nine; and Romans, eight. This brings the full count in the so-called four major epistles to 31. All this provides yet more examples, which we can add to the teaching of Jesus, for today's teacher or preacher.

---

[87] Amos N. Wilder, *Early Christian Rhetoric* (London: SCM, 1964), p. 80.

[88] Jeremias, *The Parables of Jesus*, pp. 247–8.

In addition to Paul's use of analogies, we must recall that Paul was trained in a Jewish and rabbinic tradition, but spent most of his ministry preaching either to Diaspora Jews, who were more than familiar with Hellenistic culture, or to Greeks, who at the beginning had little or no knowledge of the Old Testament. Paul's use of analogies and metaphors was not only to clarify and illustrate points, but also to provide part of his bridge to the Greek and Gentile world. There is a parallel today with preachers and teachers who are trained largely in the Church, church institutions or theological faculties, and their need to reach out into a largely secularized world.

Among many other works, W. L. Knox, Gregory Dix and F. W. Beare explore this aspect of Paul's communication: the most extensive three books are by W. L. Knox, one is a basic study by Dix, the remaining one is an essay by F. W. Beare.[89] Knox examines Hellenistic themes, with which Paul engaged, for example, he used Hellenistic or Diaspora synagogue Judaism, the concept Divine Wisdom, monotheism and other themes to find common ground. He writes, 'That the Divine Wisdom as the "image" of God was part of the regular Jewish-Hellenistic tradition; the Divine Wisdom was also the first-born of all creation.'[90] It would have been unintelligible to Gentile hearers if Paul had come preaching, 'The new age has dawned', or 'The kingdom of God is here' (Mark 1.15), even if Jewish hearers from Jerusalem would immediately have grasped the point. Paul focused in his preaching less on the kingdom of God, a ready concept for Jews, than on the lordship of Christ (1 Cor. 12.3), salvation (2 Cor. 1.6), reconciliation (2 Cor. 5.20) and turning from idols to God (1 Thess. 1.9), all of which are still related to the kingdom of God.

These images and concepts needed little explanation to the Gentiles. Paul used, as we have seen, such metaphors as 'adoption' (Rom. 8.14; Gal. 4.6; 1 Cor. 6.20), 'rescue' (Rom. 7.24; Col. 1.13; 1 Thess. 1.10) and redemption from slavery (Rom. 8.15). Dix pointed out why such terms as 'Son of God' and 'Son of Man' would be either meaningless or give rise to grave misunderstandings among Greeks.[91] Instead, Dix argues, Paul gave prominence to the term 'Lord'.

89 Wilfred L. Knox, *St Paul and the Church of the Gentiles* (Cambridge: CUP, 1939); Wilfred L. Knox, *St Paul and the Church of Jerusalem* (Cambridge: CUP, 1925); Wilfred L. Knox, *Some Hellenistic Elements in Primitive Christianity* (London: OUP, 1944); Gregory Dix, *Jew and Greek: A Study in the Primitive Church* (London: Dacre Press, 1953); and F. W. Beare and others, *The Communication of the Gospel in New Testament Times* (London: SPCK Theological Collections, 1961).

90 Knox, *St Paul and the Church of the Gentiles*, p. 159.

91 Dix, *Jew and Greek*, pp. 77–8.

1 Thessalonians provides the earliest example of Pauline sermons, although Acts also recounts Paul's early preaching. Paul says that he never came with words of flattery (1 Thess. 2.5), but 'we were gentle among you like a nurse tenderly caring for her own children' (1 Thess. 2.7). This model is so different from some preachers today who rant at, and scold, their congregations, presumably under the misapprehension that this implies their power and authority! On the contrary, J. A. Crafton argues that, far from Paul and the apostles calling attention to themselves, they sought to be like transparent windows through which their hearers could see Christ.[92] Karl Donfried also notes that Paul retained a very close friendship and personal involvement with his hearers, so much so, that he called 1 Thessalonians 'a friendship letter'.[93] In the same volume, Otto Merk argues that Paul's preaching could come only from the deep concern of a pastoral heart.[94] George Lyons anticipates Crafton's point that, far from putting the spotlight on himself, or talking about himself, Paul focuses on Christ, so that he himself can be an incarnation of Christ's gospel.[95] Again, many preachers today could learn from Paul's example.

Can we add the book of Revelation to the examples of Jesus and Paul? In Part 2, we considered the writings of all three sources, and on the book of Revelation we noted how often passages in Revelation had been misinterpreted in the post-biblical era. This means that lessons on the basis of Revelation are the polar opposite of those from Jesus and Paul. While the teaching methods of Jesus and Paul reveal the power of pictures and the need for them, interpretations of Revelation can show the seduction and speculative understanding of pictures, images and visual representations, without adequate biblical training.

We do not propose to repeat the examples discussed above, but may briefly allude to one or two notorious passages which have been understood in various ways. One such example is the millennium and the binding of Satan in Revelation 20.4–6. John Bale (1495–1563) understood the binding of the devil to take place literally over 1,000 years, from Christ's birth to AD 1000. He argued that Satan was let loose by Pope Sylvester II, and

---

92 J. A. Crafton, *The Agency of the Apostle* (JSNT Sup 51; Sheffield: Sheffield Academic Press, 1991), pp. 53–103.

93 Karl P. Donfried, 'The Christology and Rhetorical Context of 1 Thessalonians 2:1–12', in Karl P. Donfried and Johannes Beutler (eds), *The Thessalonians Debate: Methodological Discord or Methodological Synthesis?* (Grand Rapids: Eerdmans, 2000), pp. 31–60.

94 Otto Merk, '1 Thessalonians 2:1–12', in Donfried and Reutler (eds), *The Thessalonians Debate*, p. 89; cf. pp. 89–113.

95 George Leroy Lyons, *Pauline Autobiography: Toward a New Understanding* (SBLDS 73: Atlanta: Scholars Press, 1985).

that since then all the teachers of the Church had erred.[96] In England, it was argued, Satan was released through Dunstan, Archbishop of Canterbury, in the tenth century. According to Thomas Brightman (1562–1607), Satan's binding began with Constantine's Christian conversion in 306, and ended in 1300 with the invasion of the Ottoman Turks. All this is not unconnected with the popular American writer Hal Lindsey, who prophesied 'world events' in which God's sovereign acts and demonic resistance involved Russia, the USA, the Third World War and the founding of the State of Israel. The 1980s were supposedly the countdown to Armageddon.[97] Lindsey speculated that 'African nations will be united and allied with the Russians in invasion of Israel'.[98]

The identity of 'the whore of Babylon' produced many controversial interpretations. In his quest to restore a rural ideal, and attack urbanization, William Blake (1757–1827) identified the harlot of Babylon with London.[99] The *Scofield Reference Bible* identified two 'Babylons', which are to be distinguished: an 'ecclesiastical Babylon, which is apostate Christendom, headed by the papacy, and political Babylon, which is the Beast's federated empire, the last form of gentile world dominion'. 'The great whore' of the ecclesiastical Babylon is destroyed by the political Babylon (Rev. 17.15–18), so that the beast alone may now constitute 'the object of worship'.[100] Jehovah's Witnesses, Kovacs and Rowland argue, 'think the Whore of Babylon must be a world-wide religious entity (cf. Rev.17:15, 18), the entire world empire of false religion, linked with the League of Nations and the United Nations'.[101] In the Seventh-day Advent movement, most argue that the whore of Babylon is a supremely blasphemous religious system that takes in all the errors of Roman Catholicism and apostate Protestantism.

Although the book of Revelation *does not explicitly use the term 'the Antichrist'*, this term is perhaps implicit in its language about the beast and Babylon as general symbols of evil. Joachim of Fiore (*c.*1135–1202) wrote an *Exposition of the Apocalypse* in which he regarded the Antichrist as having a role in world history, and also multiple manifestations. He identified it with the heads of the dragon (Rev. 12.3), who gave its authority

---

96 Judith Kovacs and Christopher Rowland, *Revelation: The Apocalypse of Jesus Christ* (Oxford: Blackwell, 2004), p. 211.

97 Hal Lindsey, *The Late Great Planet Earth* (Grand Rapids: Zondervan, 1970), p. 55.

98 Lindsey, *Late Great Planet*, p. 68.

99 Kovacs and Rowland, *Revelation*, p. 187.

100 Kovacs and Rowland, *Revelation*, p. 187.

101 Kovacs and Rowland, *Revelation*, p. 187, and *Watchtower Bible*, p. 235.

to the beast (Rev. 13.2) in a series of political manifestations of evil. The Roman Empire, a head of the dragon, in its last phase, was identified with Babylon. The two beasts in Revelation 13, he argued, are both manifestations of the Antichrist, and were to arise at the end of a second era of world history, or at the time of the sixth seal, with the beast from the sea as a political leader, and the beast from the land as a religious leader.

Peter John Olivi (*c.*1248–98), who led the 'radical Franciscans', identified Francis of Assisi as the angel of the sixth seal, and initiated the aggressive critique of the Roman Catholic Church, including its support by secular rulers, identifying it broadly with the Antichrist. Examples of weird and wonderful interpretations of eschatological symbols could be multiplied indefinitely. Pictures and symbols, as Wittgenstein and others have warned us, can be variously interpreted, unless they are placed within an appropriate system or tradition.

We must return, however, to some positive examples of guidance on Christian preaching and teaching. Augustine considered examples of good preaching from Chrysostom and Ambrose, although these offered examples of practice rather than theory. Chrysostom avoided 'heaped up imagery'; he did *not overdo* his use of imagery, and also avoided 'bad taste'. Christ, for him, was a living reality, and he 'fully sympathizes with his hearers'. Not for nothing did he receive the nickname 'Golden-mouth' (i.e. Chrysostom).

Augustine turned to the art of preaching in Book 4 of *On Christian Doctrine.* He discussed the duty of the Christian teacher. He wrote:

> Once his hearers are friendly, attentive, and ready to learn . . . the matter treated . . . must be made fully known by means of *narrative* . . . If, however, the hearers require to be roused, rather than instructed . . . to bring their feelings into harmony with the truth . . . greater vigour of speech is needed . . . Entreaties and reproaches, exhortations and upbraidings . . . are necessary.[102]

He then quoted Cicero with approval: 'Wisdom without eloquence is of little service . . . Yet eloquence without wisdom is frequently a positive injury.'[103]

Augustine urged *perspicuity and clarity,* both in the content of speech, and in addressing emotions and will. The aim of the preacher is to teach, to delight and to move. Again he quoted Cicero: 'To teach is a necessity,

---

[102] Augustine, *On Christian Doctrine,* 4.4.6–7 (Eng., NPNF, ser. 1, vol. 2, p. 576) (my italics).

[103] Augustine, *On Christian Doctrine,* 4.5.7 (Eng., NPNF, ser. 1, vol. 2, p. 576).

to delight is a beauty, to persuade is a triumph.'[104] The preacher, said Augustine, 'must not only teach so as to give instruction . . . but he must also sway the mind so as to subdue the will'.[105] He urged prayer before preaching. The preacher, he urged, must use different styles for different occasions. Augustine strongly influenced Western mediaeval tradition, and one major example is Alan of Lille, *The Art of Preaching*.[106] By the twelfth century, preaching was based on the scholastic method, with great attention to accuracy, and it was even taught in Western universities.

At the Reformation preaching and teaching were regarded as of central importance. John Calvin discussed preaching in the context of the Church as both 'Mother' and the Communion of Saints. The aim of preaching, said Calvin, is to help believers to attain 'the measure of the stature of the fullness of Christ (Eph: 4.10–13)'.[107] He wrote:

> It proves our obedience when we listen to his [God's] ministers just as we would to himself . . . When fanatics refuse to observe [this], they entangle themselves in many fatal snares . . . meditating in private, and thus to despise public meetings, and deem preaching superfluous.[108]

In early modernity Friedrich Schleiermacher regarded preaching as a vital part of a theological syllabus.[109] In his *Speeches* he wrote, 'Preaching to the congregation to awaken faith was by far the sweetest desire of my life'; it involves 'striking up the music . . . to move the hearers' and 'to awake the slumbering spark'.[110] In the later modern era, P. T. Forsyth, James Black, John Stott and many others have written on preaching.

The history of homiletics, however, adds little to the particular argument of this book. We must return especially to Jesus and Paul to see the power of, and need for, pictures, images and analogies, which they use in abundance. To grasp the possible seduction of pictures, images and symbols, when interpreted incorrectly, we must return to the post-history of

---

104 Augustine, *On Christian Doctrine*, 4.12.27 (Eng., NPNF, ser. 1, vol. 2, p. 583).

105 Augustine, *On Christian Doctrine*, 4.13.29 (Eng., NPNF, ser. 1, vol. 2, p. 384).

106 Alan of Lille, *The Art of Preaching*, trans. Gillian R. Evans (Collegeville, MN: Liturgical Press, Cistercian Press, 1981); and *The Art of Preaching* (London: Clarke, 1939).

107 John Calvin, *Institutes of the Christian Religion*, ed. Henry Beveridge (London: James Clarke, 1957), Bk 4, ch. 1, sect. 5; vol. 2, p. 284.

108 Calvin, *Institutes*, Bk 4, ch. 1, sect. 5; vol. 2, p. 285.

109 Friedrich Schleiermacher, *A Brief Outline of the Study of Theology* (Eugene, OR: Wipf & Stock, 2007).

110 Friedrich Schleiermacher, *On Religion: Speeches to Its Cultured Despisers* (Eng., New York: Harper, 1958); quoted by Karl Barth, *The Theology of Schleiermacher* (Eng., Grand Rapids: Eerdmans, 1982), p. xviii.

the book of Revelation, with additional illustrations from Gnostic texts, some mediaeval mystics and some examples from the Charismatic movement. We may also recall our aim in such studies as *The Two Horizons*, *New Horizons in Hermeneutics*, and in related articles and essays.

Our main thesis has been that Christian preaching, teaching and communication is grossly hindered if we fail to use the mindset of Jesus and Paul, as well as the wide range of visual images used as symbols in the book of Revelation and throughout the Bible. *Pictures, illustrations and analogies strike home with vividness and power, where words alone might be less effective.* The use of pictures and images also reflects the theology of the Incarnation. On the other hand, a minority place too much confidence in the *free-standing meaning of pictures and images.* If they are interpreted in such a way as to give supposedly divine direction to a more passive or vulnerable audience, they can do great unintended harm and damage to the Church. As Crafton and others argue, Paul intended his teaching and his images and pictures to function as transparent windows through which readers or hearers could see Jesus Christ. Jesus preached and taught in order to grant us a vision and understanding of God.

Bibliography

Aageson, J. W., *Written Also for Our Sake* (Louisville: Westminster/Knox, 1993).

Advertisement for Piqua Auto Supply House, Piqua, Ohio, USA.

Alan of Lille, *The Art of Preaching*, trans. Gillian R. Evans (Collegeville, MN: Liturgical Press, Cistercian Press, 1981), and *The Art of Preaching* (London: Clarke, 1939).

Ambrose, *Of the Christian Faith* (Eng., NPNF, ser. 2, vol. 10).

Amiot, F., *The Key Concepts of St. Paul* (Eng., Freiburg: Herder, 1962).

Aquinas, Thomas, *Commentary on St Paul's First letter to the Thessalonians and Letter to the Philippians* (Albany: Magi Books, 1969).

Aquinas, Thomas, *Summa Theologiae* (Eng., 60 vols, London: Eyre and Spottiswoode, 1963).

Aristotle, *Poetics* (London: Penguin, 1996).

Auerbach, Erich, *Mimesis: The Representation of Reality in Western Literature* (Eng., Princeton: Princeton University Press, 1953).

Augustine, *City of God* (Eng., NPNF, ser. 1, vol. 2).

Augustine, *On Christian Doctrine* (Eng., NPNF, ser. 1, vol. 2).

Augustine, *On the Catechizing of the Uninstructed* (Eng., NPNF, ser. 1, vol. 3).

Augustine, *On the Trinity* (Eng., NPNF, ser. 1, vol. 3).

Augustine, *Sermons on New Testament Lessons* (Eng., NPNF, ser. 1, vol. 6).

Augustine, *Sermons on Selected Lessons of the New Testament* (Eng., NPNF, ser. 1, vol. 6).

Aune, David, *Revelation 6–16* (WBC: Nashville: Nelson, 1998).

Baillie, Donald, *God Was in Christ* (London: Faber & Faber, 1948).

Barfield, Owen, 'Poetic Diction and Legal Fiction,' in Max Black (ed.), *The Importance of Language*, pp. 51–71.

Barr, James, *The Semantics of Biblical Language* (Oxford: OUP, 1961).

Barrett, C. K., *A Commentary on the First Epistle to the Corinthians* (London: Black, 2nd edn, 1971).

Barrett, C. K., *The Epistle to the Romans* (London: Black, 1957).

Barrett, C. K., *From First Adam to Last: A Study in Pauline Theology* (London: Black, 1962).

Barrett, C. K., *The Second Epistle to the Corinthians* (London: Black, 1973).

Barth, Karl, *Church Dogmatics* (Eng., 14 vols, Edinburgh: T&T Clark, 1957–75).

Barth, Karl, *The Theology of Friedrich Schleiermacher: Lectures at Göttingen, 1923–24* (Eng., Grand Rapids: Eerdmans, 1982).

Barthes, Roland, *The Pleasure of the Text* (Eng., New York: Hill & Wang, 1975).

Bauckham, Richard, *Jesus and the Eyewitnesses: The Gospels as Eyewitness Testimony* (Grand Rapids: Eerdmans, 2006).

Bauckham, Richard, *The Theology of the Book of Revelation* (Cambridge: CUP, 1993).

Bazin, André, 'The Ontology of the Photographic Image', in Jean Renoir (ed.), *What Is Cinema?* (Berkeley: University of California Press, 1967).
Beale, G. K., *The Book of Revelation: A Commentary on the Greek Text* (Grand Rapids: Eerdmans, 1999).
Beardsley, Monroe, *Aesthetics: Problems in the Philosophy of Criticism* (Indianapolis: Harcourt, Brace & World, 1958; reprinted 1981).
Beare, F. W., and others, *The Communication of the Gospel in New Testament Times* (London: SPCK Theological Collections, 1961).
Beare, F. W., *The Epistle to the Philippians* (London: Black, 1959).
Beasley-Murray, G. R., *The Book of Revelation* (London: Oliphants, 1974).
Bede, *Excerpts from the Works of St. Augustine*, ed. David Hurst (Cistercian Publications, 1999).
Bell, Richard, *Provoked to Jealousy: The Origin and Purpose of the Jealousy Motif in Romans 9 –11* (WUNT 2, 63; Tübingen: Mohr, 1994).
Best, Ernest, *The First and Second Epistles to the Thessalonians* (London: Black, 1972).
Betz, Hans Dieter, *Galatians* (Hermeneia; Philadelphia: Fortress, 1979).
Bevan, Edwyn, *Symbolism and Belief* (London: Allen & Unwin, 1938).
Black, James, *The Mystery of Preaching* (London: James Clarke, rev. edn, 1934).
Black, Max, *Models and Metaphors: Studies in Language and Philosophy* (Ithaca: Cornell University Press, 1962).
Black, Max (ed.), *The Importance of Language* (Englewood Cliffs, NJ: Prentice-Hall, 1963).
Bligh, John, *Galatians: A Discussion of St Paul's Epistle* (London: St. Paul Publications, 1969).
Blomberg, Craig L., *Interpreting Parables* (Leicester: Apollos, 1990).
Boman, Thorlief, *Hebrew Thought Compared with Greek* (Eng., London: SCM, 1954).
Boucher, Madeleine, *The Mysterious Parable: A Literary Study* (Washington, DC: Catholic Biblical Association of America, 1977).
Brink, Gijsbert van den, *Almighty God: Study of the Doctrine of Divine Omnipotence* (Studies in Philosophical Theology; Kampen: Kok Pharos, 1993).
Broneer, Oscar, 'The Apostle Paul and the Isthmian Games', *Biblical Archaeologist* 25 (1962), pp. 2–31.
Brown, Francis, Driver, S. R., and Briggs, Charles A. (eds), *The New Hebrew and English Lexicon* (Lafayette, IN: Associated Publishers, 1980).
Bruce, A. B., *The Parabolic Teaching of Christ* (London: Hodder & Stoughton, 1882).
Bruce, F. F., *The Epistle to the Galatians: A Commentary on the Greek Text* (Grand Rapids: Eerdmans, 1982).
Bruce, F. F., *The Epistle to the Romans* (London: Tyndale Press, 1963).
Bruce, F. F., and Simpson, E. K., *The Epistles of Paul to the Ephesians and to the Colossians* (London: Marshall, Morgan & Scott, 1957).
Bryson, Norman, *Word and Image: French Painting of the Ancient Regime* (Cambridge: CUP, 1981).

Bultmann, Rudolf, 'Adam, Where Art Thou?' in Rudolf Bultmann, *Essays Philosophical and Theological* (Eng., London: SCM, 1955), pp. 119–32.

Bultmann, Rudolf, 'New Testament and Mythology', in Hans-Werner Bartsch (ed.), *Kerygma and Myth* (2 vols, London: SCM, 1953), vol. 1, pp. 1–44.

Bultmann, Rudolf, 'The Problem of Hermeneutics', in *Essays Philosophical and Theological*, pp. 243–61.

Bultmann, Rudolf, *The Second Letter to the Corinthians* (Eng., Minneapolis: Augsburg, 1985).

Bultmann, Rudolf, *Theology of the New Testament*, vol. 1 (Eng., London: SCM, 1952).

Bunyan, John, *The Pilgrim's Progress* (London: The Religious Tract Society, no date given).

Burgess, Stanley M., *The Holy Spirit: Mediaeval Roman Catholic and Reformation Traditions (*Peabody, MA: Hendrickson, 1997).

Burgess, Stanley M., and van der Mass, Eduard M. (eds), *New International Dictionary of Pentecostal and Charismatic Movements* (Grand Rapids: Zondervan, 2002).

Burton, Ernest de Witt, *The Epistle to the Galatians* (ICC; Edinburgh: T&T Clark, and New York: Scribner, 1920).

Butcher, Walter A., 'The Metaphors of St. Paul', *Baptist Quarterly* 9 (1939), pp. 484–7.

Caird, George B., *The Language and Imagery of the Bible* (London: Duckworth, 1980).

Caird, George B., *The Revelation of St. John the Divine* (London: Black, 1966).

Calvin, John, *1 and 2 Thessalonians* (Wheaton, IL: Crossway, 1999).

Calvin, John, *Institutes of the Christian Religion* (Eng., 2 vols; London: James Clarke, 1957).

Campbell, Joseph, *The Flight of the Wild Gander: Explorations in the Mythological Dimension: Selective Essays, 1944–68* (Novato, CA: New World Library, 1969).

Cassirer, Ernst, *An Essay on Man* (New Haven: Yale University Press, 1944).

Cassirer, Ernst, *Language and Myth* (Eng., New York: Harper, 1946).

Castelli, Elizabeth A., *Imitating Paul: A Discourse of Power* (Louisville: Westminster/John Knox, 1999).

Catherine of Siena, *The Dialogue of Catherine of Siena* (Eng., London: Kegan Paul, Trench, Trübner, 1907)

Catherine of Siena, *The Dialogue of Divine Presence* (London: Kegan Paul, Trench, Trübner, 1907; digitalized, 1995.)

Charles, R. H., *A Critical and Exegetical Commentary on the Revelation of St. John* (ICC; 2 vols, Edinburgh: T&T Clark, 1929).

Childs, Brevard S., *Exodus: A Commentary* (Eng., London: SCM, 1974).

Childs, Brevard S., *Myth and Reality in the Old Testament* (London: SCM, 1962).

Chladenius, Johann Martin, *Introduction to the Correct Interpretation of Reasonable Discourses and Writings* (Eng., Düsseldorf: Stern-Verlag, 1985).

Chrysostom, John, *The Gospel of Matthew* (Eng., NPNF, ser. 1, vol. 10).

Chrysostom, John, *Homilies on Thessalonians* (Eng., NPNF, vol. 13).

Clarke, Andrew D., *Secular and Christian Leadership in Corinth* (Leiden: Brill, 1993).
Clement of Alexandria, *Fragments from the Hypotyposes* (Eng., ANF, vol. 2).
Clement of Alexandria, *The Instructor* (Eng., ANF, vol. 2).
Collange, J.-F., *Enigmes de la deuxième épitre de Paul aux Corinthiens* (SNTSMS 18; Cambridge: CUP, 1972).
Congar, Yves, *The Meaning of Tradition* (San Francisco: Ignatius Press, 1964).
Conzelmann, Hans, 'On the Analysis of the Confessional Formula in 1 Cor. 15:3–5', *Int* 20 (1966), pp. 15–25.
Crafton, J. A., *The Agency of the Apostle* (JSNTSup 51; Sheffield: Sheffield Academic Press, 1991).
Craigie, Peter, *Psalms 1–50* (Waco: Word, 1983).
Cranfield, C. E. B., *A Critical and Exegetical commentary on the Epistle to the Romans*, vol. 1 (ICC; Edinburgh: T&T Clark, 1975).
Crossan, John Dominic, *Finding Is the First Act: Trove Folktales and Jesus' Treasure Parable* (Philadelphia: Fortress, and Missoula: Scholars Press, 1979).
Crossan, John Dominic, *In Parables: The Challenge of the Historical Jesus* (New York: Harper & Row, 1973).
Crossan, John Dominic, *Raid on the Articulate: Comic Eschatology in Jesus and Borges* (New York: Harper & Row, 1976).
Cullmann, Oscar, 'The Tradition', in Cullmann, Oscar, *The Early Church* (Eng., London: SCM, 1956), pp. 55–99.
Cyprian, *Treatises* (Eng., ANF, vol. 5).
Danker, Frederick W. (with Walther Bauer, W. F. Arndt and F. W. Gingrich, eds), *A Greek-English Lexicon of the New Testament and Other Early Christian Literature* (3rd edn, Chicago: University of Chicago Press, 2000).
Dean, Peter, *The Power of Symbols* (William Pitt & Foursquare Books, 2010; also e-book, 2013).
Deissmann, Adolf, *Light from the Ancient East* (London: Hodder & Stoughton, 1910).
Deluz, Gaston, *Companion to 1 Corinthians* (Eng., London: Darton, Longman & Todd, 1963).
Derrida, Jacques, 'White Mythology', in Derrida, Jacques, *Margins of Philosophy* (Eng., New York: Harvester Wheatsheaf, 1982; Fr, 1972).
Derrida, Jacques, *Writing and Difference* (Chicago: University of Chicago Press, 1978; Fr., 1967).
Descartes, René, *Discourse on Method and the Meditations* (London: Penguin, 1968).
Descartes, René, *Discourse on Method, Optics, Geometry, and Meteorology* (Cambridge, MA: Hackett Publishing, 2001).
Dillistone, Frederick W., *Christianity and Symbolism* (London: Collins, 1955).
Dillistone, Frederick W., *The Power of Symbols* (London: SCM, 1986).
Dilthey, Wilhelm, *Dilthey: Selected Writings* (Cambridge: CUP, 1976).
Dilthey, Wilhelm, *Gesammelte Schriften*, vol. 5 (Leipzig: Teuber, 1927).
Dix, Gregory, *Jew and Greek: A Study in the Primitive Church* (London: Dacre Press, 1953).

Dodd, C. H., *The Epistle of Paul to the Romans* (London: Hodder & Stoughton, 1932).

Dodd, C. H., *The Parables of the Kingdom* (London: Nisbet, 1953).

Donfried, Karl P., 'The Christology and Rhetorical Context of 1 Thessalonians 2:1–12', in Karl P. Donfried and Johannes Beutler (eds), *The Thessalonians Debate*, pp. 31–60.

Donfried, Karl P., and Beutler, Johannes (eds), *The Thessalonians Debate: Methodological Discord or Methodological Synthesis?* (Grand Rapids: Eerdmans, 2002).

Doresse, Jean, *The Secret Books of the Egyptian Gnostics* (London: Hollis and Carter, 1960).

Dudley-Smith, Timothy, *A Functional Art: Reflections of a Hymn Writer* (Oxford: OUP, 2017).

Duffy, Eamon, *The Stripping of the Altars: Traditional Religion in England c.1400–1580* (New Haven: Yale University Press, 1992).

Dunn, James D. G., *The Epistles to the Colossians and to Philemon* (NIGNT; Grand Rapids: Eerdmans, 1996).

Dunn, James D. G., *Paul and the Mosaic Law* (WUNT 89; Tübingen: Mohr, 1998).

Dunn, James D. G., *The Theology of Paul the Apostle* (Edinburgh: T&T Clark, 1998).

Dunn, James D. G., 'Was Paul Against the Law? The Law in Galatians and Romans: A Test Case of Text in Context', in T. Fornberg and D. Hellholm (eds), *Texts and Contexts: Biblical Texts in Their Textual and Situational Context* (Oslo: Scandinavian University Press, 1995) pp. 455–75.

Egan, R. B., 'Lexical Evidence on Two Pauline Passages', in *NovT* 19 (1977), pp. 34–620.

Eichrodt, Walther, *Ezekiel: A Commentary* (London: SCM, 1970).

Eichrodt, Walther, *Theology of the Old Testament*, vol. 1 (London: SCM, 1961).

Ellis, E. E., 'II Corinthians v.1–10 in Pauline Eschatology', *NTS* 6 (1959–60), pp. 211–24.

Ellul, Jacques, *The Humiliation of the Word* (Grand Rapids: Eerdmans, 1985).

Evans, Donald, *The Logic of Self-Involvement* (London: SCM, 1963).

Farbridge, Maurice H., *Studies in Biblical and Semitic Symbolism* (London: Kegan Paul, Trench, Trübner & Co., 1923).

Fawcett, Thomas, *The Symbolic Language of Religion* (London: SCM, 1970).

Findlay, G. G., 'St. Paul's First Epistle to the Corinthians', in W. R. Nicoll (ed.), *Expositor's Greek Testament* (Grand Rapids: Eerdmans, 1961; from 1900).

Fiorenza, Elisabeth Schüssler, *Revelation: Vision of a Just World* (Minneapolis: Fortress, 1991).

Fitzmyer, Joseph, *First Corinthians* (Anchor Bible; New Haven: Yale University Press, 2008).

Fitzmyer, Joseph A., *Romans: A New Translation with Introduction and Commentary* (New York: Doubleday, 1992).

Foerster, Werner, *Gnosis: A Selection of Gnostic Texts* (Oxford: Clarendon Press, 1972).

Ford, David, *Self and Salvation: Being Transformed* (Cambridge: CUP, 1999).

Foster, Richard J., and Smith, James B. (eds), *Devotional Classics: Selected Readings* (San Francisco: Harper, rev. edn, 1990), pp. 264–70.

Fuchs, Ernst, *Hermeneutik* (Tübingen: Mohr, 1970).

Fuchs, Ernst, 'The New Testament and the Hermeneutical Problem', in James M. Robinson and John B. Cobb (eds), *New Frontiers in Theology, vol. 2: The New Hermeneutic* (New York: Harper & Row, 1964), pp. 111–45.

Fuchs, Ernst, *Studies of the Historical Jesus* (London: SCM, 1964).

Funk, Robert, *Language, Hermeneutic and Word of God* (New York: Harper & Row, 1966).

Funk, Robert, 'Saying and Seeing: Phenomenology of Language and the New Testament', *Journal of Bible and Religion* 34 (1966), pp. 197–213.

Furnish, Victor P., *II Corinthians* (Anchor Bible; New York: Doubleday, 1984).

Gadamer, Hans-Georg, 'Reflections on my Philosophical Journey', in Lewis E. Hahn (ed.), *The Philosophy of Hans-Georg Gadamer* (La Salle, IL: Open Court, 1997).

Gadamer, Hans-Georg, *Truth and Method* (2nd Eng. edn, London: Sheed & Ward, 1989).

Gale, Herbert M., *The Use of Analogy in the Letters of Paul* (Philadelphia: Westminster Press, 1964).

Gärtner, Bertil, *The Theology of the Gospel of Thomas* (London: Collins, 1961).

Genova, Judith, *Wittgenstein: A Way of Seeing* (London: Routledge, 1995).

Genova, Judith, 'Wittgenstein on Thinking: Words or Pictures?' in Roberto Casati and Graham White (eds), *Philosophy and the Cognitive Sciences* (Kirchberg am Wechsel, 1993), pp. 63–167.

Gertrude, *Gertrude of Helfta: The Herald of Divine Love* (New York: Paulist Press, 1993).

Glock, Hans-Johann, 'Aspect-Perception', in *A Wittgenstein Dictionary* (Oxford: Blackwell, 1996).

Gombrich, Ernst H., *Art and Illusion: A Study in the Psychology of Pictorial Representation* (London: Phaidon Press, 1960).

Goodacre, Mark, *The Case Against Q* (London: Continuum, 2002).

Goppelt, Leonhard, '*tupos*' in G. Kittel and G. Friedrich, *TDNT*, vol. 8, pp. 236–60.

Goppelt, Leonhard, *Typos: The Typological Interpretation of the Old Testament in the New* (Eng., Grand Rapids: Eerdmans, 1982).

Gregory of Nazianzus, *Fifth Theological Oration: On the Holy Spirit* (Eng., NPNF, ser. 2, vol. 7, pp. 318–23).

Gregory of Nyssa, *Against Eunomius* (Eng., NPNF, ser. 2, vol. 5).

Gregory of Nyssa, 'On Not Three Gods' (Eng., NPNF, ser. 2, vol. 5, pp. 331–6).

Grenfell, E. P., *An Alexandrian Erotic Fragment and Other Greek Papyri* (Oxford: Clarendon Press, 1896).

Grobel, Kendrick, *The Gospel of Truth: A Valentinian Meditation on the Gospel* (London: Black, 1960).

Grosseteste, Robert, *On Six Days of Creation* (London: British Academy, 1996).

Gundry, Robert H., 'The New Jerusalem: People as Place, Not Place for People', in Robert H. Gundry, *The Old Is Better: New Testament Essays in Support of Traditional Interpretations* (WUNT 178; Tübingen: Mohr, 2005), pp. 399–411.

Hanson, Richard P. C., *Allegory and Event: A Study of the Sources and Significance of Origen's Interpretation of Scripture* (London: SCM, 1959).

Hanson, Richard P. C., *Tradition in the Early Church* (London: SCM, 1962).

Harré, Ron, *The Principles of Scientific Thinking* (London: Macmillan, 1970).

Harris, Murray, *The Second Epistle to the Corinthians* (NIGTC; Grand Rapids: Eerdmans, 2005).

Hays, Richard, *Echoes of Scripture in the Letters of Paul* (New Haven: Yale University Press, 1989).

Hays, Richard, *First Corinthians* (Interpretation; Louisville: Knox, 1997).

Hegel, Georg W. F., *Lectures on the Philosophy of Religion* (3 vols, London: Kegan Paul, Trench, Trübner, 1895).

Heidegger, Martin, *Being and Time* (Eng., Oxford: Blackwell, 1962).

Heidegger, Martin, *Introduction to Metaphysics* (Eng., New Haven: Yale University Press, 1959).

Heidegger, Martin, *On the Way to Language* (Eng., New York: Harper & Row, 1971).

Hendriksen, W., *More Than Conquerors* (London: Tyndale Press, 1962).

Hengel, Martin, *The Cross of the Son of God* (Eng., London: SCM, 1986).

Hepburn, Ronald, 'Demythologizing and the Problem of Validity', in Antony Flew and Alasdair MacIntyre (eds), *New Essays in Philosophical Theology* (London: SCM, 1955), pp. 227–42.

Héring, Jean, *First Epistle of Paul the Apostle to the Corinthians* (Eng., London: Epworth Press, 1962).

Hesse, Mary B., *Models and Analogies in Science* (Notre Dame, IN: Notre Dame University Press, 1966).

Hester, J. D., *Paul's Concept of Inheritance* (SJT Occasional Papers 14; Edinburgh: Oliver & Boyd, 1968).

Hildegard of Bingen, *Scivias* (Eng., Abbey of Regina Laudus, 1990).

Hilton, Walter, *The Ladder of Perfection* (London: Penguin, 1957).

Hilton, Walter, *The Scale of Perfection* (Kalamazoo, MI: Medieval Institute Publications, 2000).

Hock, R. F., *The Social Context of Paul's Ministry* (Philadelphia: Fortress, 1980).

Holland, Tom, *Contours of Pauline Theology* (Fearn: Mentor, 2004).

Hughes, Philip E., *Paul's Second Epistle to the Corinthians* (London: Marshall, Morgan & Scott, 1962).

Humphrey, Edith M., *And I Turned to See the Voice: The Rhetoric of Vision in the New Testament* (Grand Rapids: Baker Academic, 2007).

Hunter, A. M., *Interpreting the Parables* (Philadelphia: Westminster Press, 1960).

Inge, William Ralph, *Christian Mysticism* (London and New York: Scribner, 1899).

Irenaeus, *Against Heresies* (Eng., ANF, vol. 1).

Iser, Wolfgang, *The Act of Reading: A Theory of Aesthetic Response* (Baltimore: Johns Hopkins University Press, 1978 and 1980).

Iser, Wolfgang, *The Implied Reader* (Baltimore: Johns Hopkins University Press, 1974).

Iser, Wolfgang, 'Indeterminacy and the Reader's Response in Prose Fiction', in J. Hillis Miller (ed.), *Aspects of Narrative* (New York: Columbia University Press, 1971), pp. 1–45.

Ivins, William M., *Prints and Visual Communication* (Cambridge, MA: Harvard University Press, 1953).

Jay, Martin, *Downcast Eyes: The Denigration of Vision in Twentieth-Century French Thought* (Berkeley: University of California Press, 1993).

Jay, Martin, 'The Rise of Hermeneutics and the Crisis of Ocularcentrism', in *Force Fields: Between Intellectual History and Cultural Critique* (New York: Routledge, 1993), pp. 99–113.

Jeremias, Joachim, *The Parables of Jesus* (Eng., London: SCM, rev. edn., 1963).

Jewett, Robert, *Romans: A Commentary* (Minneapolis: Fortress, 2007).

John Chrysostom, *Homilies on the Gospel of Matthew* (Eng., NPNF, ser. 1, vol. 10).

John of the Cross, *The Dark Night of the Soul*, ed. Alison Peters (Image Books, 3rd edn, 1959).

Jonas, Hans, *The Phenomenon of Life: Toward a Philosophical Biology* (Chicago: Northwestern University Press, 1982, reprinted 2001).

Jones, Geraint Vaughan, *The Art and Truth of the Parables: A Study in Their Literary Form and Modern Interpretation* (London: SPCK, 1964).

Josephus, *Antiquities* (Eng., London: Bibliophile, 1996).

Julian of Norwich, *Revelations of Divine Love* (London: Penguin, 1998).

Julian of Norwich, *Revelations of Divine Showings*, ed. and trans. Clifton Wolters (London: Penguin, 1998).

Jülicher, Adolf, *Die Gleichnisreden Jesu* (2 vols, Freiburg: Mohr, 1888 and 1899).

Jung, Carl G., *Psychological Types* (London: Routledge, 1971).

Jüngel, Eberhard, *Collected Works* (London: Bloomsbury/Clark, 2014).

Jüngel, Eberhard, *God as the Mystery of the World* (Eng., Edinburgh: T&T Clark, 1983).

Jüngel, Eberhard, *Theological Essays* (2 vols, Edinburgh: T&T Clark, 1989).

Kelly, J. N. D., *The Pastoral Epistles* (London: Black, 1963).

Kennedy, H. A., *St. Paul's Conception of the Last Things* (London: Hodder & Stoughton, 1904).

Kenny, Anthony, *Wittgenstein* (London: Penguin, 1973).

Kent, J. H., *Corinth*, VIII/3: *The Inscriptions 1926–50* (Princeton: American School of Classical Studies at Athens, 1966).

Kiddle, Martin, *The Revelation of St John* (London: Hodder & Stoughton, 1940).

Kierkegaard, Søren, *Concluding Unscientific Postscript* (Eng., Princeton: Princeton University Press, 1974).

Kissinger, Warren S., *The Parables of Jesus: A History of Interpretation and Bibliography* (London: Scarecrow Press, 1979).

Kloppenborg, John S., *The Formation of Q Transcripts in Ancient Wisdom Collections* (Philadelphia: Fortress, 1987).

Knox, Wilfred L., *St Paul and the Church of Jerusalem* (Cambridge: CUP, 1925).

Knox, Wilfred L., *St Paul and the Church of the Gentiles* (Cambridge: CUP, 1939).

Knox, Wilfred L., *Some Hellenistic Elements in Primitive Christianity* (London: OUP, 1944).

Koester, Craig R., *Revelation: A New Translation with Introduction and Commentary* (Anchor Bible; New Haven: Yale University Press, 2014).

Koester, H., 'The Purpose of the Polemic of a Pauline Fragment (Phil. 3)', *NTS* 8 (1961–2), pp. 317–32.

Kovacs, Judith, and Rowland, Christopher, *Revelation* (Blackwell Bible Commentaries; Oxford: Blackwell, 2004).

Künneth, Walther, *The Theology of the Resurrection* (Eng., London: SCM, 1965).

Laeuchli, Samuel, *The Language of Faith: An Introduction to the Semantic Dilemma of the Early Church* (London: Epworth Press, 1965).

Lakoff, George, and Johnson, Mark, *Metaphors We Live By* (Chicago: University of Chicago Press, 1980).

Lampe, W. H. (ed.), *A Patristic Greek Lexicon* (Oxford: Clarendon Press, 1961).

Lanci, J. R., *A New Temple for Corinth: Historical and Archaeological Approaches to Pauline Imagery* (New York and Bern: Lang, 1997).

Lang, F., *Die Briefe an die Korinther* (Göttingen: Vandenhoeck & Ruprecht, 1994).

Latimer, Hugh, *Sermons* (New York: Dutton, 1906).

Leenhardt, Franz, *The Epistle to the Romans* (London: Lutterworth Press, 1961).

Lewis, C. S., 'Bluspells and Flalansferes', in Max Black (ed.), *The Importance of Language*, pp. 36–50.

Lindsey, Hal, *The Late Great Planet Earth* (Grand Rapids: Zondervan, 1970).

Linnemann, Eta, *Parables of Jesus: Introduction and Exposition* (Eng., London: SPCK, 1966).

Locke, John, *An Essay Concerning Human Understanding* (2 vols, Oxford: Clarendon Press, 1894).

Luther, Martin, *Letters of Spiritual Counsel*, ed. T. G. Tappert, (London: SCM, 1965).

Lyons, George Leroy, *Pauline Autobiography: Toward a New Understanding* (SBLDS 73; Atlanta: Scholars Press, 1985).

McGinn, Bernard, *Antichrist: Two Thousand Years of the Human Fascination with the Devil* (San Francisco: Harper, 1994).

Malherbe, Abraham, 'Gentle as a Nurse: The Cynic Background of 1 Thess. 2:2', *NovT* 12 (1970), pp. 203–17.

Malherbe, Abraham, *Paul and the Thessalonians: The Philosophic Tradition of Pastoral Care* (Philadelphia: Fortress, 1987).

Malherbe, Abraham, *The Letters to the Thessalonians* (Anchor Bible; New Haven: Yale University Press, 2000).

Margery Kempe, *The Book of Margery Kempe* (based on Robbins Digital Projects).

Marshall, P., 'A Metaphor of Social Shame: *thriambeuein* in 2 Cor. 2:14', *NovT* 25 (1983), pp. 302–17.

Martin, Dale B., *The Corinthian Body* (New Haven: Yale University Press, 1995).

Martin, Dale B., *Slavery as Salvation* (New Haven: Yale University Press, 1990).

Martin, Ralph P., *2 Corinthians* (WBC; Dallas: Word, 1986).

Martin, Ralph P., *Philippians* (NCB; London: Oliphants, 1976).

Marxsen, W., *The Resurrection of Jesus of Nazareth* (Eng., Philadelphia: Fortress, 1970).

Mathewson, David, *A New Heaven and New Earth: The Meaning and Function of the Old Testament in Revelation 21:1–22:5* (JSNTSup 238; London: Sheffield Academic Press, 2003).

Merk, Otto, '1 Thessalonians 2:1–12: An Exegetical-Theological Study', in Karl P. Donfried and Johannes Beutler (eds), *The Thessalonians Debate*, pp. 89–113.

Michel, Otto, '*naos*', in *TDNT*, vol. 4, pp. 880–90.

Milton, John, *Paradise Lost* (London: Simmons, 2017).

Mitchell, Margaret M., *Paul and the Rhetoric of Reconciliation* (Tübingen: Mohr, and Louisville: Westminster/Knox, 1992).

Mitchell, W. J. T., *Picture Theory* (Chicago: University of Chicago Press, 1994).

Mitton, C. Leslie, *The Gospel According to St Mark* (London: Epworth Press, 1957).

Mitton, C. Leslie, 'New Wine in Old Wineskins; 4: Leaven', *ExpTim* 84 (1973), pp. 339–43.

Moltmann, Jürgen, *The Crucified God: The Cross of Christ as the Foundation and Criticism of Christian Theology* (Eng., London: SCM, 1974).

Moltmann, Jürgen, *The Trinity and the Kingdom of God* (Eng., London: SCM, 1981).

Moore, Arthur L., *1 and 2 Thessalonians* (NCB; London: Nelson, 1969).

Moule, C. F. D., *The Epistles to the Colossians and to Philemon* (Cambridge: CUP, 1962).

Moulton, J. H., and Milligan, G., *The Vocabulary of the Greek Testament* (London: Hodder & Stoughton, 1952).

Moulton, W. F., and Geden, A. S., *A Concordance to the Greek Testament* (Edinburgh: T&T Clark, 1899).

Mounce, Robert H., *The Book of Revelation* (London: Marshall, Morgan & Scott, 1977).

Mounce, William D., *Pastoral Epistles* (WBC; Nashville: Nelson, 2000).

Mullins, T. Y., 'Paul's Thorn in the Flesh', *JBL* 76 (1957), pp. 299–303.

Munck, Johannes, *Paul and the Salvation of Mankind* (Eng., London: SCM, 1959).

Murphy O'Connor, Jerome, *St Paul's Corinth: Texts and Archaeology* (Wilmington: Glazier, 1983).

Nietzsche, Friedrich, *The Antichrist* (London: Penguin Classics, 1990).

Nietzsche, Friedrich, *Complete Works* (18 vols, London: Allen & Unwin, 1909–13).

Nietzsche, Friedrich, *Notebooks* (Cambridge: CUP, 2003).

Nietzsche, Friedrich, *The Portable Nietzsche*, ed. W. Kaufman (New York: Viking Press, 1968).

Nietzsche, Friedrich, *Thus Spoke Zarathustra* (London: Penguin, 1961).

Nietzsche, Friedrich, *The Twilight of the Idols* (London: Penguin Classics, 1990).

Nietzsche, Friedrich, *The Will to Power*, vol. 2, in *The Complete Works* (18 vols, London: Allen & Unwin 1909–13, vol. 15).

Nyíri, Kristóf, 'Image and Metaphor in the Philosophy of Wittgenstein', *Image and Imaging in Philosophy, Science and the Arts* (Symposium: Kirchberg, 8–14 August 2010), pp. 1–15.

Nyíri, Kristóf, 'Wittgenstein's Philosophy of Pictures', Conference Paper at the HIT Centre, University of Bergen, December 2001.

O'Brien, Peter T., *The Epistle to the Philippians* (NIGTC; Grand Rapids: Eerdmans, 1991).

O'Hear, Natasha and Anthony, *Picturing the Apocalypse: The Book of Revelation in the Arts over Two Millennia* (Oxford: OUP, 2015).

Origen, *Commentary on Matthew* (Eng., ANF, vol. 4).

Origen, *Commentary on Matthew* (Eng., New Advent, Church Fathers, *Origen's Commentary on Matthew*).

Origen, *Homilies on Luke*, Fragment 71 (described in Warren S. Kissinger, *The Parables of Jesus: A History of Interpretation and Bibliography*, London: Scarecrow Press, 1979, p. 18).

Origen, *On First Principles* (Eng., ANF, vol. 4).

Pagels, Elaine H., *The Johannine Gospel in Gnostic Exegesis: Heracleon's Commentary on John* (SBLMS 17; Nashville: Abingdon Press, 1973).

Pannenberg, Wolfhart, *Systematic Theology* (Eng., 3 vols, Edinburgh: T&T Clark, 1991–8).

Paul, Ian, 'Metaphor', in Kevin J. Vanhoozer (ed.), *Dictionary for Theological Interpretation of the Bible* (London: SPCK, and Grand Rapids: Baker Academic, 2007), pp. 507–10.

Peel, Malcolm Lee, *The Epistle to Rheginos: A Valentinian Letter on the Resurrection: Introduction, Analysis and Exposition* (London: SCM, 1969).

Perrin, Norman, *Jesus and the Language of the Kingdom: Symbol and Metaphor in New Testament Interpretation* (London: SCM, 1976).

Pfitzner, Victor, *Paul and the Agon Motif: Traditional Athletic Imagery in the Pauline Literature* (NovTSup; Leiden: Brill, 1967.

Philo, *De Plantatione* (Paris: Cerf, 1963).

Platt, Verity, 'Virtual Visions: *Phantasia* and the Perception of the Divine in the Life of Apollonius of Tyana', in E. L. Bowie and J. Elsner (eds), *Philostratus* (Cambridge: CUP, 2009).

Plummer, Alfred, *A Commentary on the Second Epistle of Paul to the Corinthians* (Edinburgh: T&T Clark, 1915).

Pogoloff, Stephen, *Logos and Sophia: The Rhetorical Situation of 1 Corinthians* (SBLDS 134; Atlanta: Scholars Press, 1992).

Prat, F., *The Theology of St. Paul* (Eng., 2 vols, London: Burns & Oates, 1945).

Ramsay, William, *Paul and Other Studies* (New York: Armstrong, 1906).

Ramsey, Ian T., *Christian Discourse* (Oxford: OUP, 1965).

Ramsey, Ian T., *Models and Mystery* (Oxford: OUP, 1964).

Ramsey, Ian T., *Models for Divine Activity* (London: SCM, 1973).

Ramsey, Ian T., *Religious Language: An Empirical Placing of Religious Belief* (London: SCM, 1957).

Reeves, Kevin, 'The Lighthouse Trail Blog', 11 May 2008.

Reid, Thomas, *An Enquiry into the Human Mind on the Principles of Common Sense* (Edinburgh: Bell & Greech, 1801).

Ricoeur, Paul, 'Biblical Hermeneutics', in *Semeia: An Experimental Journal for Biblical Criticism* (1975), pp. 29–145.

Ricoeur, Paul, *Freud and Philosophy: An Essay on Interpretation* (Eng., New Haven: Yale University Press, 1970).

Ricoeur, Paul, *Interpretation Theory: Discourse and the Surplus of Meaning* (Fort Worth: Texas Christian University Press, 1976).

Ricoeur, Paul, *Oneself as Another* (Chicago: University of Chicago Press, 1992).

Ricoeur, Paul, *The Rule of Metaphor: Multi-disciplinary Studies of the Creation of Meaning in Language* (London: Routledge & Kegan Paul, 1978).

Ricoeur, Paul, *The Symbolism of Evil* (Eng., Boston: Beacon Press, 1967 and 1969).

Ricoeur, Paul, *Time and Narrative* (Eng., 3 vols, Chicago and London: University of Chicago Press, 1984–8).

Rigaux, Beda, *Les Épitres aux Thessaloniciens* (Paris: Gabalda, 1956).

Robertson A. T., and Plummer, A., *A Critical and Exegetical Commentary on the First Epistle of St. Paul to the Corinthians* (Edinburgh: T&T Clark, 1914).

Robinson, J. Armitage, *St Paul's Epistle to the Ephesians* (London: Macmillan, 1987).

Robinson, James M., Kloppenborg, John S., and Hoffmann, Paul (eds), *The Critical Edition of Q* (Hermeneia; Minneapolis: Fortress, 2000).

Robinson, John A. T., *The Body: A Study in Pauline Theology* (London: SCM, 1952).

Rogers, Eugene F., *After the Spirit* (London: SCM, 2006).

Rorty, Richard, *Philosophy and the Mirror of Nature* (Princeton: Princeton University Press, 1979).

Rorty, Richard, *Truth and Progress: Philosophical Papers*, vol. 3 (Cambridge: CUP, 1998).

Routledge, Fleming, *The Crucifixion: Understanding the Death of Jesus Christ* (Grand Rapids: Eerdmans, 2015).

Sampley, J. Paul, *'And the Two Shall Become One Flesh': A Study of Traditions in Ephesians 5:21–33* (SNTSMS 16; Cambridge: CUP, 1971.

Sanders, E. P., *Paul, the Law, and the Jewish People* (Philadelphia: Fortress, 1983).

Sanders, Tess (ed.), 'Speakers Give Sound Advice', *Syracuse Post Standard* (28 March 1911).

Schleiermacher, Friedrich, *A Brief Outline of the Study of Theology* (Eugene, OR: Wipf & Stock, 2007).

Schleiermacher, Friedrich, *Hermeneutics: The Handwritten Manuscripts* (Eng., Missoula: Scholars Press, 1977).

Schleiermacher, Friedrich, *On Religion: Speeches to Its Cultured Despisers* (Eng., New York: Harper, 1958).

Schnackenburg, Rudolf, *Baptism in the Thought of St Paul* (Oxford: Blackwell, 1964).

Schrage, W., *Der erste Brief an die Korinther* (4 vols), vol. 1 (Zürich: Benziger Verlag, 1991).

Schroeder, Severin, 'A Tale of Two Problems: Wittgenstein's Discussion of Aspect Perception', in J. Cottingham and P. M. S. Hacker (eds), *Mind, Method, and Morality: Essays in Honour of Anthony Kenny* (Oxford: OUP, 2010) pp. 352–71.

Shanor, J., 'Paul as Master Builder: Construction Terms in 1 Corinthians', *NTS* 34 (1988), pp. 461–71.

Soskice, Janet Martin, *Metaphor and Religious Language* (Oxford: Clarendon Press, 1985).

Spurgeon, Charles Haddon, *The New Park Street Pulpit*, vol. I (1855).

Staley, Lynn (ed.), *The Book of Margery Kempe* (Kalamazoo, MI: Mediaeval Institute Publications, 1996).

Stein, Robert H., *An Introduction to the Parables of Jesus* (Philadelphia: Westminster John Knox Press, 1981).

Strack, Hermann L., and Billerbeck, Paul, *Kommentar zum Neuen Testament aus Talmud und Midrasch*, vol. 1 (Munich: C. H. Beck, 1926).

Straub, Werner, *Die Bildersprache des Apostels Paulus* (Tübingen: Mohr, 1937).

Swinburne, Richard, *The Coherence of Theism* (Oxford: Clarendon Press, 1977).

Taylor, Jeremy, *The Golden Grove* (London: Royston, 1665).

Taylor, Vincent, *The Atonement in New Testament Teaching* (London: Epworth Press, 1940).

Taylor, Vincent, 'The Original Order of Q', in A. J. B. Higgins (ed.), *New Testament Essays* (Manchester: Manchester University Press, 1959), pp. 246–69.

Teresa of Avila, *Interior Castle* (New York: Dover Publications, 1946).

Tertullian, *De Pudicitia* (Eng., ANF, vol. 4).

Tertullian, *On the Resurrection* (Eng., ANF, vol. 3).

Tertullian, *Prescription against Heretics* (Eng., ANF, vol. 3).

Teselle, Sallie McFague, *Speaking in Parables: A Study of Metaphor and Theology* (London: SCM, 1975).

Thayer, Joseph H., *Greek-English Lexicon* (Edinburgh: T&T Clark, 4th edn, 1901).

Thiselton, Anthony C., *The First Epistle to the Corinthians: A Commentary on the Greek Text* (NIGTC; Grand Rapids: Eerdmans, 2000).

Thiselton, Anthony C., *Life after Death: A New Approach to the Last Things* (Grand Rapids: Eerdmans, 2012; or *The Last Things: A New Approach* (London: SPCK, 2012).

Thiselton, Anthony C., 'The Meaning of *Sarx* in 1 Cor. 5:5: A Fresh Approach', *SJT* 26 (1973), pp. 204–28.

Thiselton, Anthony C., *New Horizons in Hermeneutics: The Theory and Practice of Transforming Biblical Reading* (London: HarperCollins, and Grand Rapids: Zondervan, 1992 and 2012).

Thiselton, Anthony C., *Systematic Theology* (Grand Rapids: Eerdmans, 2015).

Thiselton, Anthony C., *The Two Horizons: New Testament Hermeneutics and Philosophical Description* (Grand Rapids: Eerdmans, 1980.)

Thornton, L. S., *The Common Life in the Body of Christ* (London: Dacre Press, 1942 and 1950).

Tillich, Paul, *Dynamics of Faith* (London: Allen & Unwin, 1957).

Tillich, Paul, *On Art and Architecture* (New York: Crossroad, 1989).

Tillich, Paul, 'The Religious Symbol', in S. Hook (ed.), *Religious Experience and Truth* (Edinburgh: Oliver & Boyd, 1962).

Tillich, Paul, *Systematic Theology* (3 vols, Chicago: University of Chicago Press, and London: Nisbet, 1953, 1957 and 1963).

Tillich, Paul, *Theology of Culture* (Oxford: OUP, 1964).

Tolbert, Mary Ann, *Perspectives on the Parables* (Philadelphia: Fortress, 1979).

Tolbert, Mary Ann, 'The Prodigal Son: An Essay in Literary Criticism from a Psycho-Analytical Perspective', in *Semeia* 9 (1977), pp. 1–20.

Trench, Richard C., *Notes on the Parables of Our Lord* (Westwood, NJ: Revell, 1953).

Turgenev, Ivan, *Fathers and Sons* (1862; Eng., Oxford: OUP, 1991 and 2008).

Vaughan, Henry, 'The Rainbow', in H. C. Beeching (ed.), *Lyra Sacra: A Book of Religious Verse* (London: Methuen, 1903); online since 2011.

Verner, D. C., *The Household of God and the Social World of the Pastoral Epistles* (SBLDS; Chico, CA: Scholars Press, 1983).

Via, Dan Otto, 'The Parable of the Unjust Judge: A Metaphor of the Unrealized Self', in *Semiology and the Parables* (Pittsburgh: Pickwick, 1976), pp. 1–32.

Vielhauer, P., *Oikodomē. Aufsätze zum N.T.*, II: *Theologische Bücherei*, vol. 65 (Munich: Kaiser, 1979).

Voltaire, *Philosophical Dictionary* (Eng., New York: Knopf, 1924 and 1972).

Wall, Robert W., *1 & 2 Timothy and Titus* (Grand Rapids: Eerdmans, 2012).

War advertisement, *San Antonio Light* (10 January 1918).

Wenham, Gordon, *The Book of Leviticus* (Grand Rapids: Eerdmans, 1979).

Wenham, Gordon, *Genesis 1–15* (WBC 1; Texas: Word, 1987).

Westcott, Brooke F., *St Paul's Epistle to the Ephesians: Greek Text* (London: Macmillan, 1906).

Wheelwright, Philip, *The Burning Fountain: A Study in the Language of Symbolism* (Tulamore: Midland Books, 1954).

Whitaker, Robyn J., *Ekphrasis, Vision, and Persuasion in the Book of Revelation* (WUNT 2, 410; Tübingen: Mohr, 2015).

Whiteley, D. E. H., *The Theology of St. Paul* (Oxford: Blackwell, 1970).

Wickenhauser, Alfred, *Pauline Mysticism* (Edinburgh: Nelson, 1960).

Wilder, Amos N., *Early Christian Rhetoric* (London: SCM, 1964).

Williamson, L., 'Led in Triumph: Paul's Use of *Thriambeuō*', *Int* 22 (1968), pp. 317–32.

Wire, Antoinette, *The Corinthian Women Prophets* (Minneapolis: Fortress, 1990).

Witherington, Ben, III, *1 and 2 Thessalonians: A Socio-Rhetorical Commentary* (Grand Rapids: Eerdmans, 2006).

Wittgenstein, Ludwig, *The Blue and Brown Books: Preliminary Studies for the Philosophical Investigations* (Oxford: Blackwell, 2nd edn, 1969).

Wittgenstein, Ludwig, *Last Writings on the Philosophy of Psychology* (2 vols, Oxford: Blackwell, 1982 and 1992).

Wittgenstein, Ludwig, *On Certainty* (Eng. and Ger., Oxford: Blackwell, 1969).

Wittgenstein, Ludwig, *Philosophical Grammar* (Berkeley: University of California Press, 1974).

Wittgenstein, Ludwig, *Philosophical Investigations* (Eng. and Ger., Oxford: Blackwell, 1958).

Wittgenstein, Ludwig, *Remarks on the Philosophy of Psychology* (2 vols, Oxford: Blackwell, 1980).

Wittgenstein, Ludwig, *Tractatus Logico-Philosophicus* (Eng. and Ger., London: Routledge & Kegan Paul, 1922 and 1961).

Wittgenstein, Ludwig, *Zettel* (Oxford: Blackwell, 1967).

Wolff, C., *Der erste Brief des Paulus an die Korinther* (Leipzig: Evangelische Verlagsanstalt, 1996).

Wright, N. T., *Paul and the Faithfulness of God* (London: SPCK, 2013).

Wright, N. T., *The Resurrection of the Son of God* (London: SPCK, 2003).

Wycliffe, John, *On the Pastoral Office*, in Matthew Spinka (ed.), *Advocates of Reform* (LCC 214, London: SCM, 1963).

Ziesler, John, 'Paul and Arboriculture: Romans 11:17–24', *JSNT* 24 (1985), pp. 24–32.

Zimany, Roland D., *Vehicle for God: The Metaphorical Theology of Eberhard Jüngel* (Atlanta: Mercer University Press, 1994).

Zwiep, Arie W., *Christ, the Spirit, and the Community of God* (WUNT 2; Tübingen: Mohr, 2010).

Index of principal biblical references

Index of names

Note: Entries in **bold** represent names of significance.

Index of subjects

Note: Entries in **bold** represent topics of significance.